Executive Coaching in Strategic Holistic Leadership

Executive Coaching in Strategic Holistic Leadership

The Drivers and Dynamics of Vertical Development

Antoinette J. Braks

Open University Press

Open University Press
McGraw-Hill Education
8th Floor, 338 Euston Road
London
England
NW1 3BH

email: enquiries@openup.co.uk
world wide web: www.openup.co.uk

and Two Penn Plaza, New York, NY 10121-2289, USA

First edition published 2020

Head of Publishing: Laura Pacey
Associate Editor: Clara Heathcock
Content Product Manager: Ali Davis

A catalogue record of this book is available from the British Library

ISBN-13: 9780335249114
ISBN-10: 0335249116
eISBN: 9780335249121

Library of Congress Cataloging-in-Publication Data
CIP data applied for

Typeset by Transforma Pvt. Ltd., Chennai, India

Fictitious names of companies, products, people, characters and/or data that may be
used herein (in case studies or in examples) are not intended to represent any real
individual, company, product or event.

Praise page

"This is a much-needed, research-based book that shares crucial tools and techniques for coaches that are proven to move clients through the levels of developmental maturity. This book has already helped me refine my coaching!"

—Maureen Metcalf, Founder & CEO,
Innovative Leadership Institute

"If executive coaching can support the alteration from Achiever to Synergist as this book lays out, it will become much more than the support towards achieving the next goal on the career ladder, and will instead become a transformational dialogue; a holistic path that can humanise our world."

—Reinhard Stelter, Professor of Coaching Psychology,
University of Copenhagen

"In these trying times of an unprecedented global health crisis, the smooth day-to-day running of civic affairs is disrupted. Thus, it is more urgent than ever that mature leaders and visionaries are at the helm of societies and corporations. They are most likely to be able to creatively adapt strategies to the drastically changed contingencies and life circumstances. As the speed and reach of global change and challenge in all areas of life is increasing, it becomes vital that more people develop postconventional capacities: The ability to take multiple perspectives, think systemically, consider the long-term effects of decisions and base them on the best of available scientific evidence. This book offers a path to help leaders acquire these later stage characteristics."

—Susanne Cook-Greuter, Strategic Advisor and Research Director,
Vertical Development Academy

"Braks' brilliant work, supported by her research, has focused on a pivotal arc in the developmental spectrum – the capacity of our leaders and coaches to take a mature, fourth person perspective. She has accessed the most salient aspects of different developmental models to create an effective, practical and grounded approach for guiding those who are ready, opening their eyes to the next generation of coaching and leading. This is badly needed in our troubled world – a world that is hungry for new eyes that will see what is not yet seen, and heal hidden dilemmas that have not yet been identified."

—Terri O'Fallon, Founder and Partner of STAGES International

This book is dedicated to a very special aunt,
kindred spirit, and soul sister: Annie van der Horst-Braks

Annie, nog heel speciale dank voor alles! Door bij je te blijven in
je mooie en vredige huis, werd dit boek mogelijk.
Ik zal altijd heel dankbaar zijn dat het universum
ons samenbracht. Je bent geweldig!

Annie, a very special thanks for everything!
Staying with you in your beautiful and peaceful home
made this book possible. I'll always be so grateful that
the universe brought us together. You're totally awesome!

Contents

Preface   xi

PART 1 THE STAGES OF LEADERSHIP TRANSFORMATION   **1**

1   INTRODUCTION TO THE STAGES OF TRANSFORMATION   3

2   STRENGTHS AND SHADOWS OF EXECUTIVE PROTOTYPES   20

3   THE TRANSFORMATION FROM *ACHIEVIST* TO *SYNERGIST*   39

4   THE EXECUTIVE COACHING RESEARCH STUDY   54

5   THE KEY THEMES OF TRANSFORMATIVE COACHING   61

PART 2 THE DRIVERS OF LATER STAGE TRANSFORMATION   **67**

6   HOLISTIC DRIVERS 1 AND 2: CULTIVATING ONE'S BEST SELF   69

7   STRATEGIC DRIVERS 3 AND 4: UPLIFTING THE ORGANISATION   81

8   HOLISTIC DRIVERS 5 AND 6: HOLDING SAFE EMERGENT SPACE   97

9   STRATEGIC DRIVERS 7 AND 8: LEADING WIDE COLLABORATION   113

10 THE ATTITUDINAL SHIFTS IN PERCEPTION AND PERSPECTIVE   121

PART 3 THE DYNAMICS OF LATER STAGE TRANSFORMATION   **129**

11 THE 2-STEP SQUARE DANCE OF VERTICAL DEVELOPMENT   131

12 GENERATING AND HOLDING SAFE EXPANSIVE SPACE   142

13 CORRELATION WITH HUMAN FACULTIES AND ENERGY FIELDS   156

14 LINKING COACHING EFFECTIVENESS TO STAGE DEVELOPMENT   165

15 TRANSFORMATIVE STAGESHIFT™ EXECUTIVE COACHING   180

Appendix: The Multiple Case Study Research   193

References   206

Index   212

Preface

From work to play, grow to flow, calm to care, and free to love.

Many years ago when I first embarked on my career as an executive coach, I began to discern a series of mindsets or perspectives as executives developed their leadership capacity. I started out with: *from work to play, grow to flow to calm*. '*Work*' was all about turning up for work and following instructions; '*play*' concerned taking the initiative and the risk to experiment; '*grow*' involved developing the confidence to make decisions, set priorities, and take charge; '*flow*' related to trusting in the emergence of solutions as we navigate the adventure we call life; and '*calm*' was a sort of arrival in a calm, clear, open, and collaborative state of mind.

Little did I know that I had happened on vertical stage development. I had always been a fan of Maslow's Hierarchy of Needs – the shifts from physical safety, to economic security, a sense of belonging to a community, the development of self-esteem, and moving onto self-actualising in terms of realising more and more of our human potential. I was preoccupied with personal power – how could we best use our power to shape our lives and serve others?

I became an accredited coach with The Leadership Circle and developed an interest in the shift we make from being reactive to becoming more creative as leaders in organisations, as well as Richard Barrett's work that differentiated values by stage of development based on Maslow's Hierarchy. He identified a key turning point in personal power from focusing on meeting our survival needs to attending to our growth needs. I also led organisation transformations along the evolutionary arc from red, amber, and orange to green and teal (Laloux) to increasingly liberate more of our creative talents so we could serve life in more meaningful, purposeful, and fulfilling ways.

In the last decade, my persistent interest in evolution led to studying stage development with Susanne Cook-Greuter, Bill Torbert, and Terri O'Fallon. I began to read a book every Saturday to better understand leadership development and effectiveness, and organisational development and performance. My reading extended to many spiritual teachers who enriched my own journey in self-actualisation. I added: *from calm to care and free to love*, in honour of what I had come to understand as transpersonal stages. I certainly believed in a higher spiritual reality that underpinned life itself.

My personal purpose was to enable people to realise their potential, and organisations their aspirations, through conscious evolution. This was the evolution from reactive to creative, and more profoundly, from scared to sacred. It is simply the placement of the 'c' that changes the meaning of both sets of letters we refer to as words. By 'c-ing' the world with a higher, broader, and deeper perspective at a later stage of human development, we can evolve as spiritual beings.

I believe that the more we evolve, the better we are able to demonstrate integrity and inspire others as leaders, as well as enjoy increasing health, well-being, and prosperity and leave the world a better place for future generations. This series of steps: *from work to play, grow to flow, calm to care,* and *free to love,* represent the stages of vertical evolutionary development.

> *The higher our self-expression and the deeper our self-awareness, the richer our life experience and the greater our soul evolution.*
>
> Antoinette J. Braks

PART 1

The Stages of Leadership Transformation

The stages of leadership development provide an evolutionary perspective on adult development and leadership transformation. As adults, instead of being fixed, immutable identities or personalities when we physically mature, we can evolve further in terms of psychological maturation. The more we mature psychologically, the more empowered and liberated we become to lead our lives with greater wisdom and compassion.

Moreover, the further we progress through these psychological stages of development as we mature, the more effective we become as leaders. As we transform through the stages of development, we become more able and interested in taking responsibility for the care, development, and wellbeing of the people in our charge. This sense of responsibility later extends to wider communities of people, the economy and society as a whole, the health and sustainability of the environment and planet, and current and future generations.

There are five chapters in Part I, the first of which introduces you to the theoretical foundations of the stages of development. The second outlines the strengths and shadows, needs and values, of an executive prototype at each stage. Chapter 3 then zooms in on the distinctions between the predominant conventional leader at the stage of *Achievist* and the much rarer yet urgently needed postconventional leader termed *Synergist*, and otherwise more commonly known as *Strategist*. However, 'strategist' is a term that has a commonplace definition in the corporate world associated with intellectual agility in the development of strategy, whereas the stage of *Synergist* incorporates significantly greater leadership presence and substance.

Chapter 4 sets out the research project to discover if and how executive coaching could enable the transformation from *Achievist* to the intervening stage of *Catalyst* (also called *Individualist* and *Pluralist* by others) and onto *Synergist*. The surprising and inspiring results of the research project are revealed in Chapter 5. It also sets out the key themes in the coaching approach that led to the transformative shifts in stage leadership development.

Chapter 1: Introduction to the Stages of Transformation

Chapter 2: Strengths and Shadows of Executive Prototypes

Chapter 3: The Transformation from *Achievist* to *Synergist*

Chapter 4: The Executive Coaching Research Study

Chapter 5: The Key Themes of Transformative Coaching

1 INTRODUCTION TO THE STAGES OF TRANSFORMATION

Both humanistic psychology and constructive developmental psychology are concerned with evolutionary development. Abraham Maslow was the founder of humanistic psychology. He was concerned with realising our potential in terms of our motives and outcomes, while Robert Kegan, the founder of constructive developmental psychology, explored the inner capacity to see and understand more of the complexities and subtleties of life as we evolve.

After reviewing Maslow's Hierarchy of Needs and Kegan's constructive developmental psychology, we will look at the stages of development based on the research of three of the most eminent female social scientists of our time: Jane Loevinger, Susanne Cook-Greuter, and Terri O'Fallon. Their breakthrough findings lead us to critical insights into the nature and process of stage leadership development.

Maslow's Hierarchy of Needs

The concept of adult human development began with Abraham Maslow (1908–1970). He focused on how people achieved individual wellbeing and personal fulfilment in contrast to the majority of psychologists at the time such as Freud (1856–1939) and Jung (1875–1961), who were focused on the sources and symptoms of psychological dysfunction, the shadow of the human soul. Maslow preferred to give his attention to the inspiring, self-actualising lives led by some of society's most respected leaders.

Based on an empirical study of positive adult development, he identified a staged progression of growth in adulthood, which came to be widely known as the 'Hierarchy of Needs'. Maslow's Hierarchy of Needs comprised:

1 Survival needs for air, water, food, rest, shelter, and clothing;
2 Security needs for physical safety, good health, and economic security;
3 Belonging needs for family, friends, intimacy, colleagues, and community;
4 Self-esteem needs to feel confident, valuable, and worthy of respect; and
5 Self-actualising needs to be authentic, creative, and enjoy a purposeful, aspirational, and meaningful life.

Maslow determined that as each progressive need was met, the following need would demand a person's attention. For instance, once a person's ordinary physical and emotional needs were largely satisfied, they could lean towards spiritual growth with altruistic motives focused on the common good and become self-actualising. He argued that self-actualisation involved a range of distinctive perceptions and perspectives that I have clustered as becoming more aware, accepting, authentic, and astute in relation to our understanding of self and life:

More *aware*
- More perceptive of reality and more comfortable with it;
- More comfortable with detachment, and more interested in privacy and solitude;
- More able to appreciate freshly what one has experienced before;
- More frequently open to peak experiences.

More *accepting*
- More accepting of self, others, and nature;
- More deeply and profoundly experiencing of interpersonal relationships;
- More possessed of *Gemeinschaftsgefühl* (a feeling for the family-hood of man);
- More democratic.

More *authentic*
- More spontaneous, simple, and natural;
- More autonomous, independent of culture and environment, more active as an agent;
- More creative;
- More resistant to enculturation, transcendent of a particular culture.

More *astute*
- More problem centring;
- More discriminating of the differences between means and ends, good and evil;
- More resolving of dichotomies; and
- More philosophical.

These qualities reflect characteristics observed in the later stages of vertical development that I am concerned with here. Maslow suggested that self-actualisation was the pinnacle of psychological health. Later in life, Maslow added a further element, self-transcendence, to reflect the wisdom advanced by psychologist Viktor Frankl (1946), author of *Man's Search for Meaning*.

Based on his experience as a Nazi prisoner-of-war, Frankl found that the prisoners who held onto hope and consistently applied their minds to imagining a better life in the future were more likely to survive incarceration than those who did not. He concluded that people are able to transcend any situation they find themselves in, no matter how bleak, by using the power of the mind and heart. Maslow encapsulated this concept as self-transcendence, the ability to transcend one's situation in honour of the power and grace of self.

Constructive Developmental Psychology

While humanistic psychology focuses on the self in terms of motives, i.e. the 'what' – meeting one's needs in life and later maturing to realise personal growth aspirations and transcending reality – constructive developmental psychology is concerned with the means of construction of our experience of life, i.e. the 'how'. Rather than seeing life as an objective external reality, it is subjective. How we view life depends on *how* we interpret and thereby construct our life experience. We are able to do this with greater subtlety at later stages of development.

> *Constructive-developmental theory thus takes as its subject the growth and elaboration of a person's ways of understanding the self and the world.*
> (McCauley et al., 2006: 635)

Constructive developmental psychology is concerned with developing the constructive lens through which we view our world (Kegan, 1982). It explains that our capacity to perceive and interpret what we see (i.e. our meaning-making capacity) depends on the scope of our lens, on what we are able to *see*. The more we can perceive and interpret as objective reality, rather than part of our subjective identity, the greater our personal power to influence and effect our life experience. The scope of our lens develops as we consciously expand our perspective to appreciate increasing subtleties and complexities such as underlying systemic dynamics.

Kegan labels the series of lenses or meaning-making systems as Levels of Mind: the Sovereign Mind, the Socialised Mind, the Self-Authoring Mind, and the Self-Transforming Mind. The Sovereign Mind is focused on 'me', being self-willed and egotistical. The Socialised Mind is dependent on authority figures such as parents and teachers, and the rules and norms according to which we lead our lives. The Self-Authoring Mind is independent, deciding for oneself what to focus on and pursue, while the Self-Transforming Mind shifts from being concerned with self to developing interdependence with autonomous others.

> *What we mean by maturity in people's thinking is not a matter of how smart they are, but it is a matter of the order of consciousness in which they exercise their smartness or lack of it.*
> (Kegan, 1995: 130)

The level of mind contains our perception of what we can see, how we interpret what we see by way of storytelling, and thereby construct our reality. Because we have the power to develop our capacity to construct this reality, this came to be called constructive developmental psychology. It was a major departure from seeing life as an objective reality to a new understanding of human capacity in that our perception of life is a subjective reality.

> *Just as beauty is in the eye of the beholder, life is in the mind of the perceiver.*

Kegan used this subject/object paradigm to explain progression through the Levels of Mind. What was subject at one level (i.e. part of a person's identity and therefore apparently fixed) became object at a later level, separated from the self where it could be influenced, adapted, and reframed. For instance, at the level of the Socialised Mind, the work we do forms part of our identity: we are a doctor, a teacher, a lawyer, a plumber. Therefore, at this stage, we take any feedback about our work extremely personally. However, once we shift to Self-Authoring, our work becomes something objective that we do, that we have charge of, and can influence and change at will. Feedback then becomes useful in order to realise better results.

Other scientists also adopted the evolutionary pathway in human consciousness in relation to cultural memes and values development (Graves and Beck), faith development (Fowler), moral development (Kohlberg and Gilligan), and development of worldview (Gerber). All showed significant congruence identifying four substantial phases of adult development from pre-conventional to conventional, post-conventional, and the transpersonal. These overlapped with Kegan's Levels of Mind and Maslow's Hierarchy of Needs, as shown in Figure 1.1.

Figure 1.1 Early evolutionary framework

Hierarchy of Needs Maslow	Levels of Mind Kegan	Phases of Development Kohlberg
Transcendent		Transpersonal
Self-Actualising	Self-Transforming Mind	
Self-Esteem	Self-Authoring Mind	Post-conventional
Belonging	Socialised Mind	Conventional
Security	Sovereign Mind	
Survival	Impulsive Mind	Pre-conventional

The Stages of Development

Distinct from other lines of development, such as morals, values, and faith, Jane Loevinger's scientific research focused on the broader concept of ego development. The ego is a holistic construct of a person's identity, their inner psyche or way of being in the world. She found that ego development involved a continuous evolution of this personal holistic intrinsic frame of reference, a lens or mind-view, through a series of qualitatively distinctive stages that are imposed on life experiences to make sense of them, to create meaning.

To calibrate the stages of ego development, Loevinger set up an assessment exercise, the Washington University Sentence Completion Test (WUSCT). It was designed to invite a person to share their thoughts on a set of 36 sentence prompts. She analysed thousands of responses and identified a more calibrated series of qualitatively distinctive stages through the generic phases of development. She found that these perspectives were not just about more complex meaning-making in relation to cognition, but also included the affective (emotions and feelings), relational, and spiritual domains of ego development.

Loevinger found that the stages within each more expansive phase of development were sequential. It was not possible to skip a stage, and everyone followed the same stages of adult development or maturity in the same sequence. The series is also a holarchy. As we progress through the stages, our perspective expands to include our previous mind-views, strengths we have developed, and shadows not yet navigated. We raise our perspective to see more broadly through space and time and deepen our perspective to appreciate greater subtlety and the systemic nature of iterative patterns. Our identity expands to include more of our whole selves, from our egoic self to our holistic self and onto our universal self.

For each level of mind in Kegan's framework, there are two stages of development. And for each phase of development in Kohlberg's framework, there are three stages of development in Loevinger's evidence-based framework. The stages of development did come under some criticism as fuzzy prototypes. However, they constituted a quantum leap to a more precise, sequential, and holarchic way of understanding adult human development.

Susanne Cook-Greuter, a Harvard researcher who studied with Kegan, continued Loevinger's research into ego development. She added further structural understanding to the stages of ego development. Cook-Greuter identified the specific shifts from first person to second person, third person, fourth person, fifth person, and so on, as we move through the stages. We begin with the first person perspective at the early stages preoccupied with self: 'me', the Sovereign Mind. Then we shift to the second person perspective and see the other: 'you', congruent with the Socialised Mind. The third person perspective is more objective, and work becomes separate from self: 'it', and we become Self-Authoring.

The fourth person perspective of 'we' coincides with our embrace of humanity at the Self-Transforming Mind. It includes people such as cousins, immediate past and future generations, and in organisations, the levels beyond our immediate team. On this perspective we embrace diversity, psychodynamics, and inter-systemic dynamics. The fifth person perspective takes this further into several generations, civilisations, and into the transpersonal realm where space and time become increasingly boundless. The sixth person incorporates fourth dimensional reality reaching out to the cosmic transpersonal dimensions of infinite space and eternal time, emptiness of reality, and fullness of possibility.

Cook-Greuter also found that the two stages in each person perspective were quite distinctive. The first stage in each person perspective is an individuation stage and the second, an integration stage. Individuation involves discovering the new terrain, seeing things that were previously imperceptible, experimenting, and learning to navigate and influence what we begin to see more clearly. As a person gradually gains familiarity with their new subtleties of perception, they shift into integration mode and become able to apply their learning by influencing their environment and demonstrating more confident leadership. They become able to act on their world rather than be embedded in it.

This is similar to Kegan's shift from subject to object. It can be compared to shifting from seeing decisions in black and white, either/or, terms in the third person perspective to seeing decision-making in all colour variations at the fourth person perspective. At first, we see colour as separate hues as in the rainbow, as a symbol of diversity. When we start working with the expanse of colours, we learn that combining variations of blue and yellow, for instance, form multiple distinctive hues of green.

It is more comfortable to be in the secondary integration mode, as this phase denotes familiarity with one's surroundings and the capacity to prioritise, structure, integrate, resolve, and expand what is first encountered and perceived as disconnected, random data. A growing sense of mastery and self-assurance to exercise leadership manifests at the integration stage. Thus, a person 'anchors', i.e. feels comfortable and confident, in the integration phase of each couplet and may require more support and guidance during the individuation phase and into the integration phase to sustain their sense of wellbeing on their journey.

Cook-Greuter identified these two-step shifts with numerics for the stages – that is, x/y is an individuation stage from x person perspective to y person perspective, and y is the following integration stage at the y person perspective. Loevinger and Cook-Greuter also named the stages of development. These terms continue to evolve today as various researchers and practitioners select the terms that resonate with their own understanding and application of the stages of human development.

Cook-Greuter also advised that the use of more sophisticated language and sentence construction is transformed significantly through the stages of ego development. As we mature vertically, we also increase our capacity to integrate polarities, see both/and as well as either/or ends of the spectrum, and interweave complex ideas in original, multifaceted ways. She also gave a more holistic orientation to the stages of development beyond Kegan's. Cook-Greuter developed our awareness of the importance of the ever-expanding heart and higher realm of spirit in our evolution as human beings as well as expansiveness of the mind.

Figure 1.2 provides an outline of the phases, needs, and levels of development in relation to the early work on the stages of development, including that of Maslow, Kegan, Kohlberg, Loevinger, and Cook-Greuter, alongside my own phraseology (Preface). The individuation stages are shown in light grey and the integration stages in darker grey. Note that the research by Loevinger and Cook-Greuter divided the Hierarchy of Needs and Levels of Mind into these two-step stages of individuation followed by integration. The new level of need or mind is congruent with the next stage of integration.

Figure 1.2 Phases and early stages framework

Hierarchy of Needs Maslow	Levels of Adult Development Kegan	Phases of Development Kohlberg	Ego Development Loevinger	Ego Development Cook-Greuter	Self Evolution Braks
Transcendent		Transpersonal		6/7 Transpersonal	love
				6 Unitive	free
Self-Actualising	Self-Transforming Mind	Post-conventional	Integrated	5/6 Magician	care
			Autonomous	5 Strategist	calm
Self-Esteem	Self-Authoring Mind		Individualist	4/5 Individualist	flow
			Conscientious	4 Achiever	grow
Belonging	Socialised Mind	Conventional	Self-Aware	3/4 Expert	play
			Conformist	3 Diplomat	work
Security	Sovereign Mind	Pre-conventional	Self-Protective	2/3 Rule-Oriented	
				2 Opportunist	
Survival	Impulsive Mind		Impulsive	1/2 Impulsive	

Tiers and Learning Sequence

Our understanding of stage development has benefited enormously in recent years as a result of the valuable scientific research undertaken by Terri O'Fallon. She offers a ground-breaking structural framework that strengthens the systemic robustness of the vertical stages of ego development.

For decades, the stages had been viewed in the context of pre-conventional, conventional, post-conventional, and transpersonal phases of development. This placed the distinctive stages of development into groups of three as shown in Figure 1.2, albeit Cook-Greuter had pierced through this to identify the person perspectives and the two-step dance process through the stages of individuation and integration.

Through her own empirical research from an integrally informed transcendent perspective, O'Fallon re-engineered the underpinnings of stage development. By viewing the stages in groups of four set out in Tiers, she has revolutionised our understanding of the stages of development as well as the process of development through the stages.

O'Fallon offered the realisation that the trajectory of stage development involves the perception of different types of objects through the evolutionary process. At the early stages we are concerned with Concrete or physical objects – toys, clothes, possessions, houses, and buildings. Then we shift to the world of Subtle or intangible objects – goals, processes, values, relationships, systems, principles, and aspirations as we become more aware of our own identity and the unfolding adventure of life.

This is followed by what O'Fallon calls the MetAware Tier, the transpersonal, where we are aware of awareness. At this point, we have not only become self-aware and socially aware, we have developed a cosmic witnessing perspective. From here we can see and understand not only what is taking place in a situation before us but we have an awareness of the awareness of the individuals operating within a more cosmic universal frame. This enables us to inform and influence the nature of that awareness. The final Unified Tier represents the universe.

Furthermore, O'Fallon discerned a common cyclical learning sequence within each Tier, expanding on Cook-Greuter's discernment of the two-step process of individuation and integration. To explain her revelation, it is important first to have an elementary understanding of the Integral AQAL Model of All Quadrants, All Levels, designed by Ken Wilber, the founder of Integral Theory.

Wilber has undertaken the most extensive cross-cultural research of maps of evolving consciousness to date by reviewing hundreds of premodern, modern, and postmodern cultures. All Levels of individual development are represented by the stages of development described here. All Quadrants of development represent the playing fields of our life expression and experience.

The Levels you are already familiar with. They are the stages of development. However, they apply to both the Individual, as portrayed by Kegan, Loevinger, Cook-Greuter, and O'Fallon, and the Collective, as portrayed by Beck and Cowan in *Spiral Dynamics* (1996) and more recently by Laloux in

Reinventing Organisations (2014). Just as individuals shift from Opportunist to Conformist, Achievist, Catalyst and Synergist (my selection of terms), organisations shift from tribal to institutional, machine, empowered, and organic emergence (red, amber, orange, green, and teal).

In the AQAL Model, the four quadrants form a matrix. The two upper quadrants relate to the Individual and the two lower quadrants relate to the Collective. In addition, the two left-hand quadrants relate to the Interior, and the two right-hand quadrants relate to the Exterior. The Interior of the Individual therefore represents Identity, and the Exterior, Behaviour. The Interior of the Collective is symbolised by Culture, and the Exterior by Structure (see Figure 1.3).

The upper-left Individual Interior forms our inner Identity: our psychology, values, beliefs, intentions, worldview and perspective, that which is not visible to others. The upper-right Individual Exterior incorporates our Behaviour: physiology, skills, habits, responses, demonstrable capabilities, competencies, and neuroscience, elements that can be observed.

The lower-left Collective Interior forms our inner Culture, including invisible elements such as standards, norms, rituals, symbols, values, and practices. The lower-right Collective Exterior represents the Structure or the contextual framework within which we operate. It is made up of policies, laws, processes, systems, organisational design, and regimented pathways.

Figure 1.3 Adapted from the AQAL Model of Integral Theory

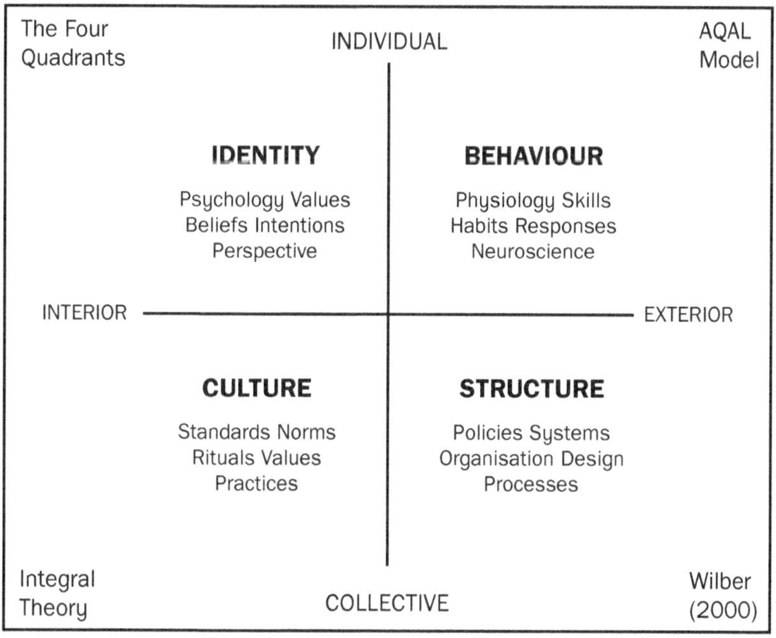

The Four Quadrants	INDIVIDUAL	AQAL Model
	IDENTITY Psychology Values Beliefs Intentions Perspective	**BEHAVIOUR** Physiology Skills Habits Responses Neuroscience
INTERIOR		EXTERIOR
	CULTURE Standards Norms Rituals Values Practices	**STRUCTURE** Policies Systems Organisation Design Processes
Integral Theory	COLLECTIVE	Wilber (2000)

The quadrants are best understood as the terrains in which our self-expression, self- and other-awareness, and our life experience take place. As we explore new terrains at consecutively higher, deeper and broader levels followed by new dimensions of spacetime, our consciousness expands to interpret, integrate, and understand more over longer time horizons and on deeper soul dimensions.

O'Fallon's point was that the stages of leadership development also move through these quadrants in successive fashion. While all four quadrants are in play at any one time, our primary preoccupation shifts from the Individual to the Collective through each Tier. The first two individuation and integration stages in each Tier have a primary focus in the Individual Quadrants of self-development. The subsequent two individuation and integration stages in the Tier primarily focus on the Collective Quadrants of mutual development.

O'Fallon terms the two stages of individuation and integration in the Individual Quadrants as Receptive and Active. At the Receptive stage, we take in all that we see and feel, hear and touch, sense and discern. At the Active stage, we develop the agility and dexterity to work with these objects and perceptions. Thus, as a *Specialist* at the Receptive stage we learn about and become skilled in our craft. As an *Achievist*, we can actively use this knowledge and our new skills to meet other people's needs and achieve specific desired results. Both these stages focus on individual development.

The next two stages in the two-step dance of individuation and integration in the Collective Quadrants are termed Reciprocal and Interpenetrative. They focus on mutual, collective, social, or organisational development. The Reciprocal learning style of the first Collective stage is where we are in relationship with others and with the system. At *Catalyst*, for instance, we begin to appreciate the dynamics of the system we occupy and the emergence that flows from the interactions within the collective. The Interpenetrative learning style of the second stage in the Collective Tier is where we have integrated much of the elements, aspects, and objects within that tier. At *Synergist* in the Subtle Tier, we realise that self and life are inevitably intertwined – i.e. that thoughts become things, that feelings have meaning, that self and other are invariably interconnected, that we play support roles in each other's life stories, and that the microcosm and macrocosm are interwoven beyond our conscious awareness of emergence.

> To understand interpenetration, you might consider the move from either/or to both/and consciousness. In the latter, two aspects remain distinct but are understood to be in a deeper kind of relationship, more interdependent. Interpenetration is the next step in this process, to a recognition of 'one within the other.' The implication of this leads to an understanding of unity beyond distinctions; one is many and many is one. Understanding subtle interpenetration, for example, one can see that, because no one is truly independent of the collectives in which they appear, they cannot truly change without a change in their relationships; likewise, no social system can transform without a transformation of the individuals involved.
>
> (Geoff Fitch, in Gunnlaugson and Brabant, 2016: 81)

Thus O'Fallon's process of stage development fine-tunes the two-step process of individuation and integration that Cook-Greuter identified through each person perspective. The two-step process becomes more of a square dance. First, we dance in the Individual Quadrants of the Concrete Tier with two steps in the first person perspective and then we add the Collective Quadrants of the Concrete Tier with two steps in the second person perspective. Now we have all four quadrants within our spectrum of stage evolution, two Individual and two Collective Quadrants.

As we step into the Individual Quadrants of the Subtle Tier to individuate and integrate the third person perspective, we retain the Concrete Collective as a backdrop while transcending our original first person perspective. Our next evolution to the Collective Quadrants of the Subtle Tier transcend and transform the Concrete Collective as we progressively master the Subtle Collective. We take our evolutionary journey onwards shifting the Individual and Collective developmental stages from primary to secondary relative to the growth edge of our developmental spectrum.

O'Fallon adapted Cook-Greuter's numbering system by identifying the individuation stage as x.0 and the integration stage as x.5, indicating the integration of the new person perspective. This numbering system confirms that the individuation stage is not just an in-between stage between stages x and y as indicated by Cook-Greuter as x/y, but the beginning of a new adventure into the next person perspective of x commencing at x.0 and consolidating at x.5.

O'Fallon's research has transformed our understanding of the stages of development and illuminated our understanding of the evolutionary process through the stages. We now appreciate the shifts through the Tiers of objects, the shifts from the Individual to the Collective, and the distinctive two-step process of individuation and integration as an iterative learning sequence within the Individual and Collective Quadrants in each Tier. Evolutionary development is a two-step square dance across a spectrum of stages through which we express ourselves and experience life simultaneously. Figure 1 4 sets out the stages as understood from earlier research through to O'Fallon's latest breakthrough insights into stage development.

To be clear in relation to the later stages of development this book is most concerned with, I would like to draw your attention to the positioning of O'Fallon's *Pluralist* (Cook-Greuter: *Individualist*; Joiner and Josephs: *Catalyst*), between *Achievist* and *Synergist*. In Kegan's framework, the *Pluralist* is consumed within the Self-Authoring Mind followed by the *Synergist* invoking the much rarer Self-Transforming Mind.

Because of this, I suggest that Kegan's framework is not as conducive to leadership development as O'Fallon's Tier-based STAGES model due to the concealment of the individuation developmental stage within the prior Level of Mind. The individuation stage is the stepping-off point that is ideally explicitly demarcated so that it is clearly seen and understood to both attract and expedite the consequent two stages of development.

Kohlberg's demarcation between Conventional and Post-conventional phases of development is more useful yet also misleading. While it marks the

Figure 1.4 From phases to tiers in stage development

Adult Development Kegan	Phases Kohlberg	Tiers O'Fallon	Quadrants O'Fallon	Learning Sequence O'Fallon	Stages O'Fallon	Stages Braks
	Transpersonal	METAWARE	Collective	Interpenetrative	6.5 Illumined	
				Reciprocal	6.0 Universal	Opportunist
			Individual	Active	5.5 Transpersonal	Rule-based
Self-Transforming Mind				Receptive	5.0 Construct-Aware	Conformist
	Post-conventional	SUBTLE	Collective	Interpenetrative	4.5 Strategist	Specialist
				Reciprocal	4.0 Pluralist	Achiever
Self-Authoring Mind			Individual	Active	3.5 Achiever	Catalyst
	Conventional			Receptive	3.0 Expert	Synergist
Socialised Mind		CONCRETE	Collective	Interpenetrative	2.5 Conformist	Constructivist
	Pre-conventional			Reciprocal	2.0 Rule-Oriented	Alchemist
Sovereign Mind			Individual	Active	1.5 Egocentric	Ironist
Impulsive Mind				Receptive	1.0 Impulsive	Holist

new adventure in post-conventional that begins at *Catalyst* and continues through to *Synergist*, it then includes and thereby conceals the next point of departure into the MetAware Tier at *Constructivist*. Thus, while the beginning of the Post-conventional phase of development coincides with the shift to the Subtle Collective, the Post-conventional phase of development also unwittingly subsumes the first stage of the MetAware Tier, hiding its significance.

A note on the term *Constructivist*, equivalent to O'Fallon's *Construct-Aware* stage, the first Receptive stage in the MetAware Individual Quadrants. Here you may encounter some confusion with previous texts as *Alchemist* is often shown as the stage following *Synergist*. However, O'Fallon's four-step approach through each tier suggests that the Active nature of the *Alchemist* must follow an interceding Receptive MetAware stage to reflect the initial evolutionary process of an individuation stage in the MetAware Tier.

In O'Fallon's Tier-based structure, the shift from *Achievist* to *Catalyst* and *Synergist* is explicit. It is marked by the shift from the Individual Quadrants to the Collective Quadrants in the Subtle Tier. This is a two-parameter stage shift in terms of Quadrant and Learning Style, i.e. from the Individual to the Collective and from Active to Reciprocal.

While you might assume, as I did at first, that O'Fallon's Learning Sequence follows each of the four quadrants, the interesting thing is that they do not. This is particularly important if we are to better understand development through the stages. To confirm, the first two stages of Receptive and Active in each Tier are set in the upper Individual Quadrants and the second set of two stages in each tier, Reciprocal and Interpenetrative, are set in the lower Collective Quadrants. However, I now invite you to take a moment to pause and open your mind for another layer of complexity.

There are zones within each quadrant, an Inner Zone of developing awareness and an Outer Zone of embodied manifestation. O'Fallon identified that the individuation stage is set in the Inner Zones of the two relevant Quadrants, and the integration stage is set in the Outer Zones in the two relevant Quadrants. The terrain of understanding, our Interior and Exterior, are interlinked. It is our agility and dexterity in the broader terrain which changes from a process of absorption, Reception and Reciprocity, in the Inner Zones of the Individual and Collective Quadrants, to a process of engagement, Active and Interpenetrative, in the Outer Zones of the Individual and Collective Quadrants, respectively (Figure 1.5).

During the individuation stages we look within. We are developing awareness of our inner world in relation to perceiving a new layer of subtle complexity in relation to the source of our Identity: our values, beliefs, and psychology, and our Behaviour: our actions, responses, and capabilities. During the individuation phase we are attempting to make sense of what we think and believe, and what we see and do. During the integration phase, we've made a lot of progress in sense-making and can act much more influentially in the Outer Zone – as leaders! This understanding is critical to understanding the developmental process from *Achievist* to *Catalyst* and onto *Synergist*.

Figure 1.5 The Zones adapted from the AQAL Model

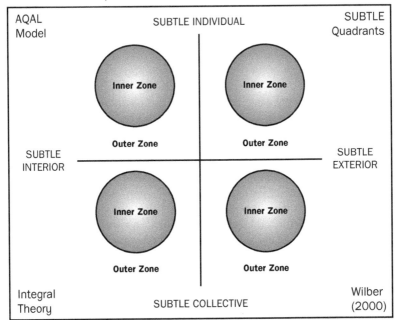

The Spectrum Stage Shift

The latest advances in constructive developmental psychology suggest that we evolve through distinctive stages of development that form a sequential holarchy, i.e. each stage follows an explicit order and is included in the following stage. Rather than form a staircase, the stages can be pictured as a trajectory on an expanding 3D spiral within a widening sphere of leadership capacity. The stages shift through the Concrete, Subtle, and MetAware Tiers and onto the Unified Tier, transitioning from the Individual to the Collective Quadrants in each Tier. The implication of this is that we each carry a spectrum of stages with us, both Individual and Collective, as we are always operating as individuals with others in a given social context as part of our self-expression and life experience.

Amongst this spectrum of stages in a profile, Cook-Greuter calibrated a person's stage of development by nominating their primary stage and secondary stage. The primary stage was where most responses were scored in the Washington University Sentence Completion Test (WUSCT) based on a weighted average, with later stages attracting increasingly higher weightings. The WUSCT was first developed by Loevinger and later enhanced by Cook-Greuter to incorporate more later stages. The secondary stage was where the next largest weighted average of responses were scored. Almost always, these were neighbouring stages: a primary and a secondary stage.

Bill Torbert, a one-time colleague of Cook-Greuter and exponent of stage development redefined as the same series of action-logics, identified three key stages in a person's profile, their Centre of Gravity, Trailing Edge, and Leading Edge. A person moves into their leading edge when they have the support and encouragement of others and may default to their trailing edge when under stress or encountering foreign situations. This led to a three-dimensional approach to comprehending a person's stage development.

O'Fallon's breakthrough research suggests that we are composed of a wider spectrum of four neighbouring stages, including both Individual and Collective Quadrants. Indeed, O'Fallon advised in one of her webinars on stage development that the average stages profile comprises four stages, which I have also found to be the case after reviewing 50+ client profiles. While profiles may also become truncated or extended at any one moment of time, it seems wise to recognise that at all times we are operating with both an Individual and Collective context in mind, one in the foreground and the other emergent.

Given the nature of individuation and integration being two steps on the one journey, it seems to me that it is not really possible to ground ourselves in an individuation stage. We remain grounded in the prior integrated stage as the individuation stage is a learning phase in the Inner Zones of the next Individual or Collective Quadrants. Thus, in my view, a person can anchor themselves i.e. have their Centre of Gravity in an integration stage (i.e. *Conformist, Achievist* or *Synergist*) but not in an individuation stage (i.e. *Specialist, Catalyst* or *Constructivist*).

The interesting thing therefore for the shift from *Achievist* to *Catalyst* and onto *Synergist*, is that, even at *Catalyst*, we are still oriented to the Concrete Collective as we have still not yet learned how to manifest in the Outer Zones of the Subtle Collective. This holds us along the four-stage spectrum axis of *Conformist–Specialist–**Achievist**–Catalyst*, anchored in the integration zone of *Achievist*. Our growth is stalled until we develop the capacity to transcend the Concrete Collective and co-create a new Subtle Collective at the final Interpenetrative stage and integrate our new identity totally within the Subtle Tier as *Achievist–Catalyst–**Synergist**–Constructivist*.

Further to the spectrum of stages within a person's profile, O'Fallon and psychotherapist colleague, Barta, also identify peak experiences to later stages and shadow crashes to earlier stages as part of our stages repertoire. Peak experiences such as a sense of unified blissful wonder with the cosmos, perceiving 4D reality or experiencing transcendent enlightenment, can arise during meditation or during normal waking life if a person is accustomed to undertaking lengthy meditations.

Shadow crashes occur when the underlying foundations of a new stage of development are insufficient to sustain further vertical development, e.g. a shadow crash from growth in the Subtle Reciprocal stage of *Catalyst* to the Concrete Reciprocal stage of *Rule-based* occurs when earlier life experiences at that stage have yet to be fully integrated. This is absolutely normal as we pass through the Concrete Tier as children and simply do not have the cognitive or emotional awareness to process or understand our life experiences at this first Tier of consciousness.

Thus, a person's stage of development is really a spectrum of developmental stages. From the above account, it could be said that we operate largely from a primary integrated stage, default to a secondary stage immediately following or preceding that stage if feeling supported or stressed respectively, a leading edge and a trailing edge that falls beyond and before these two stages, as well as a cornucopia of peak experiences and shadow crashes to fully constitute our human experience.

Chapter 1: Key Points

The world we each perceive is a subjective reality based on the lens through which we view it. The stronger and wider the lens, the more we see. This progressive series of lenses has been articulated as stages of ego or leadership development that enable us to realise our full human potential. The following key points elaborate on this.

1 Maslow's Hierarchy of Needs involves self-actualising our human potential to become more aware, accepting, authentic, and astute, and then move onto self-transcendence.
2 The trajectory towards self-actualisation is supported by constructive developmental psychology, which articulates our capacity to increasingly construct our world through distinctive and progressive stages of adult development.
3 Our capacity to construct our world by perceiving and interpreting what we see (i.e. our meaning-making capacity) depends on the scope of our lens to appreciate increasing interpersonal subtleties and complex inter-systemic dynamics.
4 Kegan articulated the progression in meaning-making capacity in terms of shifts from the Sovereign Mind, Socialised Mind, and Self-Authoring Mind to the Self-Transforming Mind.
5 Loevinger refined this progression into more discrete stages of ego development, a holistic construct incorporating cognitive, affective, relational, and spiritual domains.
6 Cook-Greuter advised that the stages are sequential and holarchic through a two-step process of individuation and integration to realise progressive person perspectives.
7 O'Fallon identified a systemic framework that underpins the stages of development incorporating four learning styles: Receptive, Active, Reciprocal and Interpenetrative, spread across four quadrants: the first two Individual and the next two Collective, in each of three tiers: Concrete, Subtle, and MetAware followed by the Unified Tier.
8 The shift from *Achievist* to *Synergist* involves a shift from the Self-Authoring to the Self-Transforming Mind, from Conventional to Postconventional,

from the third person "it" perspective to the fourth person "we" perspective, and from the Outer Zones of Individual manifestation to the Outer Zones of Collective transformation in the Subtle Tier.

9 A person's stage-spectrum includes a primary integrated stage, a secondary neighbouring stage, a leading edge, and a trailing edge, as well as peak experiences into later stages and shadow crashes into earlier stages to gradually build and strengthen a robust character where we can demonstrate consistent integrity.

10 The shift from *Achievist* to *Synergist* involves a Spectrum Stage Shift from *Conformist–Specialist–**Achievist**–Catalyst* to *Achievist–Catalyst–**Synergist**–Constructivist* –the anchoring point in each stage-spectrum being the later stage of integration in each spectrum.

Next Chapter

This chapter has introduced the theoretical foundations of stage development to provide you with a conceptual overview. In the following chapters, I offer you a synopsis of each of the distinctive stages of development, describing the parameters, strengths and shadows, and the needs and values that become important at each stage. You will gain a good understanding of the executive prototypes at each of the stages that are evident in the workplace.

2 STRENGTHS AND SHADOWS OF EXECUTIVE PROTOTYPES

Executives operate from a distinctive mindset at each stage of development. At earlier stages, leaders are more self-oriented, concerned with their personal insecurities and concerns, risk-averse, fear-based, and full of self-doubt. At later stages, leaders become more confident and increasingly oriented to the common good and the wellbeing of the broader community. This represents a shift from ego-centric to eco-centric.

I explain the strengths that executives develop at each stage of development and the types of role and role levels where a person can excel at each stage. Later stages of development have been repeatedly correlated to increased leadership responsibilities and effectiveness (Kuhnert and colleagues).

Another aspect explored at each stage are the shadow aspects. These may relate to strengths taken to excess or aspects of identity that render a person short-sighted or limited in their capacity to see and overcome personal challenges. Often they relate to the degree of emotional and spiritual intelligence of the person at each stage of development.

The following provides an outline of the needs and values of a person at each stage of development, their strengths and shadows, and a general description of a typical executive prototype with their centre of gravity at that stage.

OPPORTUNIST

The *Opportunist* is congruent with Kegan's Sovereign Mind and, in O'Fallon's framework, is the first Active driver in the Concrete Tier. It literally describes the toddler who declares 'Mine' in respect of everything that appeals to them and steals from the cookie jar. Even with crumbs on their face, they will deny that they stole anything as everything belongs to them. This is the first person perspective: life revolves around me.

Needs/Values

The *Opportunist* is concerned with survival and security, Maslow's first two needs. They are self-interested, relatively isolated, and will try to get away with whatever they can. They operate on a day-by-day or minute-by-minute basis without care for the consequences. Their view of the world is that it is unsafe, and everyone is assumed to be an enemy. They play only to their own advantage based on their impulses. Their language repertoire is very limited and polarised.

Kegan cited the example of a person who was in court for not paying their bill in a restaurant. His answers were very straightforward. Why did he do this? He dined at the restaurant because he was hungry and he was shown to a table. He didn't pay because he didn't have the money. This is an *Opportunist* perspective without the deceit that often accompanies it in adults.

Strengths

Opportunists quite simply see opportunities. They are able to scan their immediate environment and find and/or steal a good deal or a good idea. This talent is well-developed by traders, agents, and pickpockets! If they're acting on your behalf and the role does not require a lot of subtlety or nuance, then they're equipped for the role.

Shadow

The adult *Opportunist* lives in fear, trusts no one, and operates largely in fight, flight or freeze mode. However, when our safety or security is threatened by a restructure or insolvency, or we fear not getting what we want or need such as a promotion during a time when we are dealing with emotional or economic pressures, it is relatively easy to regress back to the level of the *Opportunist* as a shadow crash, and resolve our situation based on self-interest alone.

Executive Prototype

In 1995, some 4% of the executive population were anchored at *Opportunist* (Cook-Greuter, 1999), although this proportion has since fallen to 1% (PwC, 2015).

In the corporate workplace, the *Opportunist* is often deceptive and manipulative. They are the executives who steal your ideas without recognising their source, who always blame others when things go wrong, and seem to be unavailable when immediate help is needed. They will attack in self-defence when feeling threatened and are completely averse to feedback. They will go behind your back to advance their own agenda and annihilate yours. They play power politics and win–lose. They believe that they are on their own in the world and must protect their own interests at all times.

CONFORMIST   *work*

Conformists correlate with Maslow's (1962) need to belong. They also correlate with the final Interpenetrative stage in O'Fallon's (2011) Concrete Tier. At this stage, teenagers often dress alike or portray physical symbols to identify with a certain clique. Families, clubs, gangs, churches, armies, and tribes fall within the *Conformist* mentality.

They are good citizens, loyal friends, and amenable family members. Their interpenetrative sense is seen in externally visible style choices, especially as teenagers and young adults, or when they join an organisation that requires a specific uniform or style of dress. They will use their physical appearance and habits, vocabulary, and tone to look the same as the people they identify with, first their family, then their friends, and later the larger clubs, organisations or movements they become members of.

Needs/Values

The *Conformist* decides to play it safe. While they still view the world as a very challenging place to inhabit, they believe that if they abide by all the rules and do what people in higher authority ask or tell them to do, they will be safe. Therefore, they conform. They hold a fully formed second person perspective and are aware of me and you as separate people, and also very much resonate with "us and them" i.e., people like us, and them, people who look and sound different and therefore are not to be trusted.

Strengths

The *Conformist* is superb with day-to-day familiar routines and processes that require little customisation or adaptation. They enjoy the sameness and gain in self-confidence from their ability to execute or implement the same processes effectively to their manager's satisfaction. Provided they do not need to negotiate their manager's time or navigate people concerns, the *Conformist* can be a superb executive assistant, coordinator, or administrator.

Shadow

Conformists use reactive emotional strategies to get what they want. The three key strategies are appeasing others by being nice to them and bending over backwards to fit in – usually in relation to more senior people; controlling others by criticising, berating, and offending others – usually in relation to more junior people; or otherwise withdrawing from people altogether by avoiding all communication and even eye contact. If a *Conformist* does not feel accepted, they will generally react in one of these ways in an attempt to stay safe.

All of these are unconscious, emotionally manipulative techniques that produce workplace drama in the form of passive-aggressive behaviour manifesting in bullies and victims. We subconsciously base our boss-subordinate and peer-based interpersonal strategies on those we employed to get what we wanted as a child within the comparable context of parent–child and sibling dynamics. By unravelling the psychodynamics of past family-based relationships, it is possible to source and resolve the cause of a person's fears and concerns.

Executive Prototype

As executives, *Conformists* are risk-averse and will only take action if instructed to do so. Most will need a step-by-step approach mapped out for them so that there are no surprises. Voluntary participation will be relatively limited but they will put the effort in during work hours.

In complying, *Conformists* give away their personal authentic power to positional authority. This leads to a sense of personal ineptitude that moves them to complain. In other words, when we give our personal power away to comply with others, we address this imbalance by complaining about others. If you know anyone in your workplace who complains a lot, they will be operating from a *Conformist* mindset.

Around 10% of the executive population were anchored at *Conformist* in 1995 (Cook-Greuter, 1999), but this has now fallen to just 1% (PwC, 2015). It is a common fall-back position when executives are uncertain about the integrity of their managers. They become obliging and obedient to remain safe and sure, keeping evidence of their compliance to stay out of trouble.

SPECIALIST   *play*

The *Specialist* is a novice. Based on O'Fallon's STAGES model (2011), this is a three-parameter quantum shift into a completely new worldview. It is an entirely new orientation from the Concrete to the Subtle Tier, from the prior

Collective to the new Individual, and from the predictability and mastery of Interpenetrative to the unknown and uncertainty at Receptive.

The *Specialist* embarks on their individual development emerging from the rules-based, authoritarian Collective of the *Conformist*. They experience the desire to develop their own independent identity and role in life beyond the group or groups to which they belong. It can be quite a disorienting period, as much of everything that is now perceived is new, intangible, and barely distinguishable.

Needs/Values

At this stage, the *Specialist* develops their own craft or expertise, often working with lots of data and detail, techniques and processes to gain a better understanding of how things work. The focus is on developing excellence in their domain of interest, work or study that facilitates the emergence of their own competence and self-esteem. This stage develops post-secondary school as young adults take up their first job, undertake an apprenticeship or internship, or move into tertiary education. All their traditional and comforting structures such as home, school, and local community often fall away.

There is significant neurological development at this time in that a person begins to experience beta brain wave activity – commonly described as 'busy beta'. The average age for this brain wave change is 19 (Amen, 1998). This stage can continue well into a person's twenties and beyond as they polish and perfect their skills and capabilities. Many *Specialists* are in specialist, technical, and functional roles.

Strengths

The *Specialist* develops a third person perspective that enables them to observe others in transactional relationships with each other, as well as look at information objectively and critically. While a second person perspective can stand alongside another person and explain what they might do in their situation, a third person perspective enables a person to look objectively at a situation and view multiple options for decision-making in a rational way.

They are able to argue their own position, sometimes in oppositional fashion dismissing others' views and concerns. The *Specialist* prides themselves on being 'right', having the last word and standing out from others. They seek and enjoy recognition from highly respected subject matter experts for their individual talents and accomplishments, and no longer gain as much satisfaction from the approval of those in authority. They want to be seen and respected for their differences and special talents that set them apart rather than for what they have in common with others.

Shadow

Specialists taken to extreme can become argumentative, opinionated, and oppositional. 'Yes, but' is a common phrase used by *Specialists*. They can show contempt for the views of those perceived to be less expert and may even ridicule them to feel 'better than'. This can lead to a distancing from others and arrogance. Logic rules. They hold high ethical and moral standards in relation to rules and responsibilities, and will label non-compliant behaviours as simply 'wrong'.

However, when their work or behaviour fails to meet their own exacting standards, they are just as critical of themselves. The universal shadow of being 'not good enough' is found here. It is a psychological response related to the fact that the *Specialist* identifies with their work. If their work falls short, they feel that they are personally falling short.

In other words, in Kegan's subject/object framework, they are 'subject' to their work, while rules and norms have become 'object'. This leads to many *Specialists* becoming perfectionists, constantly striving for higher standards of excellence. The mantra 'do your best' is symbolic of the *Specialist*.

Executive Prototype

In an organisational setting, the *Specialist's* focus on continuous improvement and finding alternative solutions is an asset in relation to the enhancement of standard business operating processes. Their logical presentation based on scientifically rigorous evidence enables them to gain consensus and win approval for business proposals. This preoccupation with perfection can also become a flaw. Their endless pursuit of micro improvement leads to missed deadlines, higher costs, and potentially unneeded or impractical additions.

As leaders, they can become micro-managers as they are so focused on the details and doing things the 'one, right way', they can take a 'my way or the highway' type of approach. This leads to many a frustrated employee also wishing to find their own 'best way' to carry out a particular activity.

Because a person is Receptive at this point, providing a range of options instigates the empowering process of making one's own choices and then seeing how they pan out. However, this is not easy for *Specialists*. They only learn to categorise, sort, and prioritise as they progress towards the next integration stage of *Achievist*. It helps to set priorities for them and then with them as they develop their self-esteem and learn to become more objective and decisive.

Their sense of time is moment-by-moment. *Specialists* can easily be pulled in multiple directions at once, maintaining a smiling exterior while struggling to work out what to do next and for whom. They have not yet developed a sense of priorities. Unless these are identified for them and they are visually and clearly articulated, a *Specialist* can easily become overwhelmed and very confused as to what their role really is. Some cut themselves off from all the disruptive noise and continue to work on the one thing that most interests them.

A key challenge for the *Specialist* is their relationship with time. At this stage of their development, timeliness is less important than the excellence and completeness of their work. Thus, while they may juggle many tasks, they will not necessarily complete them on time, or indeed appreciate any deadlines or milestones that they are actively working towards. Their awareness of time is still very much the same day, week or perhaps month, so they are very focused on what is current and their need to perfect their work.

Today, *Specialists* comprise some 10% of the executive population (PwC, 2015), at least from among those who are investing in stage leadership development. In 1995, they made up the majority of executives at around 38% (Cook-Greuter, 1999), just prior to the *Achievist* orientation becoming prevalent.

ACHIEVIST   *grow*

The *Achievist* represents the final stage in the conventional world. It is a consolidation mode where the person feels comfortable, a sense of having arrived and pride in having developed a certain mastery of life. In O'Fallon's Tier model, the *Achievist* moves into the Active modality within the Subtle Tier still focused largely on themselves as an individual contributor, team, or divisional or organisational leader.

Regardless of their relationships and responsibilities, their view of the world is largely still constituted by 'me' and my team, division, business, or organisation. This stage of development is their opportunity to find out what they can achieve in the world. From Kegan's (1982) perspective, the *Achievist* is Self-Authoring for the first time. They feel confident setting goals, making decisions, and directing others.

Needs/Values

The *Achievist* sets specific goals and strives to achieve the results they want. Time horizons open up for them into the future in that they are able to set goals three to five years hence and create a specific step-by-step action plan as to how those goals will be achieved. Their mature third person perspective enables them to prioritise both goals and activities, and create feedback loops by way of milestones, deadlines, and key performance indicators that enable them to measure and monitor performance over time.

While the *Specialist* was able to work towards a blurry possible future, the *Achievist* begins to envisage their most desired future outcomes and can contrast this with the past. They learn to understand and appreciate more why things went the way they did historically and what to do differently in the time ahead to create a better future. They are active learners and agile doers.

Strengths

Achievists work incredibly hard to achieve their goals. Their developing ability to set goals, make plans, focus attention, juggle priorities, create strategies, implement initiatives, take risks, and monitor progress enables many *Achievists* to become high performers in their industry. The *Achievist* can manage the downside of things going wrong, resolve problems as they arise, and anticipate rival activities that might threaten their own success. This enables them to become effective and efficient competitors. The *Achievist* competes side by side with others to win market share. They are happy to play win–lose. 'When the going gets tough, the tough get going' is an apt representation of the *Achievist*.

They focus on effectiveness rather than excellence, and fit for purpose rather than perfection. Efficiency becomes important and 'good enough' is indeed good enough if the work meets clearly set expectations. Their best work is not defined by its high quality but by realising a competitive standard on time within budget that ensures client and customer satisfaction. Time is money. The audience, not the author, is the arbiter, after clarifying set goals and expectations from the outset in the form of informal or contractual agreements.

This is the first stage at which the feedback loop on work quality and output by both customers and managers is not taken personally. The *Achievist* no longer identifies with their work; their work is now 'object'. Feedback on their work is gratefully received and valued by the *Achievist* with a view to responding actively to better match expectations and agreed performance outcomes in the future.

The *Achievist's* ability to take an objective third person perspective on their work also applies to their thoughts, feelings, behaviours, and impulses. This meta-cognitive facility that emerged at *Specialist* is mastered by the *Achievist*. They come to realise that their thoughts, feelings, actions, and impulses form a linear causal thread and, most importantly, that they can intervene and rearrange or reconstitute their thoughts, feelings, and impulses to realise better outcomes.

Cognitive behaviour coaching approaches are therefore highly effective. Affirmations, thinking through their emotional responses to emotions they have experienced, also become tools and techniques *Achievists* can learn and activate to generate higher individual performance. Their perspective lifts from a downward blinkered silo focus to a forward-looking goal focus.

Shadow

The *Achievist* is driven to succeed and gives everything they have to their work. Their identification with the results they achieve and the fact that there are more targets next week, next month, and next year sets them on a trajectory of enterprise, creativity, and ongoing compulsion to achieve and do more. They can easily become bound up into being continuously and frantically busy on the treadmill of work and become a workaholic.

This form of addiction is very typical of the *Achievist*. Their constant wish is to do more, achieve more, have more, and give more. 'More' shouts loud and clear. This is particularly so if there is little sense of completion or celebration following lots of effort for the sometimes worn out, and occasionally burnt out, high-performing *Achievist*.

The *Achievist's* relationships are transactional. They will bring people along through what is appropriately called 'buy-in'. This means that people will generally have the opportunity to share their views but will nevertheless be unilaterally told what is going to happen and given limited choices either to get on board with the new plan or to get off the bus. Profits, market share, technology shifts, and other new threats and opportunities will take priority over people, whether it be their livelihood, family, health, or wellbeing.

At some point, some *Achievists* wonder if there might be more to life than more material goods and better results. They begin to feel burnt out, dissatisfied with their most intimate relationships, and consider taking time-out to relate genuinely to others. Sometimes they experience a mid-life crisis, a serious setback, divorce, or health issue. At this point, they question life and begin to look for new answers.

However, there are also many *Achievists* who enjoy their dominance in the corporate landscape and world affairs. They prefer to protect their positional authority and maintain the status quo as it serves them well, at least on the surface.

Executive Prototype

Achievists form the largest proportion of the executive population: close to 33% in 1995 (Cook-Greuter, 1999) and 60% in 2005, and still over 50% in 2015 (PwC, 2015). They are the archetypal hunter and committed capitalist.

They are very happy to work with others and their team members, and they can lead divisions and organisations extremely effectively and efficiently although not always ethically. *Achievists* focus on creating a positive atmosphere contrasting a positive outlook with the 'not good enough' worldview of the *Specialist* and leveraging people's strengths with a keen eye on deliverables and results.

In discussing issues with their peers or other stakeholders, *Achievists* are happy to 'agree to disagree' rather than take time to explore the concerns of others. They are in charge and enjoy controlling others by giving directions and advice. There is no need to compromise unless the other person happens to be an important customer who could move to a competitor, or a more senior executive who has the power to impact their career.

Achievists tend to be strong negotiators and highly commercially focused. In counterpoint, when *Achievists* realise that a conflict will inhibit progress, they can and do engage with others with some sensitivity and endeavour to influence them in positive ways to overcome the current obstacle and realise the desired results (Rooke and Torbert, 2005). However, this is still largely a rational response to the extent necessary to break through a business challenge. Genuine mutual relationships only emerge at the next stage of Reciprocity.

Achievists make great project managers, change managers, salespeople, and sales managers; they are the quintessential manager extraordinaire. Their decision-making, planning, and delegating skills become finely tuned at this stage of development.

CATALYST   *flow*

The *Catalyst* is the first post-conventional individuation stage and, in O'Fallon's model, is moving from the Individual Active phase into the Collective domain of Reciprocity, a two-parameter shift. It represents a leap into a new growth zone and another unfamiliar world. The *Catalyst* is focused on understanding their inner world: their thoughts and feelings, motives and fears, reactions and responses, and their deepest desires and aspirations in relationship with others.

By exploring their inner world, and inquiring into others' experiences and perceptions, they become more intuitive and understanding, more insightful and purposeful. *Catalysts* ask existential questions: 'Why?', 'Why am I here?', 'Who am I?', and 'What is the meaning of life?'

Needs/Values

The *Catalyst* is no longer driven by deficiency needs but by growth needs. A person at *Catalyst* moves into their personal growth zone where growing and evolving becomes their natural way of being. Even though the challenges they encounter along the way may be unfamiliar and disconcerting, for the participant, life is forever enriched.

A person shifts from being satisfied with a life based on cause and effect to feeling their way forward in the world despite uncertainty and adversity in order to lead a more purposeful and fulfilling life based on conscious intention, committed action, and ethical considerations. The implications of commercial results are considered more broadly beyond shareholder returns in terms of their impact on health and wellbeing, environmental sustainability, social impact, and community interests.

The *Catalyst* wishes to explore different ways of living life with reference to values, morals, and ethics. They become concerned about others and the environment. Their interest in others and appreciation of the value of others' perceptions enables them to recognise the uniqueness of others and the importance of diversity. They advocate for human rights in all forms.

With their new fourth person perspective, *Catalysts* can see into the dynamic interplay of people as an objective bystander. They see the dynamics across different generations and across many levels within the organisation. They begin to tune into the systemic context at work and learn to appreciate the normative effect of culture. They come to see how the past influences the present with repeating patterns of behaviour and interpersonal dynamics.

Strengths

Awareness is a key word for the *Catalyst*, as is respect: both self-respect and respect for others. This is a key shift from implementing the transactional means to achieve specific ends to ensuring that the means employed are mutually respectful and appreciative of others, regardless of their capabilities. Their attention extends from 'what', to 'how' and 'why'. Their focus expands from forward to inward.

In their view, everyone is entitled to a voice, and they realise that collaboration – thinking together, learning together, exploring together, and then deciding together – is essential to generate new solutions and accomplish mutually beneficial outcomes. The *Catalyst* talks 'with' people rather than 'at' them, sees assumptions that others are making, and is cognisant of the defensive behaviours that people adopt to avoid emotional issues. However, they have yet to realise the extent of their influence and power in shaping the collective. This only emerges at the next stage. For now, they learn to navigate.

Shadow

The shadow of the *Catalyst* is in their uncertainty and confusion. They can still adopt the forward propulsion of the *Achievist*, but they are becoming much more mindful of 'how' work is accomplished rather than driving for results. At this first post-conventional stage they break out of the conventional capitalist model of the world and seek to develop personal alignment with values that they are only beginning to understand the impact and implications of.

This makes a *Catalyst* more of an inquirer and facilitator, rather than a manager. They will now be bored as project managers yet adept as change leaders but not yet ready to become divisional, organisational, industry or socially transformative leaders. At early *Catalyst* they are very self-preoccupied and then gradually lean into genuine emotionally intimate relationships in order to better understand differences amongst self and others. As a leader they can therefore be best charged with cross-boundary engagement processes and cross-sector discovery projects rather than typical results-oriented workplace assignments.

Executive Prototype

Catalysts enjoy bringing about change as change leaders – in contrast to change managers who model *Achievists*. *Catalysts* are focused on genuinely engaging others, getting and using their input, igniting change, and working across boundaries. Their focus turns from the impact of their work on customers and clients to the input into the design and nature of the work itself through active early and continuous engagement with all stakeholders. Empowering processes are extremely important to them. They are attuned to leveraging strengths, investing in personal growth, and collaborating with others to begin to exercise mutual power to co-create the best possible outcomes for the whole community. This aspect matures further at the next stage.

Catalysts are the fastest growing proportion of the executive population. The inward focus of authentic leadership programs are geared to develop *Catalyst* capacity. While comprising just 10% of the executive population in 1995 (Cook-Greuter, 1999), they increased to 23% in 2005 and reached 33% in 2015 (PwC, 2015). This reflects the need for organisations to collaborate more across boundaries, innovate across product and service categories, and shift beyond shareholders to the conscious capitalist mindset of meeting the needs of multiple diverse stakeholders.

The capacity to genuinely innovate and collaborate is initiated at *Catalyst*. With this mindset, the inner world of the individual becomes more important than the external world within which they operate. In other words, they heed their intuition and feelings to make decisions and generate new insights and ideas. They begin to think more radically and gradually feel their way into confidently taking inspired action rather than relying purely on their rational logic.

They also listen from a much deeper place of inquiry and can therefore create a deeper connection with others and develop the ability to build genuine trust with others. This authentic way of relating initiates change in the Collective context they engage in. Many words beginning with 'In' are associated with the *Catalyst* worldview as they begin to explore their inner world: insight, innovation, intrinsic, innate, inquiry, introspection, intricate, inclusive, inquisitive, interest, intimacy, intuition, interweaving, interpretation and inspiration. They experiment with the value and opportunity of interdependence.

SYNERGIST   *calm*

The *Synergist* consolidates their journey through the Subtle Tier. They integrate their identity at the new inter-systemic, interpenetrative collective and are now able to transcend and transform the previous Concrete collective. This is a significant culmination of deep personal work in relation to cultivating their identity and integrity. They have developed an expanded capacity to integrate the broader organisational and industry context they are surrounded by and yet an integral part of.

Once the many experiences and objects in the Subtle Tier are categorised, prioritised, and situated in the wider mind-space, the *Synergist* becomes very agile at zooming-in and zooming-out on situations to interpenetrate them and choose the right action in the moment, perceptively appreciating the opportunity, subtlety, systemic complexity, and wider context simultaneously.

The *Synergist* has adopted the Self-Transforming Mind defined by Kegan. They are a masterpiece-in-progress, in every moment understanding how they need to be to accommodate yet influence and advocate the diverse needs and goals of all people involved in any given situation. Thus, they are transforming their intention and attention to generate increasing alignment amongst multiple interests and different time horizons. Their broader, deeper, and longer-term perspective, along with higher aspirations enables them to bring many people together to gain and build momentum towards realising synergistic outcomes.

Needs/Values

The *Synergist* is defined by their capacity to engage more collaboratively, think more systemically, demonstrate more curiosity in relation to other people's viewpoints, actively step in to resolve conflict more readily, and look into situations with greater insight and discernment. They show a genuine interest in developing others and capitalising on the interconnections across situations, regions, and cultures.

Brown's (2012) research illustrated that the new and enhanced capacities that emerge from the broader and deeper post-conventional mindset enable leaders to better appreciate, resolve, and transcend sophisticated, ambiguous, and complex challenges during volatile, uncertain times in sustainable, successful ways.

The post-conventional stages are less and less implicit frames that limit one's choices, and more and more become explicit frames that highlight the multiplicity of action-logics and the developing freedom and what we call the response-ability to choose one's action-logic on each occasion (Torbert et al., 2004: 93).

Synergists develop the capacity to think inter-systemically in relation to how the multiple stages and their implicit strengths and shadows mutually influence one another in action. Causation is recognised as circular, relational, and systemic. The interpenetrative nature of life is perceived through projections, transference, and psychodynamics. The Subtle Interpenetrative realisation is that people share a common humanity, the same breadth and depth of emotions, dreams, hopes, and fears within, that make us a single human community.

Strengths

At this point in their journey of increasing expanding consciousness, Synergists have become self-aware and other-aware and have the ability to be discerning and self-validating. They do not seek approval or permission from others. They have developed strength of character and their integrity is evident. *Synergists* have the vision, conviction, and presence to generate and sustain transformative change by standing up for what they believe in and articulating their perspective graciously and wisely. They have adopted the mantle of personal authentic power and integrated this with their positional authority in the interests of serving their community as a whole in the decades ahead and not just selected interest groups.

The *Synergist* adopts a late fourth person perspective. In addition to seeing through the interconnections of system dynamics, they are also able to discern these interactions through multiple generations, past and future. This makes them incredibly adept at understanding the intangible and emotional contextual implications of human growth and social evolution. Most of this is simply unconscious to others and therefore out of their scope. However, for the *Synergist*, this is their opportunity to illuminate, transcend, and even heal past patterns in families over generations and for organisations, in relation to their history of mergers and acquisitions, lineage of CEOs, and corporate cultures.

Shadow

The shadow of the *Synergist* reflects their expanding leadership capacity. While they can be seen to demonstrate a shared humanity and embrace diversity, they are not yet renowned for their humility. That doesn't emerge until a leader embarks on their voyage into the MetAware Tier. Instead, they have a tendency towards being directive and even arrogant as they bring people together. Their generosity can dissipate when they become exasperated by their own impatience with others as they learn to develop the patience of timelessness.

Synergists learn to appreciate the organic stretch and collapse of time and to trust in their inner guidance system. This process can make the *Synergist* appear to be a little other-worldly occasionally, although the evident strength of their leadership integrity generally wins them much support, admiration, and respect.

Executive Prototype

Executives anchored at *Synergist* remain rare. They comprised just 5% of the executive population in 1995 (Cook-Greuter, 1999), 7% in 2005, and 8% in 2015 (PwC, 2015). The proportion of *Synergists* is increasing at a snail's pace at the rate of 1% in each of the last two decades. The fact that the development of executive leaders seems to be stalled at *Catalyst* is one of the key motives to undertaking my research study to discover the developmental drivers to *Synergist*.

The collective perspective is fully manifested at *Synergist* when the leader acts to transform the previous conventional collective based on rules and authority to a post-conventional collective based on shared eco-centric values, respect for personal autonomy, equity and diversity, and the intention and capacity to re-engineer the collective to organically generate greater community wellbeing and shared prosperity.

When led by a *Synergist*, the organisation shifts from being customer-centric to community-centric, that is, eco-centric. It succeeds in achieving medium- to long-term sustainable outcomes that make a real, significant, and beneficial impact on the people they serve and affect now and in future generations. They generate a new world through their convictions and intentions, living by their principles and high ethical standards, in tune with their life purpose while embracing others with compassion and enthusiasm.

The mature *Synergist* is an inspiring, collaborative, visionary leader. They lead confidently from the 'inside out'. They are able to consistently stand and hold their ground in the moment while holding a nurturing space for the emergence of a transformed world. They are extremely mindful, highly considered, and passionately articulate in their advocacy for a better world. They are able to take purposeful action over the long term to raise conscious awareness and keep everyone on course and in meaningful relationship with each other.

CONSTRUCTIVIST   *care*

The next stage is another quantum shift of all three parameters into a new Tier, a Tier that is unknown to 99% of people today. The MetAware Tier is awareness of awareness, a metacognition that begins to identify with source, or cosmic energy forces. The first stage in this tier is of course an individual receptive stage where a person once again encounters an entirely new world of energy dynamics and perceptible dimensions of reality.

Needs/Values

This stage encounters the loss of identity and surrender of self. After investing significant time, energy, and commitment to defining and understanding self and other, the step into MetAware is to step into the void of emptiness and fullness, where nothing is and all is possible.

While the journey through *Catalyst* and *Synergist* can be compared to the archetypal Hero's Journey, the transition through *Constructivist* and *Alchemist* is akin to a voyage to the bottom of the sea. There is a sense of immersion in a wholeness that cannot yet be understood or fathomed.

Strengths

There is a new perception of time and space, or spacetime evolves as being boundaryless, eternal, and infinite, the power of now. Patience and humility, tenderness and gentleness, acceptance and faith, modesty and selflessness, become embodied following an immersion into deep despair and disillusionment.

Shadow

This transition takes a deeper dive into emotions that have hitherto not been experienced in the same way. People are known to experience the dark night of the soul, a time of desolation, as their appreciation of century-old patterns of world evolution and regression can be seen and begin to be understood. The opportunity for humanity to retrieve light and love in the world suddenly becomes quite hopeless, even futile.

Collective shadow emerges. Experiences include encountering people from all walks of life who have suffered from tragic and abusive experiences in their lives; a complete reprieve from rational thought while reflecting on, learning from, and healing endemic regrets and the most incoherent human errors of judgment; and an immersion into grief and despair. This type of shadow experience leads to unconditional acceptance, endless patience, deep compassion, and a sense of surrender to cosmic evolution. Will is transmuted, and the mind becomes the instrument of spirit.

Executive Prototype

Executives at this stage would benefit most from a sabbatical! Any drive and commitment dissipate temporarily as the cosmic universe peers through into one's conscious awareness. It is a great time to rewind and reflect, ponder and wonder, and consider human evolution and devolution, involution and revolution.

ALCHEMIST   *free*

The *Alchemist* enjoys the 5th person perspective. In the MetAware Tier, they become Active and are aware of multi-generational, iterative individual and collective shadow through the ages and epochs of human civilisation. The final stage that can be observed in the post-conventional world is the *Alchemist*. They account for just 1% of the executive population.

Needs/Values

At the stage of *Alchemist*, the evolution of society to enable greater peace and goodwill becomes salient. The *Alchemist* embodies their own intuitive guidance and employs mutually collaborative power to generate transformative shifts in the world that lead to a more sustainable, healthy and equitable world where everyone, the planet and all of life is supported and nurtured to thrive and flourish, grow and evolve. Rather than carry this out through planning or stewardship, it is a matter of rising to the opportunity as it presents itself.

Alchemists are able to hold and embrace wonderful future possibilities while standing firmly in the present accepting and embracing all that is, and being cognisant of all that has preceded and led to the current situation. They look at events symbolically and value both the shadow and the light in the systemic psychodynamics of common human interactions.

Strengths

The *Alchemist* can have a far-reaching impact on their world. They feel free to be uniquely themselves, liberated from any social or cultural conventions, and can feel both delighted and tormented as they perceive, attend to, and process the vast cacophony of thought and emotion that swirls around them while their interior mind is quiet and still. They are able to be fully vulnerable yet vitally alive and vigorous as they give their conscious, compassionate attention to the dynamic interplay in each and every moment to exercise wisdom and compassion in action.

Shadow

The *Alchemist* has released the shadow of their ego through grief, understanding, and forgiveness and has surrendered their personal will to be an instrument in the divine orchestra on earth. They live to evolve in tune with the cosmos, listening into the dark and the deep recesses of their soul's voyage in life.

The shadow that manifests at *Alchemist* is the collective shadow of families, countries, regions, religions, cultures, societies, even civilisations. This is explored through energy dynamics such as constellation work.

Executive Prototype

Alchemists are the iconic leaders who ignite and generate social evolution as well as transform global industries. However, there are also many *Alchemists* who are amazingly effective behind the scenes in niche markets and uniquely tailored roles such as strategic consulting, brand design, sustainability initiatives, and executive coaching. They can juggle multiple responsibilities, intervene very briefly yet with significant strategic impact, and live their lives with passion and purpose.

Chapter 2: Key Points

While we are each a spectrum of neighbouring stages, we also each have a centre of gravity and accompanying stage that typify our leadership mindset and the qualities we bring to challenges and opportunities, dilemmas and possibilities. The following key points encapsulate each stage.

1   The *Opportunist* executive leader feels threatened by life, acts in self-interest, steals ideas, blames others, attacks to defend yet sees opportunities. (mature 1st person perspective)
2   The *Conformist* executive leader sees life as a struggle yet enjoys belonging to a specific collective. They follow directives, comply with people in authority, regularly complain about others, and distrust people who are unlike them. (mature 2nd person perspective)
3   The *Specialist* executive leader sees life as an effort and enjoys investing their efforts into developing technical and functional expertise and skills. They enjoy continuous improvement yet can be highly critical, perfectionist, and take feedback personally. (early 3rd person perspective)
4   The *Achievist* executive leader enjoys striving in life and reaping the results of their efforts. They are positive, pragmatic, and can juggle priorities to achieve team goals. They always want 'more' and wear being continuously busy as a badge of honour. (mature 3rd person perspective)
5   The *Catalyst* executive leader sees life as a journey. They are a collaborative change leader, reflective and insightful, innovative and intuitive, interweaving across stakeholders, boundaries, divisions, and sectors. (early 4th person perspective)
6   The *Synergist* executive leader sees the interpenetrative nature of life as a projection and reflection of self. They embrace diversity and conflicting perspectives to resolve issues and lead transformative and revolutionary change to usher in a new order. (mature 4th person perspective)
7   The *Constructivist* executive leader realises the futility of effort as generations of humanity evolve and devolve, progress and regress. They surrender to the shadow of the soul to embrace a MetAware cosmic perspective. (early 5th person perspective)
8   The *Alchemist* executive leader sees life as a theatre with an empty mind committed to social evolution integrating material and spiritual spheres. They can lead social evolution through symbolic actions. (mature 5th person perspective)

Next Chapter

This chapter has reviewed the emerging strengths, shadows, and idiosyncrasies of each stage of development. In the next chapter, we explore the distribution of the executive population based on their primary stage of development with reference to statistics based on WUSCT assessments. You will also gain a good understanding of the nature and validation of the assessment. Moreover, I will explore the features that distinguish the *Achievist* from the *Synergist* and why and how the latter have been found to be more effective leaders. We also review the factors that appear to prompt later stage development.

3 THE TRANSFORMATION FROM *ACHIEVIST* TO *SYNERGIST*

Now that you're familiar with the stages of development, it becomes interesting to better understand what distinguishes high-performing *Achievists* from wise transforming *Synergists*. This chapter also reviews the evidence on the correlation between later stages and leadership effectiveness and explores the mechanism and validity of stage assessment. It then goes on to review various research findings and claims by thought leaders on the processes and environment that seem to prompt and enable later stage vertical development.

The Key Distinctions between *Achievists* and *Synergists*

While relationships are largely transactional at the *Achievist* stage, people at *Catalyst* explore relationships with a view to understanding self, particularly one's inner world and the diversity of human expression amongst others. They appreciate reciprocity in a genuine sense that nurtures mutual understanding.

A *Catalyst* also begins to realise that they have the autonomy, the self-authorship, to choose who they wish to become in terms of their identity in contrast to the external manifestations of their strengths and talents.

At the stage of *Synergist*, a person is no longer captive to the Self-Authoring Mind. They realise that they can transform themselves on an ongoing basis to embrace more and more of who they are, including all that is before them, that is most instrumental in showing understanding of others in order to realise shared desirable outcomes and meaningful aspirations. They become the transforming self, operating inter-independently with others.

Torbert's typology of action-logics suggests that the focus on results, effectiveness, and success in a single highly productive high-performance system at the *Achievist* stage, shifts to relativism at *Catalyst*. The focus turns to the self and others interacting with the system in a more dynamic change-oriented way. An appreciation of the complex adaptive system dawns with the realisation that everything is in constant flux and that change in one element affects the whole.

At the stage of *Synergist*, an understanding of multiple dynamic systemic interactions emerges as a person's perspective expands to encompass greater diversity, subtlety, and complexity. There is a shift from relativism to a prioritisation of the principles that best serve mutually beneficial longer-term sustainable outcomes.

In addition to inter-systemic awareness, *Synergists* also have a primary focus on development in terms of self-exploration and the evolution of others. Conflict is embraced as providing an opportunity for dynamic mutual transformation. Their exercise of leadership is designed to facilitate the development of others (Kegan et al., 2014).

Kegan (1995) asserts that leadership processes that invite leaders to fully engage others in developing a collective vision demands leadership capacity at *Synergist*. A leader at *Synergist* invites and challenges everyone to become leaders too.

It would seem valuable for *Synergist* leaders who wish to engage others in the development of a shared vision and values, to facilitate the development of their followers to the level of *Achievist*. At that point they are self-governing and self-defining, and accordingly expect to engage as autonomous individuals to set a shared vision of the future reflecting their aspirational intent.

Values come into play as an important dimension to seek alignment with others and thereby lead more authentically. *Catalysts* risk interpersonal harmony to be true to their inner values. At *Synergist*, there is a shift from personal values to more uplifting values and universally held principles of broader entities such as organisations and society.

Only at the stage of *Synergist* is a leader able to reflect on contradictions and paradoxes and weigh different paradigms against higher-order values and principles during turbulent times. This enables the *Synergist* to forge unifying pathways that allow for full expression. Through openness to new possibilities and fostering the emergence of mutual understanding, they are able to transform self and lead transformative change for others in the interests of generating sustainable synergistic outcomes.

Not only does a person at *Synergist* take an all-encompassing, interpenetrative, and integrative view of their external context, they have the realisation that all that is perceived externally is also present internally. That which they have made peace with internally is able to be embraced externally. Their reconciliation of combative forces and conflicting voices from within gives rise to their comfort with external conflict. The self-transforming leader at *Synergist* has the 'capacity to meet others of any station in their life in their full height and depth' (Torbert, 1994: 186).

In summary, *Synergists* are inter-systemic thinkers and long-term synergistic decision-makers who are able to conceive and construct empowering strategic architectures in collaboration with diverse stakeholders to create shared prosperity and wellbeing for current and future generations. They are able to integrate the complexity of diversity across all social demographics and take a fifth person multi-generational perspective to lead the emergence of evolutionary, transformative social structures that can serve economic, social, and environmental sustainability. They also embody respect for uplifting universal principles and elevated ethical practices to enable the full and equitable participation of all people.

The above research findings suggest that the *Synergist* is defined by their newly emergent capacity to think more strategically, synergistically and systemically over the longer term. They can look into situations with greater insight and discernment, engage more curiously and collaboratively with people's diverse viewpoints, and actively step in to resolve conflict more readily. They show a genuine interest in developing others while capitalising on the interconnections across situations, regions, and cultures.

As Brown (2012) discovered in his study of later stage global sustainability leaders, the new and enhanced capacities that emerge from the broader and deeper meaning-making perspective at *Synergist*, enable leaders to better appreciate, resolve, and transcend sophisticated, ambiguous, and complex challenges during volatile, uncertain times in sustainable, synergistic ways.

Increased Leadership Effectiveness at Later Stages

Later stages have also been correlated with increased leadership effectiveness. Evidence indicates that executives at later stages with more complex meaning-making systems are more effective leaders. Holding a deeper understanding of themselves, the people around them and their strategic context, in other words intrapersonal, interpersonal, systems and cognitive skills and capabilities, helps leaders to be more effective.

Bill Torbert undertook many of the early research studies. He is the creator of the term 'action-logic' for stages and was one of the most outstanding practitioners in stage development for executives and organisations in the 1980s and 1990s.

In a problem-solving test, he found that the 32 conventional leaders at *Specialist* and *Achievist* tended to respond to the problems independently with a first-order response e.g. tackle the issue as an isolated event. In contrast, the 17 post-conventional leaders at *Catalyst* and *Synergist* sought out the underlying causes of the symptom in more collaborative ways to resolve the problem at cause rather than effect. This affirmed the theory that later stage leaders look below the surface and the face-value of events to see patterns, inquire further, and engage with others to reset the norms and values, processes and practices, that otherwise lead to problems. *Synergists* were found to be the most effective (Merron et al. 1987).

In a later study of 17 managers, of whom 7 were at *Specialist* and *Achievist* and 10 at *Catalyst* and *Synergist*, the *Synergists* in particular worked with their subordinates to generate synergy and exercise mutual power with them, while the *Achievists* worked with their subordinates to impose solutions on them through the exercise of unilateral power. The *Synergists* also articulated and followed principles in defiance of set rules, whereas the *Achievists* did not. Torbert concluded that the *Synergist* action-logic is needed to create the context within which people and organisations can transform in emergent, empowering ways (Fisher and Torbert, 1991).

Professor Karl Kuhnert, previously Chair of Organisational Psychology at the University of Georgia, has also overseen a number of research studies on leadership effectiveness in relation to the stages of development with various colleagues. They undertook a study of 21 CEOs and executive leaders and 21 middle managers, all of a similar age operating in 17 large American public companies with average gross revenues of US$5 billion across a wide range of industries. They found that a leader's stage of development was positively and significantly correlated to their leadership level. Their responses to leadership themes such as conflict, success, and vision were also positively and significantly related to their level of stage development (Eigel, 1998).

Another study found that the stage of development of a group of 41 executives in C-suite to management roles, with an average age of 46, was positively and significantly correlated with their 360 performance ratings. In later studies of similar but larger groups of 67 and 74 executives, it was found that the level of stage development was able to predict overall leadership effectiveness across all 360 ratings (Harris and Kuhnert, 2008; Strang and Kuhnert, 2009).

A further study found a strong correlation between leaders' stage of development and the effectiveness of their responses to demanding challenges. Only leaders at *Catalyst* and later offered responses that were considered very effective or exceptional, while those at *Synergist* provided the most effective responses overall (Eigel and Kuhnert, 2005).

Through their consulting work in organisations, Rooke and Torbert (1998, 2005) found that only at *Synergist* was an executive able to lead and sustain whole-system organisational transformation, including transforming the core beliefs, values, practices, and culture of the organisation. *Synergist* leaders were uniquely open to reconsidering their assumptions and synthesising with others to enable synergistic collaborative momentum towards fulfilling a purpose. This involved personal and organisational double-loop learning where they questioned and reformulated the strategy and structure, the contextual framework and not just their actions, to encourage voluntary engagement to accomplish overarching goals.

Leaders at earlier stages relied on hierarchical authority and the unilateral exercise of power that failed to generate personal or organisational transformation. Change efforts were limited to a sense of obligatory buy-in rather than the voluntary engagement of vulnerable authentic power widely distributed amongst all people involved. The paradox of tapping into this vulnerable power of diverse interests and not knowing yet trusting in emergence was only appreciated by leaders at *Synergist* and beyond.

This was endorsed by another study that found that 11 of 64 internal consultants measuring at *Synergist* were assessed as being more effective as transformative change leaders than the other consultants at earlier stages of development (Bushe and Gibbs, 1990).

David Rooke and Bill Torbert, two of the most active stage development consultants in the 1980s and 1990s, also integrated a research inquiry as part of their significant and substantial consulting assignments with organisational clients. In a total of ten longitudinal studies of organisational transformation with an average duration of 4.2 years, seven prospered significantly to go on to become unique industry leaders and three did not. The organisations included five corporations and five not-for-profits with between 5 and 1019 employees and an average of 485 employees each.

The CEOs at the successful organisations undertook a total of 18 business transformations and significantly increased their size, efficiency, service quality, people engagement, profitability, corporate reputation, and systems-logic. These seven CEOs either measured at *Synergist* or built trust with external consultants at *Synergist* and *Alchemist*, treating them as close confidantes. The other three CEOs were pre-*Synergist* and distanced themselves from *Synergist* colleagues and consultants (Rooke and Torbert, 1998).

Rooke and Torbert concluded that CEOs at *Synergist* and beyond or those who collaborated closely with colleagues, consultants, and coaches at *Synergist* and beyond, could not only lead successive organisational transformations effectively but extraordinarily so.

The Measurement of Stage Development

This spectrum of stages is best understood by how you express yourself, and the values and beliefs that underlie your feelings, thoughts, words, and actions. Jane Loevinger dedicated decades of research to developing the Washington University Sentence Completion Test (WUSCT) to elicit aspects of adult development. The WUSCT is a qualitatively based yet quantitatively measured yardstick of a person's level of stage development.

It involves 36 open sentence stems which you complete in your own words, sharing your perspective as fully as you consider appropriate to express yourself authentically. It is a projective test, as you are projecting your thoughts, feelings, and beliefs by expressing yourself in words in relation to a particular prompt, such as: 'Change is …', 'I feel sorry …', 'My mother and I …', 'Crime and delinquency could be halted if …'.

People complete these sentence prompts in their own words, unconsciously projecting their underlying conceptual framework (Cook-Greuter, 1995). They cover the ambit of cognitive, behavioural, affective, relationship, and systems responses that we engage in during the normal course of life.

The WUSCT is one of the most widely used and arguably the most extensively validated in the field of personality assessment (Cook-Greuter, 1999; Lilienfeld et al., 2000; Redmore and Waldman, 1975). It has been used in more than 300 studies, translated into at least 11 languages, and administered to more than 11,000 individuals (Cohn, 1998). Later, Cook-Greuter, in collaboration with Torbert, revised and expanded the WUSCT to enhance its capacity in transpersonal stage evaluation and better capture professionals and executives in organisational contexts.

A range of relevant correlations has been identified with moral behaviour, ideological values, delinquency, wariness, conformity, tolerance, personality characteristics, preoccupations, and personal concerns expressed to be typical of pre-conventional, conventional, and post-conventional stages of development (Cohn and Westenberg, 2004; Kohlberg, 1981). This gives weight to the measurement validity of the stages of development based on levels of increasing conscious self-awareness due to greater psychological insight and perspective-taking.

While projective techniques have caused some controversy in the past (Torbert and Livne-Tarandach, 2009), the WUSCT is more akin to a projective test rather than a technique as it involves standard testing instructions, a systematic process for scoring responses to sentence stems based on extensive empirical data, and well calibrated norms to compare responses amongst participants (Lilienfeld et al., 2000).

Pure modernists suggest that the methodologies for measuring the stages are not sufficiently precise because they require too high-level interpretation to be considered scientifically sound (Manners and Durkin, 2001; McCauley et al., 2006). However, the research into language construction and use of specific vocabulary at progressive stages is substantial and fully documented in the assessment methodologies used by the leading researchers (Cook-Greuter, 1995; O'Fallon, 2020).

Highly qualified, trained, and certified evaluators compare each sentence completion to an extensive compendium of scoring indicators in terms of language used, sentence construction, and other features that have become more visible over time to researchers scoring and reviewing the scored assessments (Loevinger and Wessler, 1970). Each sentence then receives a numerical score indicating the stage projected in each particular sentence completion. Inter-rater reliability has been shown to be extremely robust at 94% (Torbert and Livne-Tarandach, 2009).

Once all 36 sentences have been scored, it is clear how many sentences score at each stage of development. Sentences at increasingly later stages attract a higher weighting due to their increasing scarcity with the use of a standard algorithm. A weighted majority rather than a simple majority of sentence prompts leads to the person's stage assessment. The stage with the highest total weighted score (TWS) is referred to as their primary stage. The surrounding stages are indicative of secondary stages, trailing and leading edges.

The quantitative TWS provides an ideal mechanism to accurately measure the change in stage capacity of executives on a longitudinal basis. It provides more granular insight into the spectrum of stages in a person's profile to both quantify and better understand the nuances of a person's development over time. The WUSCT is therefore suggested as a highly relevant and exceptionally objective pre- and post-measure of the effectiveness of executive coaching in leadership development.

Statistical Evidence of Executive Distribution

Statistics published by the leading researchers and practitioners in stage leadership development, suggest that there has been a shift in the primary stage of executives over the last few decades. In 1995, based on Cook-Greuter's data, the primary stage for most executives was at *Specialist* (38%) with a strong cohort at the next stage of *Achievist* (30%). Less than 15% of executives had their primary stage in the post-conventional stages beyond *Achievist*.

In 2005, ten years later, Rooke and Torbert published their statistical data in the *Harvard Business Review* as part of their iconic article, 'Seven Transformations of Leadership'. Their combined statistics were based on Cook-Greuter's statistics over the previous 25 years and therefore showed a very similar picture to those published in 1995.

The most recent statistical data were published in 2015 thanks to PwC's collaboration with David Rooke, Founder of Harthill Consulting. The Harthill data for 2005 show a different trend. There is a definite shift to a prevailing *Achievist* orientation with 52% anchored there, and the proportion of executives with their primary stage at *Specialist* has reduced to 9%. The percentage of *Catalysts* is shown to have more than doubled from 10% to 23% (see Figure 3.1).

The 2015 data show the beginning of a diminishing proportion of executives at *Achievist*, albeit still predominant, and a consistently growing proportion at *Catalyst*, now at 33%. This augurs well, suggesting that executives are continuing to mature in their leadership capacity. If the average aggregate is viewed as a whole (i.e. a single person), then there is a clear albeit declining majority of executives with their primary stage at *Achievist* and their secondary stage at *Catalyst*. Taken as a whole, they have a leading edge at *Synergist* and a trailing edge at *Specialist*.

All in all, it would appear that the proportion of *Catalysts* has been growing at a healthy rate of 11% in each of the last two decades. This is very encouraging, as the later the stage, the more effective the leader. They develop new engagement capabilities that add to their existing strengths as high-performing

Figure 3.1 The distribution of the executive population

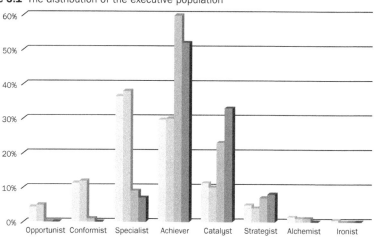

1995 Cook-Greuter USA   2005 HBR Rooke & Torbert   2005 PwC Harthill UK   2015 PwC Harthill UK

Achievists. However, the proportion of *Synergists* has largely stalled. Their number has been increasing at a snail's pace of just 1% in each of the last two decades. This is concerning.

Cook-Greuter and O'Fallon have published other statistical samples. They indicate that the more senior the leaders and the more consultants included in the sample, the greater the proportion of later stages. O'Fallon's samples of data taken from attendees at and following their participation at integral leadership transformation programs, show a much higher proportion of people at *Synergist* and the more mature MetAware stages. However, it is fair to say that this is an extraordinarily skewed sample of later stage executives, consultants, and executive coaches drawn purposefully to the integral programs due to their third Tier transpersonal growth value proposition.

Evidence of Later Stage Development

A person's stage is understood to be relatively stable. It is thought that we progress incrementally through the stages and it has been said to take years to mature to later stages as there are so few people modelling later stages of leadership capacity. However, there is some evidence that this developmental process can be accelerated through participation in deliberate conscious vertical leadership development programs.

Stage development reflects vertical learning through the stages in contrast to lateral or horizontal learning within each stage. While both are essential and important, only vertical learning by shifting our centre of gravity to the stage of *Synergist* will enable us to transcend the inter-systemic complexity of our times and lead the transformation of the VUCA (volatile, uncertain, complex, and ambiguous) world we currently occupy. 'For leaders who face the challenge of triple-bottom-line mandates or large-scale multi-stakeholder engagement to advance sophisticated social and/or environmental initiatives, later stage consciousness may indeed be a discreet advantage' (Brown, 2012a: 30).

Studies show that there are a number of individual and group interventions that can give rise to the development of leadership capacity at *Synergist*. In an early study, Torbert and Fisher (1992) assessed 15 Master of Business Administration (MBA) graduates at graduation and approximately five years after their graduation. Six had participated in a voluntary action inquiry group that met every three weeks over five years to reflect collectively on their life experiences. The average stage of these six had lifted a full stage, with 88% of their profile shifting to *Synergist* whereas the other nine graduates had only developed their leadership capacity by approximately 5%, a difference that was statistically significant.

Thus, collective action inquiry into disorienting life experiences, albeit over a lengthy period of time, five years, is a valuable developmental intervention in the shift to *Synergist*. This action inquiry process has since been advanced by Torbert et al. (2004) and is known as Collaborative Developmental Action

Inquiry today. Similar interventions that have been found to contribute to later stage development include exploring inner conflicts with peers who hold a more complex worldview (Laloux, 2014) and formal peer-based learning groups (Kaiser and Kaplan, 2006).

Exploring the drivers of development, Manners and Durkin (2001) built on Mezirow's (2003) concept of 'disorientating dilemmas' to identify the potential for stage growth. They found that having a personal disposition that was curious and open to attracting personally salient life experiences that were interpersonal in nature and emotionally engaging and challenging, was likely to generate later stage development. However, most studies were of student populations at *Conformist/Specialist* participating in relatively brief interventions. For example, 76% (16/21) of *Specialists* advanced one stage to *Achievist* following a ten-week group program of one 90-minute workshop per week. However, only one of the ten *Achievists* in the study shifted to a later stage, and this person regressed at retest four months later (Manners and Durkin, 2001).

Vincent et al. (2015) undertook a comprehensive study of 335 adults with an average age of 40 taking part in one of seven enhanced ten-month community leadership programs (CLPs), four standard CLPs, and two management programs (control). The enhanced CLPs included the equivalent of two to three full-day sessions per month as well as multi-day retreats and fields trips. The total development days per enhanced CLP is estimated at 25 to 40 days.

While there was no deliberate intent to develop consciousness levels among participants, the CLPs did include disequilibrating experiences that could be interpersonally challenging and personally salient for participants, as described in Manners and Durkin's (2000) conceptual model. Participants were confronted with major economic, environmental, social, and cultural issues affecting their communities, such as serving meals in a homeless centre and talking to prisoners, indigenous elders, and farmers facing drought. These were highly interactive and experiential sessions followed by group debriefs, a form of collective inquiry, facilitated by the program leaders, guest facilitators, or the participants themselves.

The enhanced CLPs also included psychosocial components and challenges that had the potential to promote stage development. These included the opportunity and support to self-reflect, undertake a group strategic initiative and learn from the experience, work with diverse perspectives, offer 360 feedback and invite feedforward, become more aware of group psychodynamic patterns, receive group input on personal case studies in leadership, and participate in outward-bound experiences in the wilderness. Two of the enhanced CLP programs specified a minimum of two or four individual coaching sessions.

The enhanced CLPs were found to be significantly more successful in triggering stage development than the standard CLPs and the management programs. A total of 28% (55/197) of *Achievists* and *Catalysts* progressed to the next stage: 23% (9/40) shifted from *Catalyst* to *Synergist* and 29% (46/157) shifted from *Achievist* to *Catalyst*; while 69% (22/32) transitioned from *Specialist* to *Achievist*. This research study suggests that approximately a quarter of participants attending an intensive, psychosocially disequilibrating 25-40-day leadership program over 12 months, can be expected to shift one stage to the later post-conventional stages of *Catalyst* and *Synergist*.

Studies suggest that executive leadership programs based on integral theory focused explicitly on expediting vertical learning to later stage development, such as the Integral Generating Transformative Change Program, are significantly more effective: 'Typically, it takes 5 years for a leader to shift a full action logic, or developmental stage, if they shift at all. Leaders in these programs [MetaIntegral Associates, Pacific Integral, JFK University] shifted as much as an entire stage or two in vertical learning programs lasting 1–2 years' (Brown, 2014: 21, n. 13).

While these single- and double-stage shifts manifest in a short space of time, integral leadership programs also tend to be highly intensive, e.g. participation in four 5-day residential retreats over a period of nine months. Geoff Fitch (in Gunnlaugson and Brabant, 2016), Founder of Pacific Integral, suggests that the intimate collective holding space co-created during MetAware retreats is significant in liberating this later stage transpersonal development. All facilitators at these retreats are anchored at the Transpersonal stage of *Alchemist* (5.5) and beyond.

The success of integral leadership development programs suggests that the intimate collective holding space may have significantly more developmental impact than the challenge invoked by psychosocially disequilibrating experiences. In other words, it is not the 'heat experiences' (Petrie, 2015) themselves that enable or even ignite later stage post-conventional development but the open, responsive later stage deeper inquiry into the experience of the participants within a psychologically safe and sacred space that invokes vertical growth.

Rooke and Torbert (2005) advised that, in addition to one individual making the shift from *Specialist* to *Achievist* to *Catalyst* and then on to *Synergist* over a period of three years, '[w]e have had only two other instances in which a leader has transformed twice in less than four years' (Rooke and Torbert, 2005: 73).

Petriglieri et al. (2011) undertook a research study of students participating in the highly popular Personal Development Elective in Insead's MBA program. They endorsed the importance of exploring identity advising that transformational learning took place 'through a process of personalization by which individuals examine their experiences and revisit their life stories' (2011: 436). One of the features that was thought to ignite and sustain the personalisation of management learning was the social context of the MBA program, described as a 'regressive domain' that provoked emotional distress due to performance and social anxiety (i.e. a heat experience).

The other feature was existential puzzlement caused by open questions on direction, purpose, and behaviours. Problematic experiences were reframed as learning opportunities through psychotherapy, enabling the participants to examine and revise the ways they interpreted, responded emotionally to, and acted upon their experiences. 'Within the PDE [Personal Development Elective], participants engaged in a combination of self-clarification, emotional processing, and planning behavioural experiments that fostered reflective engagement in every aspect of the MBA program' (Petriglieri et al., 2011: 436)

This suggests that reflection and resolution of identity issues may facilitate transformational learning, although the research did not specify or calibrate later stage vertical development.

Pfaffenberger et al. (2011) compared the written narratives and interview transcripts concerning the growth process of 22 post-conventional participants with those of a control group of six conventional participants. The three major themes that distinguished the two groups were complexity, interiority, and intentionality. The complexity could be conceived as an outcome. It was evident from the post-conventional participants' coherent articulation of multiple diverse perspectives on disparate developmental life events, their differentiation of subtleties, and demonstration of a high degree of deep cognitive–emotional integration.

The interiority came through personal inquiry into inner awareness, purposefully seeking inner congruence to resolve the inner disquiet that arose from incidents and dilemmas. The integration process of the self emerged from new insights into interconnections. Pffaffenberger and colleagues' (2011) third differentiating dimension, intentionality, referred to the commitment to prioritise personal growth despite the discomfort and increasing sensitivity. Interiority and intentionality appear to be developmental drivers also closely associated with the development of a coherent inner identity and the intentional resolution of disorientating dilemmas and tensions at a deeper level.

Post-conventional participants described their outcomes as new inner awareness rather than a change in behaviour. *Synergist* participants translated their increasing awareness into an embodied presence, an expanded capacity for self-expression and being-ness in the midst and moment of life situations. They joined like-minded people for dialogue, cognitive learning, and emotional support, and maintained personal practices such as meditation, psychotherapy, coaching, and martial arts. The post-conventional participants also frequently cited giftedness, early intellectual interests, self-employment, unconventionality, attending retreats and cross cultural experiences in contrast to the control group, but rejected social activism as a part of their development.

> Postconventional *growth emerges from this study as a highly individualized process ... Another aspect that distinguished the postconventional participants were their positive emotional and mental skills, apparent freedom from regret, resentment, cynicism and anger, and their interpersonal warmth and great social skills.*
>
> (Pfaffenberger et al., 2011: 5)

It would appear that by reflecting on, inquiring into, and processing their dilemmas and moments of disquiet in relation to their inner identity, the post-conventional participants were able to release past grievances and meet the world with a positive and warm interpersonal demeanour engaging heart and mind. This perspective is endorsed by Quatro et al. (2007), who advise that a person develops to later stages by taking a more holistic view of the self and integrating one's analytical, conceptual, emotional, and spiritual dimensions.

Sharma and Cook-Greuter (2012) suggest that working with polarities facilitates later stage vertical development. When only one pole is preferred, the other is seen only for its downside and therefore becomes something to avoid.

> Each pole in a polarity carries a wisdom or value (upside). In the polarity of firm and yielding, being assertive and strong are upsides of being firm, being cooperative and flexible are upsides of being yielding. When we overfocus on being firm to the exclusion of being yielding, we get a downside: we are seen as rigid and unbending. By the same token, if we overfocus on being yielding to the exclusion of being firm, we get a downside: we may be judged as being irresolute and push-overs.
>
> (Sharma and Cook-Greuter, 2012: 10)

These shifts from 'either–or' to 'both–and', and then to 'both–and' *and* 'either–or', are undertaken in the transformation from *Catalyst* to *Synergist*.

Polarities come to be seen as interdependent pairs of values, strengths, constructs, or concepts. Once the full spectrum is seen as a whole, and the benefits of the less valued pole are understood, polarities can be transcended and become interpenetrative where the microcosm is the macrocosm and vice versa. They come to be seen as manifestations of a unified field.

Sharma and Cook-Greuter also suggested that the questioning of assumptions and the re-evaluation of interpretations to reframe reality in more comprehensive ways are at the heart of the developmental process. 'The psychodynamic process of owning the disowned releases developmental energy. It allows one to make new meaning by having greater choice and more power to explain a situation than privileging one side of a polarity over the other' (Sharma and Cook-Greuter, 2012: 25). The mastery of self leads to expanded leadership presence.

Others attribute post-conventional development to organisational settings. Torbert (1987: 216–217), for instance, suggests that liberating organisational disciplines, 'structures that would simultaneously make sense to organizational members at various stages of development and invite developmental transformation', could be conducive to vertical leadership development. He argues that personal leadership development is most conducive in the context of a safe holding space designed for growth (Scharmer, 2018; Torbert and Fisher, 1992) in a deliberately developmental organisation (Kegan et al., 2014) or with an accomplished facilitator (Scharmer, 2018) or expert therapist (Petriglieri et al., 2011).

Rooke and Torbert explain that: 'What sets [*Catalysts*] apart from *Achievists* is their awareness of a possible conflict between their principles and their actions, or between the organization's values and its implementation of those values. This conflict becomes the source of tension, creativity, and a growing desire for further development' (2005: 71)

Scharmer (2018) encourages organisations to demonstrate more effective leadership by generating a holding space that sets and sustains the intention to co-create the best possible emerging future. He suggests that attention be given to what is arising at the heart of the collective, and cultivate deep listening with an open mind, heart, and will while suspending judgement, cynicism, and fear.

Kegan et al. (2014) advocate deliberately developmental organisations to adopt a primary focus on vertical learning on a day-by-day basis as the key to business growth. 'What can be done is to create environments that are conducive to growing into later stages ... When someone is surrounded by peers who already see the world from a more complex perspective, in a context safe enough to explore inner conflicts, chances are higher that the person will make the leap' (Laloux, 2014: 1039–1043).

The shifts in organisational development from an orderly top-down command/control hierarchy (orange) to a learning, experimental values-led organisation (green), and on to the understanding that an organisation is a complex adaptive system that liberates peer-based organic collaboration (teal) (Laloux, 2014) reflect the individual stages of development from *Achievist* (orange) to *Catalyst* (green) and *Synergist* (teal). Executives leading evolved teal organisations, presumably *Synergists* who can hold and trust the organic emergence, lead co-creation with an evolutionary purpose, empowering processes, and by generating a sense of community and freedom.

Teal organisational leaders at *Synergist* unite everyone through an aspirational evolutionary purpose, e.g. 'whole foods, whole people, whole planet' (Hamel, 2007). Laloux (2014) advises that purpose emerges from listening into the organisation in response to profound questions, such as 'Why does the organisation exist?', 'What is it best able to contribute?', 'What is wanting to grow?', 'What could an inspiring future look like?' This establishes a dialogue in the collective field that brings forth an evolutionary purpose aligned with the source of our cosmic evolution, however that source might be termed. The organic process itself supports alignment with individual vocation and purpose. This is in direct contrast to the conventional orange business focus on financial outcomes such as increasing profits, market share, and business growth.

Teal organisations are more empowering. They prefer to trust rather than control, and the systems, processes, and information flows are designed to support everyone's growth and success. For instance, whole-foods teams make their own hiring and procurement decisions; they operate as independent entrepreneurial business units, all united behind the same overriding purpose focused on a sustainable healthy local food value chain (Hamel, 2007).

By providing leaders and teams with the information to make wise decisions, the autonomy to make those business decisions, and accountability for the results through incentives based on business outcomes, everyone is empowered to learn and grow, succeed, and prosper in sustainable, healthy ways. In W.L. Gore, a peer-based process drawing people from across the organisation was used for making funding decisions (Hamel, 2007). Teal organisations replace power hierarchies with self-managing teams. Trusting others generates shared responsibility for all.

Synergists leading evolved teal organisations also create a sense of community. For instance, Google opened up the strategy process to include all employees, respected diversity as a stimulus of creativity, and encouraged dissent to ignite innovation (Hamel, 2007). All stakeholders are treated equally rather than advancing the interests of shareholders only. People genuinely care for each other and build personal relationships at work.

The most innovative companies have created a community of volunteers by enabling voluntary participation in the ideas and projects that most interest them. They have enabled the redeployment of resources to future-focused strategic initiatives in the same way that Kotter (2014) has advanced the building of a second operating system in an organisation, resourced from the main hierarchical operating system but formed by peer networks focused on creating the future.

Another foundation of Laloux's (2014) teal organisation is an appreciation of the wholeness of people. Their authenticity and growth is of the essence and therefore storytelling, real conversations, and building mutual understanding in a psychologically safe space are an essential element to the development of a thriving and flourishing, more soulful community.

Finally, *Synergists* create a sense of freedom in their teal organisations. For instance, W.L. Gore (Hamel, 2007) accommodates a lattice of self-organising teams across the organisation that are free to experiment. Team members are free to move around as their interests coincide with the emergence of new needs for their particular set of talents. Innovation is sponsored throughout the organisation by giving teams explicit permission to experiment by prototyping and testing new ideas on the market early in the creative process. It is standard practice for 10% of everyone's time to be devoted to new, non-mandated initiatives.

Google also proliferate rapid, low-cost experimentation and handsomely reward game-changing innovations (Hamel, 2007). Rather than trying to predict and control, teal organisations try to sense and respond (Laloux, 2014). They view a desired future 20 years ahead and then sense their way forward following intuitive and embodied guidance. It is an emergent process.

Chapter 3: Key Points

1 While high-performing *Achievists* are transactional, competitive, and focused on business results and growth over 3–5 years, *Synergists* are transformative, collaborative, and focused on leadership and organisational development. They are able to embrace conflict, resolve paradoxes, and integrate polarities to generate synthesis, synergy, and sustainable solutions over longer-term time horizons.

2 Later stage leaders are correlated with more senior roles, increased leadership effectiveness, and the capacity to explore and resolve the source of problems rather than the symptoms. Only *Synergists* or CEOs with trusted *Synergist*[+] advisers, can lead and sustain whole-system successive organisational transformations to become industry leaders.

3 The WUSCT is a projective test that is one of the most extensively validated personality assessments scored by highly qualified and trained assessors with reference to an extensive compendium with a 94% inter-rater reliability. The total weighted score is an objective pre- and post-measure of the effectiveness of executive coaching in leadership development.

4 While the development of authentic leaders at *Catalyst* has increased at a rate of 11% in each of the last two decades, the development of leaders to *Synergist* has stalled.

5 Shifts to later post-conventional stages of development such as *Catalyst* and especially *Synergist*, can take place over five years through monthly collaborative developmental action inquiry with later stage peers.

6 Without a later stage facilitator who can hold and sustain a psychologically safe space to explore and resolve inner conflicts, disorientating dilemmas, and disequilibrating events, only a quarter of executives can be expected to shift to these later stages while participating in 25- to 40-day intensive leadership development programs over 12 months.

7 With MetAware facilitators who consistently hold a psychologically safe emergent space over the course of a 20-day intensive and intimate 9-month integral program, later stage participants are able to shift one and occasionally two vertical stages in the one year.

8 It is not the disorienting, challenging, or incongruent experiences *per se* that generate vertical development, but the subsequent personal inquiry into inner conflict, inner disquiet, the analytical, conceptual, emotional, and spiritual dimensions of one's personal identity and life stories that generates greater inner coherence, which results in later stage development.

9 This process of personal inquiry focused on increasing self-awareness rather than changing behaviour, involves processing and thereby releasing regret, resentment, cynicism, and anger so the person ends up exuding more interpersonal warmth.

10 Evolutionary purpose, empowering processes, liberating disciplines, cultivating deep open listening to become aware of what is arising in the heart of the collective, enabling wide decision-making, and trusting in proactive community participation leads to a vertical developmental environment where businesses and people can flourish in healthy and sustainable ways.

Next Chapter

Given that there is an urgent and critical need for more *Synergists* in society today to transcend the turmoil, navigate complex adaptive systems, liberate latent potential, and generate synergy, I wondered what could be done to break through the lack of developmental evolution to *Synergist*. This led to the design of a research study to explore if and how executive coaching might expedite this shift to *Synergist*, given that most development programs were clearly falling short.

4 THE EXECUTIVE COACHING RESEARCH STUDY

The Research Question

How might Transformative Executive Coaching with a later stage coach at *Synergist⁺* enable vertical leadership development for senior executives at the predominant conventional stage of *Achievist* to the less commonly held later post-conventional stages of *Catalyst* and *Synergist*?

The Nine Initial Coachees

I began the research study with nine participants. The selection of participants was one of the most important initial decisions. I decided to include only coachees with their primary stage at or below *Achievist* in order to investigate the ability of transformative executive coaching to enable, in terms of both igniting and expediting, later stage development.

I was involved in an Executive Development Program for 400 of the most senior leaders in the Senior Executive Public Service of New South Wales, Australia. They included deputy secretaries, C-suite leaders, agency heads, executive directors, and directors. The Program was specifically designed to assess and strengthen the strategic leadership capabilities needed to deliver major reform and take up positions as chief executives in the future.

In its second year, the Public Service Commission offered to fund a leadership assessment and executive coaching program for all interested participants. I took this opportunity to invite 25 of these senior leaders to participate in the research project. Of these, 19 accepted and undertook the WUSCT-based assessment. Susanne Cook-Greuter, one of the most expert and experienced assessors in the world, kindly agreed to assess their profiles.

The total weighted score (TWS) of 250 marked a clear delineation between two groups of potential participants. The primary stage for 12 of the 19 executives was at the conventional stages of *Achievist* or *Specialist*. They each had more than 80%, and an average aggregate of 92%, of their sentence completions profiling up to and including *Achievist*. The other group of seven held emergent post-conventional stage profiles.

The first group of 12 executives were ideal for the research study in terms of purposive sampling. Their largely conventional perspectives would test the capacity of executive coaching to both ignite and expedite later stage leadership development from *Achievist* to the post-conventional stages of *Catalyst* and *Synergist*. The assessment data is presented in full in the Appendix.

Each of the 12 executives with a TWS below 250 was invited to participate in the research study at the end of their individual coaching debrief. The other executives were also invited to continue with a coaching program outside of the research study if they wished.

Nine of the 12 executives who were invited to participate in the research study agreed to go ahead. The initial average profile of these nine participants across the pre- to post-conventional stages of *Opportunist, Conformist, Specialist,* and *Achievist* was also 92%. Please note that I am not suggesting that these participants represent a sample to reflect the universe of conventional executive leaders, but rather as a sufficient number of strategic leaders whose participation would generate directly relevant empirical data to explore the effectiveness of transformative executive coaching in later stage leadership development.

Of the nine, there were three women and six men. Given the gender bias at this level of leadership, this was an adequate gender balance. Three were under 50 and six were over 50 with an overall average age of 52. Three had graduate degrees and six had postgraduate degrees. They included one deputy secretary, one chief information officer, one agency head, three executive directors, one program director, and two other directors leading strategic org-wide functions.

The seniority of their positions, level of responsibilities, maturity in years, higher degree education, and desire to invest dedicated time into an executive coaching program explicitly intended to foster later stage leadership development suggested that they had the potential, readiness, desire, and commitment to develop later stage leadership capacity.

The Coaching Programs

Twelve 90-minute coaching meetings were scheduled every four weeks in advance for the full 12-month period ahead. Attendance varied relative to unpredictable work commitments and holidays. I was very happy to reschedule meetings as needed and extend the total time period during which the series of coaching meetings could run. It turned out that the average number of coaching sessions within the 12-month period for all nine participants was eight, with a range of five to eleven.

No other stakeholders were involved. While the public sector funded the assessments and coaching programs, there was no explicit review of the coaching. Rather, the Public Service Commission intended to hold a further Leadership Review two years later. They were relatively volatile times for the public sector given the iterative restructures that ensued. Readiness for future promotions was always a motivating factor for the coachees.

As the executive coach, I showed up each time as best as I was able. I always scheduled 30 minutes between coaching meetings so that I had time to reflect on and let go of one coaching meeting, before reviewing the notes and meditating prior to the next coaching meeting.

My coaching was not premeditated. I did not have any agenda outside of the intention to support, guide, and encourage later stage development. It was up to the coachee to bring their agenda to the coaching meeting. At the beginning of each coaching meeting, I would simply listen with an open and warm presence excited to hear about their previous month and what was bubbling to the surface for them today. Once we had reconnected and the coachee had debriefed me on their current situation, the collaborative coaching conversation followed.

I had become an executive coach more by way of natural talent, inclination, and serendipity than as a result of significant study in coaching. In my career I had been a management consultant in executive selection and search, management assessment, leadership development and organisational development, a regional human resources executive, an executive general manager of people and culture, a facilitator of strategic planning events for executive teams, and a director of organisational transformation. I had worked with national and global corporations across Asia Pacific, Europe, Africa, and Latin America. My sweet spot seemed to be leading and transforming organisations or divisions numbering some 1,000 people.

My educational background included an honours degree in International Law, a BA in Political Science, a diploma in International Marketing (Hons), an MBA from London Business School, and an MA in Management Research. I had been reading a book every Saturday for the last five or so years. I was a student of life and business and my reading ranged broadly across bestsellers by thought leaders, business texts by world-leading consultants, and other books in the fields of psychology, spirituality, shadow, energy, personal power, and quantum leadership (Zohar, 2016). I had also been an avid reader of the *Harvard Business Review* for decades.

I had first undertaken the Stages Assessment in February 2010 while undertaking a Stages Development Program with Susanne Cook-Greuter. I had been assessed at *Synergist* with 72% of sentence completions at post-conventional levels, and 42% at *Synergist* and *Alchemist* (today this would be considered *Constructivist*). My stage-spectrum was *Specialist–Achievist–Catalyst–Synergist–Constructivist*. The first nine coaching programs took place from 2013 to 2014.

I undertook another assessment with Terri O'Fallon at Stages International in February 2018. I was assessed at 5.5 with 100% of sentence completions at *Synergist* and beyond, and 36% in the MetAware Tier. My stage-spectrum was *Synergist–Constructivist–Alchemist*. It may be helpful to note that I underwent a significantly despairing period in my life during most of 2015 when everything seemed meaningless and I was immersed in grief for quite some time. This is indicative of the transition from the Subtle Tier into the MetAware Tier. The second set of coaching programs included in the research study took place from 2016 to 2018.

I had been working as an executive coach and strategic transformation consultant since 2010 and had delivered over 2,000 coaching hours, approximately

80% with individual strategic leaders and 20% with senior executive teams or groups of senior leaders. I have since almost doubled that quota of coaching hours and have also undertaken a wide range of coaching programs, including organisational coaching, ontological coaching, stakeholder coaching and, notably, coaching supervision at Oxford Brookes University while continuing my studies in Developmental Psychology and Coaching Psychology as part of my PhD.

Post-Program Assessments

All of the nine participants undertook a second WUSCT stages assessment 12 months later. They were submitted as blind profiles and were again assessed by Susanne Cook-Greuter.

Given the research findings set out in Chapter 3, it was not anticipated that the participants would shift a full stage in the one year. The period of time was not long enough (five years) nor intensive enough (20+ days) to suggest a potential stage shift. However, I did hope that some participants might shift more than others and that there might be some features or aspects that distinguished the content of their coaching programs from the rest.

I anticipated that most of the participants might increase their leadership capacity in incremental ways within the same stage, that is, lateral or horizontal learning. This would be clear from changes in their TWS or potentially a shift in their secondary stage or leading and trailing edges. I anticipated that the research analysis could at best compare and contrast the coaching interventions and the coachees' unique individual developmental journeys to illuminate the research question.

I was completely surprised to discover that 100% of the participants had shifted a full stage in their centre of gravity in the 12-month period! Seven of the nine participants (78%) shifted from *Achievist/Specialist* to a primary later stage perspective at *Catalyst/Achievist*. One of the nine participants (11%) transformed twice to *Synergist/Catalyst*. The TWS of a second participant also indicated the same double shift but their total protocol rating (TPR) was demoted from *Synergist* to *Catalyst* on the basis of the assessor's holistic consideration of their sentence completions. The ninth participant made the stage shift from *Specialist* to *Achievist*.

Each one of the first nine participants in the research study shifted either one or two stages in their leadership development after an average of eight 90-minute coaching meetings over a 12-month period.

Three More Participants and Assessments

I then added a further three coachees to test the original findings and I invited the original coachees to complete a third assessment three years after their second assessment to incorporate a longitudinal dimension to the research.

Of the three additional participants, one was also from the public sector and the other two were senior executives in the financial services sector. Two of the participants also had at least 80% of their initial stage profiles in conventional stages, one 94%, and the other 83%. The third participant was included in the research study by way of exception to test the shift from *Catalyst* to *Synergist*. That person began with 47% of their profile at *Catalyst*.

These three supplementary coachees undertook an average of nine coaching sessions each. The order of transformation was similar to the initial nine participants. Two shifted one stage each and the third transformed twice from *Achievist* to *Synergist*.

To add the longitudinal dimension to the research, all of the original nine coachees were also invited to undertake a third assessment three years after their second assessment to ascertain the sustainability of their transformative vertical development. Three agreed to do so. The results were unanimous. All three participants now had their centre of gravity at *Synergist*.

The participant who had vaulted their way to *Synergist/Catalyst* earlier sustained this profile. Now 100% of their profile was at later stages (previously 81%) with 63% at *Synergist* and *Constructivist* (previously 25%). The second repeat participant who had quantitatively but not qualitatively been at *Synergist* at the end of the initial 12-month period was now operating at *Synergist/Catalyst*. Their later stage profile had increased from 64% to 90%. The third participant had also shifted to *Synergist/Catalyst* with 73% of their responses at these two later stages compared to 50% three years previously. Not only had the three participants sustained their development, but they had continued to progress their individual transformations to significantly strengthen their post-conventional leadership capacity at *Synergist*.

Over the four-year time period the research took place, the average aggregate post-conventional profile of all 12 participants shifted from 12% to 46% and, for three, onto 88%, in Years 0, 1, and 4 (Figure 4.1). Figure 4.2 provides a summary of the demographics together with the coaching history for each of the 12 participants in the research study.

These findings are most valid for executive coachees who are graduates, aged between 36 and 56 years (the age range of the participants), and who hold senior executive positions with significant and substantial strategic leadership responsibilities.

The mean of the difference in the before and after scores was 28.7, approximately the ambit of a full stage. The difference in the before and after scores ranged from 14 to 48 points. There were no outliers (Tukey Fence). The standard deviation of the difference was 8.7. A matched sample paired t-test showed that there was a highly significant statistical difference between the before and after TWSs. The R^2 of this shift was 0.519 with a single tail p-value of 0.00001 at a 95% confidence interval.

The Hedges g score showed that the number of coaching sessions undertaken by the participants during the research project, had no significant effect on the scope of the shift in each participant's profile. Some coaching sessions

Figure 4.1 The research study results

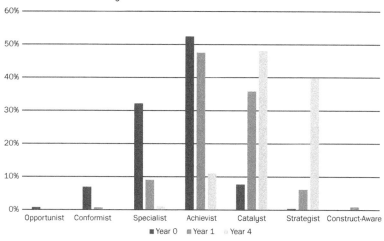

Figure 4.2 Participants' profiles and coaching programs

	Gender	Age	Degree	Prior Sessions	MAP Year 1	Coaching Sessions	MAP Year 2	Post Sessions
A	F	54	PhD	7	7 Jun 13	8	10 Jul 14	7
B	F	48	M	3	9 Apr 13	7	11 Jul 14	1
C	M	53	M	6	23 May 13	8	12 Jul 14	9
D	F	56	B	3	12 Apr 13	5	6 Aug 14	0
E	M	56	B	5	20 Jun 13	9	5 Aug 14	1
F	M	53	MBA	6	23 May 13	10	4 Aug 14	9
G	M	46	M	5	7 Jun 13	9	5 Aug 14	1
H	M	44	B	1	11 Apr 13	11	11 Aug 14	1
I	M	56	M	4	7 Jun 13	5	5 Aug 14	1
J	M	50	M	2	1 Apr 13	5	1 Apr 16	1
K	F	42	B	1	23 Mar 17	12	21 Mar 18	1
L	F	36	B	1	24 Mar 17	12	01 Jun 18	1
Avg	42% F	50	58% M	3.7	Coaching	8.4	Sessions	2.8

The empirical evidence offered by the stage assessments before and after executive coaching with 12 strategic leaders with an average age of 50 years and a later stage coach, indicates that an average of eight 90-minute monthly coaching sessions over a 12-month period was instrumental in igniting, expediting, and sustaining ten single (83%) and two double shifts (17%), almost all (92%) to later stage post-conventional leadership capacity at *Catalyst* and *Synergist*.

were also taken prior to the research project, and those that undertook the third assessment had continued with an average of six coaching sessions following the project. The Hedges g score showed that the total number of coaching sessions undertaken had no significant effect on the results. The average number of coaching sessions undertaken by those who shifted two stages in one year from Achievist to Synergist was eight.

Chapter 4: Key Points

The pre- and post-coaching program stage assessments indicate that:

1 The transformative executive coaching approach deliberately intended to liberate later stage development generated a vertical shift in stage for 100% of the coachees in the 12-month research study.

2 An average of eight 90-minute monthly coaching sessions spread throughout one year was sufficient to generate a shift to later stage post-conventional leadership capacity for 100% of the coaches, i.e. just 2 days in total, in contrast to 20-day leadership programs.

3 The transformative executive coaching approach also has the potential to enable a double shift from *Achievist* to *Synergist* (2/11 or 18% of participants with a third very close) also with just eight 90-minute monthly coaching sessions in one year.

4 The longitudinal sample indicates that once a person has shifted to *Catalyst* or *Synergist* as a primary centre of gravity, their journey continues to consolidate at *Synergist* as suggested by the two-step sequence of individuation followed by integration, indicating that once transformative shifts are attained, they are sustained, based on 100% of a sample of three participants three years later.

5 The equivalent coaching approach appears to be just as relevant in expediting the subsequent integration at *Synergist* (5/12 or 42%) as it is in igniting individuation to *Catalyst* (11/12 or 92%).

6 Over the four-year time period the research took place, the average aggregate post-conventional profile (*Catalyst*+) of the 12 participants shifted from 12% to 46% and, for three, onto 88%, in years 0, 1, and 4.

Next Chapter

This chapter reviewed the quantitatively measured research results of the coaching outcomes after a 12-month executive coaching program. The next chapter begins to explore the qualitative analysis of the coaching programs to explore how the executive coaching led to such dramatic and surprising results. Parts II and III explore these findings further and examine the coaching approach in greater depth.

5 THE KEY THEMES OF TRANSFORMATIVE COACHING

This chapter sets out the thematic analysis of the content of the coaching conversations. It sets out how the data was investigated and analysed to arrive at the key drivers in post-conventional development from *Achievist* to *Catalyst* and *Synergist*.

Thematic Analysis

The executive coaching had been shown to be effective in igniting and expediting later stage development. The next step was to discover 'how?', an ideal key question for case study research. My initial approach to answer this question was to excavate the coaching content by way of thematic analysis, i.e. to identify the key themes that took up most of our attention during the coaching conversations.

I wanted to find out what the coachees had discovered in our coaching conversations. What may have prompted their growth? In what ways did I share a later stage perspective with them that may have facilitated their vertical development? What important aspects did the coaching conversations have in common?

I was aware that I had spent time with the coachees on strategic business planning and performance frameworks, as well as on intimate personal matters concerning their own attitudes and experiences in relationship to others. This also became apparent from Leximancer's quantitative content analysis. I plugged 75,000 words of notes from the coaching conversations with the initial nine participants into the Leximancer software program. This immediately brought categories to light. Two led the field: People and Strategic.

Figure 5.1 is a Leximancer bubble diagram showing the relational analysis amongst words commonly found together, with the size of the bubbles indicating their frequency. Figure 5.2 provides a list of the words most commonly repeated throughout the coaching transcripts.

The topics resonated with me. The next step was to take a more disciplined and in-depth approach to identifying the actual coaching interventions or turning points in coaching conversations that appeared to be most helpful to the coachees.

Figure 5.1 Leximancer thematic relational analysis

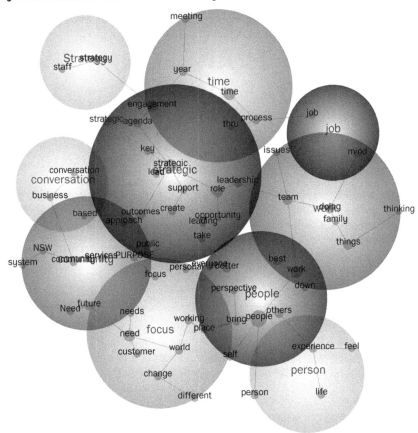

Figure 5.2 Leximancer word cluster analysis

Theme	Hits
people	784
strategic	732
focus	536
community	472
work	470
time	416
person	260
conversation	117
strategy	114
job	95

Clustering Topics of Conversation

I went through all the data sorting it into topics of conversation. My initial categories were quite broad. They included understanding self, leading change, leading people, business leadership, industry leadership, meetings and time management, through to generic terms such as practices, experiences, dreams, observations, and judgements.

To create a clear chain of evidence, I placed this data by topic of conversation (rows) and coachees (columns) into an Excel spreadsheet. This enabled me to compare and contrast the nature of the conversations in each topic looking along each row.

After many iterations reviewing and reflecting on the data and making a few adjustments in topics so that they better encapsulated the nature of the coaching conversations taking place along each row, I ended up with seven business-oriented topics related to strategic and management issues and nine personal topics related to self-awareness and self-mastery. However, this list still seemed to be rather long and incoherent to be able to articulate more value than a simple list of items.

After taking time away from the data, I re-approached it once more. I continued with the two key categories, now labelled Strategic (business) and Holistic (personal) and took another look at the range of topics within them. It dawned on me that some of the topics were very self-oriented, the coachee's thoughts and aspirations, their feelings and subconscious shadow. They fell into the Intrapersonal category – 'From Within'. Other topics concerned active engagement with others that were clearly more of an Interpersonal nature – 'With Others'.

This led to clustering all the topics into eight clear drivers across a matrix of four integrated categories. The drivers included all the key coaching topics, clustering like with like, and represented most (guestimate of > 90%) of the substantive coaching conversations held. They certainly reflected the recurring ideas that often came up more than once for each coachee. Their repetition and reporting of progress in relation to these items indicated that the coachees also considered them to be very important in their development as inspiring, strategic leaders.

A Matrix of Eight Key Drivers

The order of the drivers is identified by the numbers in the StageSHIFT Matrix. This order was commonly found across all coaching programs. It so happened that the nine coaching programs began at the beginning of the financial year and therefore required the development of strategic business performance frameworks to engage others effectively.

The eight StageSHIFT Drivers in order are (Figure 5.3):

- Setting inspiring evolutionary purposeful personal aspirations;
- Expressing oneself with a positive, open, kind, and compassionate mind;
- Engaging everyone in setting shared purposeful strategic direction;

- A dynamic approach to distributing time to orchestrate flow;
- Exploring psychodynamics to appreciate, heal, and release shadow;
- Sustaining standards with courageous caring conversations;
- Articulating a unique signature inspiring living presentation;
- Collaborating widely with stakeholders to generate synergy.

Many had a lot of resonance with the research findings and suggestions from thought leaders presented in Chapter 5.

Driver 1, setting inspiring evolutionary purposeful personal aspirations, was a key first stepping-stone that was advocated by Laloux. Driver 3, engaging everyone in setting shared purposeful strategic direction, was also focused on developing an inspiring evolutionary purpose for the division or organisation led by the coachee. These were developed through the emergent coaching dialogue, first during the coaching sessions as a type of rehearsal so that the coachee could gain confidence with the principles and process, and then by the coachee with their people.

Driver 2, expressing oneself with a positive, open, kind, and compassionate mind and heart, is a synthesis of positive psychology, heart-based research, and neuroscience. It is based on much of the research undertaken by Martin Seligman, Barbara Fredrickson, the HeartMath Institute, and the many breakthrough findings on the neuroplasticity of the brain.

Driver 4 enabled a highly empowering strategic scaffolding to be engineered and transposed on top of more typically bureaucratic organisational processes and policies. In many ways, this liberated the latent talents of the people reporting to the coachees. They developed the trusted relationships and sense of community that Hamel, Kegan, Laloux, and Scharmer espoused albeit within an *Achievist*-oriented framework.

Driver 6, holding courageous caring conversations, emerged repeatedly over time to enable the gracious exercise of personal power, both assertive and

Figure 5.3 The StageSHIFT Executive Coaching Matrix

SELF	FROM WITHIN	WITH OTHERS
HOLISTIC	1. Set Evolutionary Personal Aspirations	2. Positive Kindness and Open Mindfulness
	5. Release Shadow Psychodynamics	6. Hold Courageous Caring Conversations
STRATEGIC	3. Shared Purposeful Strategic Direction	4. Distribute Time to Orchestrate Flow
	7. A Unique Signature Living Presentation	8. Collabotate Widely to Generate Synergy

vulnerable power. It was one of the most common interventions across all the coaching conversations.

The reflective and resolution work with disorientating dilemmas and challenging life experiences was undertaken as part of Driver 5: exploring psychodynamics and their source to appreciate, heal, and integrate shadow. This included a life review and reframing of personal story to develop a more empowering interpretation of their narrative along with sharing insights to create the opportunity for soul evolution.

The holding of the psychologically safe and supportive space was essential for this type of dialogue to occur. The confidentiality of the conversation also would have contributed to its intimacy, directness, and depth. Typical business or even developmental coaching conversations don't tend to explore shadow.

Drivers 7 and 8 arose in response to coachee needs to make presentations and engage external stakeholders. They became an extension of earlier work that we travelled to later in the year after most of the coachees had already implemented or applied the first six drivers. They led to the consolidation of the *Synergist* perspective while reaching into the transpersonal space.

Each of these drivers came into play during the coaching conversations as a response to the issues, concerns, dilemmas, challenges, opportunities, and threats experienced and articulated by the coachees. They are also a reflection of a coach's stage of development, proven expertise, and career experience. Together, these aspects synchronised to build momentum in vertical development to later stages, to *Catalyst* and more remarkably, to the development of the transformative leadership capacity of a *Synergist*.

Chapter 5: Key Points

1   The data from the coaching conversations with the first nine research participants was based on over 100 hours of executive coaching and consisted of 75,000 words.
2   The data was first analysed using Leximancer computer software to gain some initial insights into key themes.
3   The data was then evaluated from the ground-up to fine-tune the themes as specific categories by pasting it into a large spreadsheet by column/participant and row/category.
4   Over time and iterative reviews of the data, it became evident that both strategic and holistic leadership were equally influential, and that each had an inner component of self-realisation or awareness within self, and an outer component of the application or implementation of the coachees' new and emerging perspective on leadership.
5   This led to the articulation of eight key drivers in later stage development from *Achievist* to *Catalyst* and *Synergist*.
6   These eight key drivers were found to be just as effective when employed with three new participants.

Next Part

This concludes Part I, the Stages of Leadership Transformation. Part II provides you with an in-depth explanation of each of the eight drivers of development in relation to the experience of the coachees. It concludes with their key changes in perception during the coaching program.

PART 2

The Drivers of Later Stage Transformation

Part II sets out the eight drivers of later stage development from *Achievist* to *Catalyst* and *Synergist*. It looks at each driver in turn and explains how it arose in response to coachee challenges and dilemmas, what it involves, and how it was implemented or applied to their life at work. We also begin to look beneath the surface to explore the experience of the coachee and the impact of the driver on their presence, reputation, and career.

Chapters 6–9 set out two drivers each. They offer the two steps in couplet form, the inner dimension of awareness, attention, and intention in the Inner Zone, followed by the outer dimension of demonstrating this understanding in the midst of challenging or demanding interpersonal situations in the Outer Zone. This reflects the two-step process of individuation and integration through the stages.

Part II concludes with Chapter 10, which outlines a number of shifts in perception. These were repeated often during all of the case studies and apply across the eight drivers. I believe they were of significant influence in transforming beliefs, values, and perceptions while navigating the shift in perspective from *Achievist* to *Synergist*.

Chapter 6: Holistic Drivers 1 and 2: Cultivating One's Best Self

Chapter 7: Strategic Drivers 3 and 4: Uplifting the Organisation

Chapter 8: Holistic Drivers 5 and 6: Holding Safe Emergent Space

Chapter 9: Strategic Drivers 7 and 8: Leading Wide Collaboration

Chapter 10: The Attitudinal Shifts in Perception and Perspective

6 HOLISTIC DRIVERS 1 AND 2: CULTIVATING ONE'S BEST SELF

DRIVER 1: Setting Inspiring Evolutionary Purposeful Personal Aspirations

The problem or need the driver addressed

The question that forms at the beginning of any coaching program is 'why?' Why is the coachee embarking on a coaching program at this time? What do they hope to gain? What do they wish to overcome? What do they aspire to? What are their developmental goals? In the words of one coachee: I want 'to step beyond my current role with a wider field of interests, to become perceived as a strategic thinker beyond technical and government knowledge'.

The beginning of a coaching program is the ideal time to set clear direction. For me, this entailed setting inspiring evolutionary personal aspirations for the self. This, in my mind, was much more transformative than setting developmental goals in terms of specific capabilities. Intentions resonate at a level higher than goals, and aspirations, another level higher again. I believe that the more aspirational the goals, the more we stimulate vertical growth.

Goals require taking actions to achieve them – they are very performance orientated. Intentions require mindful endeavour and focused attention. They relate less to achievement and more to one person's impact on another person. They require paying close conscious personal attention to the cultivation of self-expression. Aspirations, if they are sufficiently inspiring and the person is fully committed to them, demand the transformation of the self. They are set at a level that is currently out of a person's reach and have the power to pull a person towards fulfilling those aspirations. If we are committed to realising our greatest potential, prepared to learn from our mistakes and follow our inner GPS, we can and will ultimately arrive at that aspirational destination.

What the driver involves

Each coachee was invited to develop what came to be known as an Aspirational Leadership Brand Declaration (ALBD – mnemonic: A Little Black Dress). It was aspirational so that it would be truly inspiring and offer a significant reach for the coachee. Note the subtle difference between the words 'reach' and 'stretch', in the context of far-reaching intentions and stretch goals. Reach suggests vertical learning, to transform oneself, while stretch suggests lateral learning, to use all the resources one already has available. I wanted coachees to reach out for who they truly wanted to become in order to tap into their intrinsic potential and inner sources of power.

The ALBD focused on leadership, as that was the point of my transformative coaching program: stage leadership development to the later stages of *Catalyst* and *Synergist*. It involved their brand, what made them distinctive, unique, the qualities that others would identify them with, values they would model for others. And it was a declaration. A little like the Declaration of Independence, it was intended to be an announcement, an explicit unilateral proclamation to oneself.

How the driver is implemented

Each coachee crafts their own statement during the coaching meeting. The initial frame is: 'I am becoming a . . . leader who . . .'. They articulate the type of leader they would like to become and complete the statement with their highest intrinsic purpose. This takes a little time and iteration. I invite the coachee to simply ponder out loud, I take notes and offer back to them what they have said. I often invite the coachee to uplift their statement and make it even more aspirational.

I encourage the coachee to continue to draft their ALBD until they are happy with it. I suggest that it be succinct enough to be memorable, yet distinctive enough to be inspiring. Most coachees bring their revised and refined ALBD to the next coaching meeting for discussion. Sometimes a little more fine-tuning is required.

I then invite them to memorise it, say it daily when they first start their work-day, and bring it to mind during the day in an unobtrusive way, such as when entering a room, at the beginning of a meeting, or when waiting at a pedestrian crossing or red light. The ALBD for each coachee becomes a clear, succinct, mindful, and heartfelt intentional statement of the type of leader they aspire to become, at work and at home.

This driver is enriched by creating a vision board of the future, journaling life in five years' time on the basis that things turn out much better than the coachee could ever imagine, or simply imagining the future in their mind. A favourite formula of mine is my first ever MAGIC reflection. It involves simply pondering each element one at a time, setting the scene for more magic to enter your life (Figure 6.1).

Figure 6.1 The MAGIC affirmation process to create the future

M is for Mastery . . . I am the master of my life, the captain of my ship . . .

A is for Abundance . . . There are infinite resources and possibilities available to me . . .

G is for Gratitude . . . I am grateful for all the blessings in my life, past, present, and future . . . *and then go through as many as you can think of while opening the Heart.*

I is for Imagination . . . *Imagine yourself in the most wonderful future . . . play out the future until you're overjoyed with your imagined dream . . . the Mind is very powerful.*

C is for Celebration . . . *Celebrate how wonderful life is with an inspired sense of joy!*

Here are some ALBD examples at various stages in the development process.

I am a strong strategic leader who forges bold strategic direction and empowers leaders holding them to account. More tough love.

I lead with vision, I influence key stakeholders, and honour authenticity over and above authority.

I am a visionary leader with a clear strategic agenda and an orchestrated focus. I am confident, calm, and centred.

I am a visionary leader in society who inspires and empowers others to do their best and develops their capacity to contribute. I am a genius with communications. I love intellectual challenge. I create order out of chaos. I evolve through my life experience. As a leader, I generate wonderful results that help others. I am happy having fun, enjoying life with people while having an enriching, wonderful life experience. I am gracious and wise. There is joy in my life.

I am positive, ethical, honest, concerned for people and the environment. I am a fantastic parent and partner who is strategic, responsible, and sensitive to others.

I am courageous, valiant and decisive, objective and pragmatic, diligent and strategic.

I am a globally recognised strategic leader pursuing the salience of science in the community.

I am a balanced, innovative, and visionary leader who inspires the team and organisation. I am a fabulous husband and father. I serve my family with wisdom and kindness.

The coachees' experience with it

The coachees often brought up aspects of their development during the coaching program in broader reference to their changing life experience.

It feels sometimes like I'm floating a bit, re this development I'm doing. It feels as if I was quite attached to what I was doing, and it was all stable, cause and effect and it will happen. And then to come up that notch, it's like being in water where you can't touch the bottom, I'm still floating, and it's ok, yet I feel nervous sometimes when I can't touch the bottom. Treading water is reinforcing that I'd better get used to this feeling. I'm even enjoying the process, it's not painful, just disconcerting, I think I've got more energy because of it, I'm feeling great!

Even in terms of being 'authentic', that word resonates with me really strongly, even if I'm feeling a bit fake . . . I tend to speak of myself now. For instance, my son's friend asked me on the weekend while we were at an art gallery, 'What do I do?' I said, 'I'm a leader, of about 400 people'. A really different answer from what I would've said before. I would've described myself as a technical expert, project manager or program director, or a leader of a community-wide strategic initiative.

The impact of this driver on the coachees

Coachees developed a sense of faith in their own purposeful leadership intentions. The sense of authentic affirmation from a deep sense of vocation and contribution held many of the participants steady through the turmoils of interpersonal battles and organisational restructures. Indeed, their sense of self-validation increased over the course of the year as their intentions manifested in the external world.

Defining an ALBD initiated the process of articulating new thought streams that transcended anxieties, shifting their thoughts away from what they found insulting and offensive to what they desired and deserved. Their passion and enthusiasm for their own 'hero's journey' grew over time as evidence of their new emerging identity accumulated.

The underlying principles of the driver

From the *Synergist* perspective of an individually constructed interpenetrative world, our repeated thoughts, deep feelings, and clear intentions have the power to set up a chain of events in our life experience, both opportunities and challenges, that manifest our thoughts, feelings, wishes, and concerns. Thus, setting aspirational intent attracts personal growth – both lessons and blessings.

A clear aspirational intention is like a homing device or an inner compass that will attract the very challenges and opportunities to realise those aspirations – and learn how to do better and understand implications more deeply, each time. Scharmer (2018) advocated connecting to source to uncover one's highest future potential and to inquire into questions of identity and purpose: What is my Self? What is my Work? Intentional change involves envisioning the ideal self: who you wish to be and what you want to do.

Setting an aspirational intention to be a certain type of leader is a deliberately developmental intervention to cultivate the self, to open oneself up to learning how we might become that type of leader, not through striving and driving for results as an *Achievist* does, but by opening oneself up to organic emergent growth in reciprocity with others at *Catalyst*. This is a distinction between being on a proven path to achieve results and being on a journey to become a stronger and better person or leader. As Ralph Waldo Emerson revealed, 'Do not go where the path may lead, go instead where there is no path and leave a trail'.

I would like to emphasise that the ALBD needs to be both aspirational and inspiring. An aspiration is a far-reaching intention that is an ideal, a dream, to which there is no logical path but a deep fervent desire to become so, something that would give life meaning and purpose. It is inspiring if it resonates deeply within, if it warms the heart, invites the spirit to soar, and compels a person to think twice and change their default autopilot way of being or behaving, to make their dream come true.

Neuroscience is continually providing new evidence of the power of the mind, introspection, interpretation, and imagination to re-engineer our habits of mind and neural pathways.

The nature of the shift that was activated

Coachees commonly expressed developmental goals around wishing to become more strategic leaders. This is typical of *Achievists*. While they are adept at setting goals, creating strategies, getting things done, and achieving results, they are much less confident exercising visionary strategic leadership to shape the world around them. They have not yet invested significant time in considering how they would prefer the world to be. They are simply highly effective in playing the current game to their advantage, being winners rather than losers.

Becoming a more strategic leader is not enough to activate a vertical shift. It is possible to contemplate being more strategic as being more manipulative, astute, wily, or canny. Setting an ALBD changed the nature of the game from one of rivalry, competition, survival, and manipulation in the corporate trenches, to one of spiritual evolution to rise above the fray, transcend the turmoil, become one's best self, and exercise integrity based on principles.

Inviting the commitment to become one's best and most inspiring unique and distinctive self in order to exercise more courageous and authentic leadership in a win-win-win world, is a game-changer. The focus shifted from struggling and thriving to transcending the noise and clutter to do justice to self, to become a more courageous person and flourish. This marked a critical shift in mindset at the level of identity from the calculating *Achievist* to demonstrating the integrity of character that emerges at *Catalyst* and manifests at *Synergist*.

DRIVER 2: Cultivating a Positive, Open, Kind, and Compassionate Mind

The problem or need the driver addressed

Another key element that arose repeatedly across all the case studies in one form or another was the coachees' criticism and judgement of others. Calling other people 'idiots' and 'useless', or otherwise venting about their annoying qualities is common practice amongst people at the stages of the sensitive *Specialist* and competitive *Achievist*.

However, on the realisation from an interpenetrative point of view that this is transference (i.e. that whatever we accuse another of is a criticism of oneself), the participants began to alter their way of thinking and speaking. The same is true for talents we admire in others. These are also latent within us. Thus, when developing their ALBDs, it was helpful for the participants to consider the leadership traits of people they admired. Similarly, it was helpful in their development to realise that the flaws they saw in others around them were also within them. The very fact that they noticed these flaws in others and found them unappealing indicated that they were precisely the character traits to address within themselves.

> *I'd like to be more 'good'. It's easy for me to criticise people and I want to stop that, I want to care for people more . . . be less encumbered to drop a bag that I've been carrying . . . it's easy to criticise and ridicule them . . . enjoyable at that moment, but can leave a bad aftertaste . . . How you're not very high up that spiral if that's what you're doing . . . It's fun to ridicule others, but do I want the pleasure of that ridicule or do I want to be up the spiral? I'll give up the lower pleasures to take up the higher ground . . . Hence, I'm willing to change.*

Criticism of others is often a form of defensiveness and self-protection when feeling fearful or exposed. The busy senior executives were assailed by many fears and self-doubts, just like everyone else at conventional stages of adult development. For instance:

> *I'm terrified about the day or my ability to work as an executive; the executive team is messy, there is no clear mission.*

> *I'm concerned about what people may think . . . wondering how to reshape myself to embrace more perspectives . . . Have conformed . . . Made situations easier than made hard decisions . . . New ideas were frowned upon . . . I've been institutionalised . . . felt out on a limb.*

> *I have three key fear factors [in relation to speaking up]: 1, people with higher authority; 2, embarrassment if decisions go against my point of view; and 3, there's all the extra work, why should I bother?*

What the driver involves

This driver involves a range of elements integrating self-awareness and self-expression.

- To recognise transference as a learning opportunity to cultivate the self;
- To recognise automatic negative thoughts (ants) in self-talk as simply thoughts that are often parents' or teachers' voices from youth that have become embedded unconsciously in the mind and can now be consciously deleted;
- To discipline one's self-expression to only use positive vocabulary at all times;
- To pay attention to one's throw-away lines at the end of sentences, conversations, or other interactions as they reveal one's subconscious beliefs;
- To choose to inquire of another to genuinely wish to understand them better rather than immediately telling one's own story;

- To revise unfavourable situations that happen during the day by reprogramming the mind with a new memory of a more empowering imagined drama that has a more favourable outcome; and
- To add and multiply positive wellbeing practices to our daily lives to live and enjoy a better and more satisfying, beneficial, fulfilling life.

How the driver is implemented

The implementation of this driver is focused on increasing self-awareness by becoming aware of self-expression, both internally and externally. Once more aware, attention turns to enhancing and enriching one's self-expression by cultivating positivity, discernment, personal empowerment, compassion, and using the power of mindful imagination.

Acknowledgement of transference led to self-reflection, first during a coaching session, and later as a standard form of inquiry for the coachee. If I see this in another person, where is that in me? This reflects the interpenetrative perspective of the *Synergist*.

Conscious deletion of negative thoughts is also an important strategy to become aware of and deliberately clear the mind of obsolete phrases from childhood that are simply the projections of parents, teachers, relatives, and elders associated with childhood friends. I have found this is possible when combined with a physical motion, such as a control-alt-delete thought while pinching fingers and thumb together like you would to close the mouth of a hand puppet, a waving of the hand as you would to shoo away a fly, or a flick of the fingers! I do not know if there is any science around this but I do believe in mind–body energy integration, so in my belief system, the physical actions with the thought work! I've found that the conscious deletion thought and action does need to be repeated and then it simply disappears: 'third time's a charm'.

If the negative thought is associated with negative emotion, then a simple flick will not work. Negative emotions are covered in the next driver on exploring psychodynamics.

Case study examples

As most people hold onto negativity at earlier stages, I incorporated some positive psychology techniques (Seligman, 2007), mindfulness practices, and respectful communications to facilitate the development of a stronger and more robust positive growth mindset (Dweck, 2008). There were 12 key elements commonly found across the coaching transcripts:

1 To consciously adopt an optimistic mood, even if it is contrived, to look forward to the day ahead, invite wonderful surprises and new opportunities, to smile with anticipation and remind yourself to smile throughout the day.

2 To use positive language *always*, using the preface 'not' to communicate when things are not so good. This strategy helps the listener to embrace the communication much more positively, including constructive feedback.

3 To replace specific key words and phrases: e.g. 'I worry that' thinking the worst that could happen to 'I wonder if' inviting the finest possibilities in life; to exchange 'should' for 'could' to replace compliance with choice; and to use 'and' instead of 'but' to consider a fuller spectrum of views rather than oppositional polarising views.

4 To refine and memorise one's ALBD and recall it three times a day, as well as repeating heartfelt affirmations to oneself to counter obsolete inhibiting beliefs.

5 To listen to others with an open mind, seeking to understand them rather than formulating your own view and waiting to speak next. To always inquire into another person's point of view immediately after it is articulated rather than advocating and advancing one's own perspective. This creates dialogue instead of argument. To consciously stop 'telling' behaviour such as pointing your finger and demonstrate listening behaviour by nodding your head when someone is talking to you.

6 To delete negative thoughts as they arise with a physical action of some kind such as pressing the fingers and thumb together, flicking the wrist or fingers while thinking control-alt-delete.

7 To become aware of throwaway lines, the things we say when we're not thinking about what we're saying, as these illuminate our limiting beliefs. Once we're aware of them, we have the power to change them e.g. from scarcity to abundance. One participant discovered that her view that 'You're only as good as your last gig' was inhibiting her confidence despite a very successful career track record.

8 To engage in spontaneous daily acts of kindness whenever the opportunity arises.

9 To consciously undertake one-minute, heart-based meditations (the Loving Kindness Meditation is advocated by the HearthMath Institute), sending gratitude and love to specific people and out into the world generally, ideal during lapse time such as when queuing or waiting. This has been proven to lower your heart rate and relieve stress. To meditate daily using silence, music, structured meditations, or customised applications.

10 By 3.00pm each day, to

a) Hold one active constructive conversation (Seligman, 2011), encouraging and validating another person on their life's journey;

b) Praise two people explaining exactly what they've done well and why it is such an important contribution; and

c) Say an inspiring 'Thank you' three times to three different people with a generous heart.

11 To ask at the end of the day, 'What went well today?' by way of conversation or journaling (Seligman, 2011).

12 To practise the 3 R's of rewind, rehearse, and record to reframe any less than optimal events that occurred that day and replace the existing memory with a new imagined memory where you intervene in a more empowering way that generates more beneficial outcomes. Based on the neuroplasticity of the brain, this new memory is then available to draw on when a similar situation occurs in the future, rather than the unfavourable memory stored during the actual event (Doidge, 2010). This is also a very effective strategy when you find yourself stuck for words. I invite coachees to articulate what they could say graciously next time something similar occurs and to simply create a pause when feeling challenged by something someone else has said, potentially revealing their unconscious bias, e.g. 'What did you just say?', 'What do you mean by that?'

The coachees' experience with it

All coachees found that giving attention to self-expression, internally and externally, was of great value to them. There was a certain relief that undesirable situations could be completely transformed by first transforming their perspective on it by valuing life's lessons, and then transforming the self in relation to it.

> Doing the Aspirational Brand Statement, the method of scripting, helped me to be aware of what I've been thinking . . . Now . . . in the morning . . . I realised I'd scripted myself to say 'I'm tired' and I was concerned that this is a bit debilitating . . . So I switched it to 'I'm ready' in the week leading up to Easter. The week I rescripted my autopilot was the week I decluttered my desk . . . I'm beginning to exercise mindfulness, aware of what I think, why I think it, what I say, what I do . . . Instead of feeling despondent, I feel excited about the day ahead.

> 'You didn't look like you were rattled'. But I felt rattled. I had to stay positive holding the standard for all staff members. My staff used to react and I've coached them on how to respond to people positively.

> 5–10 minutes on the train dreaming of the future, imagining the future . . . 3 goals . . . 100% people trained, 100% people going to work joyfully, a happy workplace, 100% of trains working perfectly . . . 3 goals . . . Perfect retirement, wonderful family relationships, lots of travel.

> 'Tell me more about that' has become my auto responder. Listening with genuine empathy and concern.

> At work, we were moving from 105 to just 40 people, with many people looking for the future in their careers. I managed it really well, how to be positive about facing change. I stopped being a micro-manager, and empowered people. It was very satisfying to get the feedback I did when I left.

Cleared my desk, decluttered and now have amazing clarity of thought . . . it's working on a metaphysical level . . . I'm much more organised . . . also tackled my study at home and cleaned up the garage, blew the leaves in the garden, totally on a roll . . .

Engage first, means ask questions, put people into a process of engagement. I'm acting more as a colleague than as a parent now.

Seeing the person in terms of strengths . . . When people feel seen, they respond. Wasn't doing this 6 months ago . . . Physically moved back from the table, made a few observations, not sure what I was going to say next, something was going on with the space . . .

The impact of this driver on the coachees

The sense of fear of being outed as 'not good enough', being exposed for making unwise decisions, or being imposed upon by more senior executives and then made to feel small, was replaced to a large extent by positive reframing, re-imagining, and re-engineering oneself. The new sense of personal power gave many coachees profound moments of illumination.

I remember one day I began a coaching session by describing how irritated I had been by a hygienist cleaning my teeth – including her New Zealand accent. [Antoinette is from New Zealand.] I was just wanting to vent and remove this experience from my state of mind. Little did I know that Antoinette would turn this into a teaching moment for me. She provided a life-changing reflection back to me – did I want to be reactive to situations? She told me that my reaction was as much about me as it was about her. Did I want to be an irritable or irritated person, or did I want to be a different type of person in the world? I did not believe it was possible to change my personality, and then I realised I could. I wasn't that type of person; I could be whoever I wanted to be. I've never forgotten that moment.

I was always intolerant of fools and cranky, idiotic people behaving badly . . . Realising that whatever happens in their life, they are trying to do the best they can. Maybe a bit more understanding from my point of view rather than creating relationship issues with them . . . Not getting personally stressed about it. Huge shift . . . Biggest shift of all!

Noticing my language and self-correcting in the moment, I have more energy in what I'm doing, confluence of factors helping me to stride into the role I need to take . . . Defining my role and striding into it . . .

The underlying principles of the driver

We are all human, and one of the universally adopted shadow human conditions that is prevalent at *Specialist* is the psychological state of being not good enough (NGE). Because we feel NGE, we accuse others of being NGE. Also, because a person identifies with their work at *Specialist* – '*I am* a teacher', '*I am* a doctor', '*I am* an executive leader' – they take feedback on their work extremely personally. Their identity is their work. Therefore, if there is any suggestion that their work is NGE, then this immediately raises the universal spectre of feeling not good enough as deserving of a life.

At *Achievist*, a person begins to endorse the psychological notion of 'You're okay, I'm okay'. The underlying principle that transmutes NGE available at *Catalyst* is an appreciation that everyone is doing the best they can with their current breadth and depth of awareness. This builds compassion for self and others. This understanding seemed to be a vital contributor to the release of the *Specialist* shadow and the adoption of the *Catalyst* appreciative mindset.

By no longer criticising, judging, or deprecating others, and simultaneously interpreting their frustrations as alerts to discover the character flaws within themselves, the participants released aspects of their shadow at *Specialist* and cultivated their leadership capacity at *Catalyst*. They were no longer NGE, nor even a work-in-progress, but an evolving human masterpiece-in-progress.

Other underlying principles are the scientific research findings of positive psychology, neuroscience, the HeartMath Institute, and a greater appreciation of what it is to be an evolving human being. From a stage perspective, the interpenetrative transforming self comes into full view with this driver.

The nature of the shift that was activated

In the conventional world, *Conformists* are largely absent, *Specialists* are highly sensitive and critical of others, and *Achievists* are very competitive and can be dismissive of others. The heart has not really opened to embrace others, understand them, and empathise with their experience of the trials and tribulations of life.

As a person becomes aware of their judgements and criticisms, and views them as a mirror of their own flawed identity, personal growth is instigated. Shifting from a fixed to a growth mindset begins at *Achievist*, but an understanding of transference takes this mindset to a deeper personal level at *Catalyst*.

The introduction of positive psychology shifted the participants' focus from negative to positive, and the coaching in the development of a growth mindset integrating transference shifted the participants' focus to personal growth and interpersonal kindness and appreciation.

Inviting participants to open up their hearts to others, to 'bring their heart to meetings', and to see life as a movie – a projection of the conscious mind, and a mirror – a reflection of the subconscious mind, was thought to contribute significantly to the shift in conscious awareness as a witness of one's self-expression and consequent life experience at *Catalyst* and *Synergist*.

This driver has a lot of congruence with becoming a more mindful leader. Someone who embodies leadership presence cultivates focus, clarity, creativity, and compassion (Marturano, 2014). The interpenetrative world of the *Synergist* identifies with all emotions, experiences, and impulses within the human condition with a compassionate and discerning mind.

Chapter 6: Key Points

1 It's important to set clear, purposeful, far-reaching aspirations, not just goals or intentions, to activate the Hero's Journey to *Synergist*.
2 An Aspirational Leadership Brand Declaration can be activated as a powerful GPS signalling system by memorising and repeating it.
3 Creating an aspirational future can be augmented with the creation of a Vision Board, the power of imagination, and the MAGIC formula.
4 The qualities we criticise in others are undesirable qualities of our own character that are coming to our attention so that we can change to become the person we wish to be.
5 Automatic negative thoughts are unconsciously adopted when we were young; we can delete them and create new positive thoughts with conscious attention.
6 Notice throw-away lines and revelations to reveal and consciously change limiting beliefs.
7 Everything we say reflects what we believe and are trying to understand about ourselves and others – listen to self, become aware and shift to positive language only while seeking to understand why we say what we say and do what we do.
8 Reprogram the mind with the 3 R's of rewind, rehearse, and record to formulate new, more empowering memories to draw on in the future and help to generate better outcomes when a similar situation presents itself next time.
9 Create multiple wellbeing practices and rituals in daily life to live a more fulfilling life, e.g. acts of kindness, gratitude, meditation, praise, 'what went well today?'
10 Listen to others with open mindfulness always following through with a further question to better understand them and give them the opportunity to express themselves further. This can lead to an active constructive conversation where a person can feel seen, heard, and understood in a remarkably empowering way.

Next Chapter

This chapter has reviewed the first two drivers in holistic leadership development related to aspirational intent and positive mindfulness. These two drivers created an uplifting personal direction for each of the coachees and invited them to become extremely vigilant in the language they used and their attitude to situations. It also reframed criticism of others as a way to develop awareness of self from an interpenetrative perspective. The next chapter looks at the first two strategic business drivers.

7 STRATEGIC DRIVERS 3 AND 4: UPLIFTING THE ORGANISATION

DRIVER 3: Engaging Everyone in Setting Shared Purposeful Strategic Direction

The problem or need the driver addressed

It was the beginning of the financial year. All coachees led divisions i.e. had at least two levels of people reporting to them, and there was therefore a need to set strategic direction. There was little knowledge amongst the coachees on how to go about establishing an outcomes-oriented strategic agenda that would be shared by all of their people. This was perhaps due to the public sector's and financial institutions' preoccupation with top-down planning and resource allocation rather than engaging employees in a more empowering, emergent way to realise purposeful shared and agreed outcomes. I have found this to be the case in many large corporations.

I recommended that the coachees set strategic direction in such a way that empowered their division or team, increased accountability and engagement, and uplifted their culture. My background included consulting in organisational development, and I had led organisational transformations three times in my career. In one instance, people engagement increased by 30% in six months; in another, leadership effectiveness increased by 20% in 12 months; and in another small trading company, revenues increased by over 100% in just three weeks.

I had used these empowering strategic frameworks to facilitate many strategic planning offsites for executive teams. The framework created an empowering team context (green in Laloux's model) for employees to have the opportunity to become high-performing *Achievists* and authentic, values-based *Catalysts*. The addition of cross-boundary Key Strategic Initiatives provided the opportunity for those already at *Achievist* to shift to engaging, redefining *Catalysts* as in Kotter's second networked organisation. Simultaneously, if the teams were effective, the coachee who was already in a highly responsible strategic role would have the opportunity to shift to *Synergist* and engage more outwardly and strategically with stakeholders within and beyond the organisation.

I wanted to share proven approaches with the coachees so they could realise their aspirations to become more inspiring, strategic, and empowering leaders. I felt it was important to integrate the role of consultant or mentor within my role as executive coach in order to offer as much support and expertise that I was capable of. I offered an outline of an engagement process that became more sophisticated over time. It enabled the coachees to set shared strategic direction with their people in order to empower and uplift their people and improve business performance.

What the driver involves

To uplift broader strategic engagement, I offered guidance to all coachees on how to develop a Strategic Business charter. It involved a significant chunk of work, including:

- An aspirational evolutionary purpose statement where key words were activated as annual themes over the timeline of the charter, e.g. build, thrive, and sustain;
- Key team performance outcomes with associated measures, benchmarks, and targets based on a simple EQUIP (Efficiency, Quality, User, Income, People) scorecard with no more than 10 key performance indicators;
- Three strategic shifts in performance outcomes and three strategic shifts in culture outcomes, thoughtfully sequenced over a three- to five-year time horizon; this demanded strategic thinking around satisfaction with overall performance and how best to generate greater focus on areas of challenge or opportunity, in contrast to incremental performance improvement across all indicators;
- Key strategic initiatives that would enable the strategic shifts in performance and culture to take place and would be led by executives on a voluntary basis in addition to their principal responsibilities, enacting Kotter's (2014) secondary networked organisation of cross-boundary teams who lead transformative change;
- An agreed set of uplifting values that formed a significant acronym to set standards of behaviour to facilitate respectful communications, uplift people engagement and the culture (e.g. I-CARE: Integrity, Courage, Accountability, Respect, Energy), and initiate stage development to *Catalyst* as values become embodied as well as espoused; and
- A set of operating norms that orchestrated engagement with regular one-on-one meetings, team, divisional and stakeholder meetings, generating a Dynamic Operating Rhythm of engagement over the year ahead (see Driver 4).

How the driver is implemented

Generating a Strategic Business Charter involved developing initial ideas around the draft content of the coachee's charter during a coaching meeting, and then sharing a process with them on how to lead an engagement with their people to collaborate on the creation of a shared charter. The initial work during the coaching session gave coachees the opportunity to articulate their ideas and experience the creative process. In this way, they gained the confidence to repeat the exercise with their people.

An outline of the charter was first developed during the coaching meeting to provide each coachee with the opportunity to think through their own thoughts on purpose and key strategic outcomes. The coach then provided the participant with a series of open questions that they could use when engaging their people to create the charter.

At the next session, the coachee reported their progress, and they talked through the next two elements: strategic shifts and key strategic initiatives. I then collaborated with the coachee on how they could lead an engagement with their people to complete the second tranche of strategic creative work.

In the third session, we talked through the development of values. I must admit I was quite specific about the desired outcomes of the process, and the step-by-step outcomes of the engagement to co-create and produce the end result. However, work of this type was new to all the coachees, so they gladly sought and accepted advice on how to lead an effective engagement process that would generate shared strategic direction and reliable outcomes.

As a coach with lots of corporate and consulting experience in creating Strategic Business Charters, and a proven track record in lifting people engagement and business performance, I believe my confidence in the suggested approach came through. I collaborated with coachees on the specifics, e.g. their selection of outcomes for their divisions, and the different options for measuring those outcomes: the key performance shifts, their sequence, and the types of strategic initiatives that could activate those shifts. This prior collaborative thinking enabled the coachees to demonstrate confidence when engaging their people. They had had the opportunity to think things through strategically and could therefore ask relevant questions and suggest ideas with their people.

Case study examples

> Key Outcomes we Aspire to are:
> Agile workforce
> Social trust
> Prevention of crime
> Investing wisely
> Reduction of crime
> Ethical treatment
>
> Draft work on Strategic Shifts in
> a. Operational effectiveness – more strategic and efficient, quality outcomes
> b. Shift to a new paradigm for evaluating outcomes of education
>   i. Educational outcomes by market segment, school type, etc.

    c. *Cultural transformation, capacity building, research and education, empower everyone to be leaders, be accountable . . . collaborate*
      i. *Leadership capacity – values-based leadership model, % capability match to role requirements*
      ii. *Experience of students and parents and teachers in the school . . .*

A CLIP set of strategic outcomes were based on the Customer, Leadership, Integrated (with other stakeholders), and Project deliverables – time, cost, and quality.

A set of SCIENCE Values were based on being Strategic, Collaborative, demonstrating Integrity, Excellence, being Networked, Creative, and showing Enthusiasm.

The coachees' experience with it

As a framework I think it's exceptionally powerful. Even if you implemented bits of it, it still makes an enormous difference.

I've a sense that leadership in a group is to tease things out of people. If I propose and then support others, we have everyone in the game, creating solutions. My strategic leadership capability has been enhanced.

Having a strategic vision is not an action plan; it's bigger than that. It's a strategic journey. You can see the next steps but not all of them to take you towards the broadest conception of the future for your career. It's up to me to create the future, so that's how life is to me. By systematising what I do, I can embed the ideas I'm happy to embrace in the way I live.

My role is to set higher-order strategic outcomes . . . and advance a strategic, scientifically based perspective along with effective and accountable probing governance with greater integrity . . . in such a way that everyone feels engaged, identifying with and owning a longer-term strategic vision so that the return on the investment for the Australian public and industry sponsors generates tangible, breakthrough solutions that create a healthier environment for life and future generations.

I'm getting a sense of achieving more through others, by leading more effectively, generating more presence, a strong resource backing that can be directed into new directions to take advantage of opportunities.

Team members are starting to collaborate . . . and starting to listen more and consulting more.

People first . . . Doing it with them not to them.

The impact of this driver on the coachees

Eleven of the twelve participants (92%) implemented it, and six presented their charters to me at later coaching meetings. A few brought a resulting A3 document or fully printed brochure to a later coaching meeting, showing great pride in their work. It was an absolute delight to see the fruits of their endeavours and the meticulous care they had given to presenting the final versions!

For some coachees, the document was also immeasurably helpful in their meetings with ministers and C-suite executives. One coachee advised that this was the first time the minister said they could see the big picture. Some coachees were congratulated for their impressive work. The publication of the Strategic Business Charter changed their relationships with their managers and trans-formed their conversations from earlier expressions of concern and risk, to new words of encouragement and recognition.

It is interesting to note that the two participants who did the most work co-creating and implementing their Strategic Business Charter were the same two participants who advanced their leadership development the furthest to *Synergist*.

The underlying principles of the driver

The implementation of a Strategic Business Charter was designed to transcend a collective culture of conformity and compliance with plans. Without a charter, the coachees were responsible for ensuring the timely completion of strategic projects and initiatives based on the public policy statements and management commitments. These activities with deadlines became their objectives.

While this initiated a goal orientation to achieve those deadlines within bud-get, it reflected a top-down imposition of sometimes impossible targets. With-out any goals concerning people engagement, customer satisfaction and their experience, and the quality of the outcomes being achieved to balance task and people, efficiency and effectiveness, organisations become soulless machines.

The shift to a very simple Strategic Business Charter, including an important purpose statement to bring everyone together, and a simple and therefore doable EQUIP scorecard of key strategic outcomes for the whole team, changed the game in very critical ways. The charter brought people together. It tran-scended individual job descriptions and offered everyone the opportunity to think about purpose and outcomes and develop a shared focus.

People's minds and hearts were activated, engaged, and focused. They brought renewed commitment to their work. There evolved a shared under-standing not just on what was to be achieved, but how. Values had been articu-lated and agreed – and would be discussed each month as you will see in the next driver, and there was an important People Engagement target to be achieved by each team within the division.

The nature of the shift that was activated

My reflections on this intervention from a developmental perspective is that leading an engagement on setting strategic direction is both demanding and transformative for the participant, as they are leading the transformation of the strategic context for their division, a collective, which is a *Synergist* capacity.

This requires them to exercise courage to lead something aspirational for perhaps the first time, to demonstrate the commitment and confidence to their people that, together, by uplifting their strategic thinking and imagining aspirational eco-centric outcomes, they can realise strategic outcomes and co-create a better future. Casting the coachee into the role of steward of the future significantly expanded their strategic horizons.

Furthermore, inviting them to realise shared aspirational outcomes in addition to short-term results by building an outcomes-oriented, synergistic, collective performance framework set up the structure, the strategic scaffolding, for their people to make the shift from task-driven *Specialists* to proactive *Achievers* and onto change *Catalysts*. Their direct reports were given the new opportunity to lead the development of a high-performing team!

Individuals within those teams had a new and more expansive container within which to shift from being *Specialists* with a downward focus on their individual tasks and a silo mentality, to becoming *Achievists*, with an outward focus on their combined results and a customer mentality.

This had significant implications for the coachees. Not only did the teams achieve more, engage more, and become more creative and proactive in their work (noted during coaching sessions), but the coachees were freed to rise above their *Achievist* mindset because the achievement of their division's goals and targets was being taken care of by their people.

Because their people were trusted to become high-performing teams at *Achievist* as a result of the new more empowering performance context and regular outcome feedback, the coachees gained the time and mental space to think more strategically beyond immediate performance outcomes. They could give consideration to reforming (*Catalyst*) and transforming (*Synergist*) their wider strategic context across the organisation and with external diverse stakeholders in their industry and wider community.

DRIVER 4: Distributing Time to Generate Dynamic Flow

The problem or need the driver addressed

Long days of work was also a prominent topic that came up repeatedly during all coaching programs. Near the beginning of a meeting, coachees would share their time pressures. For example:

> I'm working 12-hour days.
>
> I'm working big days, to 8.30pm; it's affecting my home life.
>
> I'm feeling a bit worn out as the diary got smashed.

Some coachees also felt that they were not contributing to meetings effectively.

> *I would like to be able to operate differently . . . I would like to be more confident . . . more strategic and bring more strategic material to the agenda for our strategy and culture meetings.*

Coachees were visibly stressed and sometimes feeling anxious, fatigued, or in despair. They were not always enjoying their role in what was often seen as a tumultuous, ever-changing unpredictable work environment.

Time management is regarded as one of the most essential skills in a busy corporate environment. Most executives are on a treadmill of meetings, emails, and reports. If you ask any executive during a typical day: 'How are you?', the most frequent response, often worn as a badge of honour, is: 'I'm really busy. How about you?'

Organisational leaders managing divisions, functions, or regions spend most of their time at work in meetings. Because most conventional organisations are based on a power hierarchy, if someone more senior wishes to hold a meeting, other meetings are shifted to accommodate them. This has a domino effect causing multiple meeting changes each day.

The meetings an executive has most control over are meetings with their own team, together, and one-on-one. These meetings are accordingly most often changed to make way for apparently more important meetings with higher-ups due to the hierarchical code, and sometimes they're cancelled altogether. This common practice depresses teamwork and team performance, diminishes empowerment and development, and turns a senior executive from being proactive to becoming largely reactive.

In conclusion, there were three key issues to address in relation to time: long hours, work–home life balance, and constant change to meeting times. If these could be addressed, executives would be happier in their roles, enjoy more wellbeing in life, build relationships with their team and encourage team performance, be more proactive on a strategic level, and feel that there was more to life and work than being in a constant state of busy-ness.

What the driver involves

There are many standard time management guidelines. One is to 'do, delegate, delete, or delay' a particular task until a person is able to manage their workload within a standard executive business day, which is perhaps typically from 8.00am to 6.00pm or ten hours long. Another is to get rid of all distractions, clutter, and bad habits such as constantly looking at emails or procrastination of difficult tasks. Others focus on making lists and setting time limits and priorities.

Covey's (1994) advice was to give priority to the important, non-urgent strategic initiatives first, the 'big rocks', to invest 80% of one's time on important strategic work rather than urgent reactive work as most organisations do. And then of course it's important to take breaks to refresh the mind.

These types of standard time management tools do not meet the needs of strategic leaders. Their focus is not so much on getting the work done, as they spend most of their time in meetings. Their role is to delegate almost everything except the engagement of all people inside and outside the organisation to activate and accomplish their shared strategic and culture aspirations and more immediately pressing performance goals.

Another dimension of time is that the time it takes to accomplish any activity is not fixed, and the quality of output is not always related to the time invested or available. Rather, the value of the insights we can offer and the strategic perspective we can advance is based on the quality of our thinking, not the quantity of time we have to give to reflection or imagination. The quality of our thinking and the degree of creativity we bring to a situation at any given time is dependent on our stage of development.

As a *Synergist* who had learnt how to become enormously productive by pre-programming the mind and setting up an emergent state of flow to foster high-quality, highly efficient creative thinking, I offered an innovative way of thinking about and managing time. Rather than focusing on the work to be done and chasing one's tail to complete everything in time, the focus shifted to the distribution of time through which value was created. Instead of focusing on the content, the work itself, it was more valuable to turn to the channel through which the content flowed, time.

By managing oneself well over the course of the day, a person could also sustain the energy and creativity to contribute effectively throughout a recurring ten- to twelve-hour day.

How the driver is implemented

The channel is the days of the week. Coachees were invited to consider the days of the week like the individual lanes on a five-lane highway. The work was the traffic that drove across the highway. By distributing the days of the week, the lanes of the highway, to specific types of traffic or streams of work, a strategic leader was able to automatically set strategic priorities on workflow.

Instead of juggling disorderly traffic, the coachees were invited to become traffic controllers. For instance, a standard week consisted of Mondays: strategic, Tuesdays: team and one-on-one meetings, Wednesdays: project meetings, Thursdays: stakeholder meetings, and Fridays: pre-scheduled 10-minute phone call catchups, doing favours, building goodwill, and completing the week's work. No meetings take place on Monday mornings when a person is fresh. They are set aside for creative strategic thinking. Friday afternoons are always held open for tidying up loose ends.

The structure of each day was also significant. A generative flow state at alpha brain wave frequency is enhanced by holding 90-minute meetings to make time for genuine inquiry, authentic collaboration, inspiring insights, and the opportunity to develop mutual understanding in accordance with a person's natural ultradian rhythm (Ericsson, 2009; Kleitman, 1982; Schwartz, 2010). The 30-minute break in between each meeting allows time for travel, emails, calls, meeting preparation, and, very importantly, time for the brain to process what has just taken place.

To compensate for the 90-minute time allocation instead of the routine 60-minute meeting cycle, meetings are held less frequently, i.e. fortnightly instead of weekly. Team and one-on-one meetings can be optimised by getting together for a half-day fortnightly and alternating team members across the weeks. Because the meetings were more engaging, they were also more productive and generative. The diary times for meetings that the coachees found to be most effective were 9.00am, 11.00am, 2.00pm, and 4.00pm.

The principal role of their executive assistants shifted from accommodating multiple changes in meeting schedules to maintaining diary consistency. The coachees who were able to do this most effectively also began to orchestrate their meetings with external stakeholders in advance nearer the end of the 12-month coaching period. Together we thought through how to set up clusters of stakeholders to meet together in a series of forums each year over a 3- to 5-year time horizon as a channel for collaboration and exploration of key strategic priorities. This approach is set out in Driver 8.

The key was to set up the Dynamic Operating Rhythm (DOR) well in advance. After three months of piloting and fine-tuning an orchestrated approach, while influencing changes to other meetings to align with their new series of highways, meetings were set up 12 months in advance and refined and extended every six months. That way the calendar was always scheduled 12 months in advance and enhanced every six. In summary, the eight principles of a DOR are:

1 Distributing different types of work to different days of the week.

2 Always keeping Monday mornings and Friday afternoons free for strategic work and completing work respectively.

3 Holding fewer, longer 90-minute meetings to engage creatively and collaboratively followed by 30-minute breaks to respond to emails, review work, travel, and prepare for other meetings.

4 Scheduling meetings at 9.00am, 11.00am, 2.00pm, and 4.00pm and leaving the office at 6.00pm (some executives also left 4.00pm open to be available for ad hoc meetings or to leave the office earlier).

5 Setting up a repeating, consistent cycle of team and one-on-one meetings on Tuesdays, project meetings on Wednesdays, and external meetings on Thursdays.

6 Focusing on maintaining consistency, especially family first, by coaching your executive assistant to speak up courageously: 'I'm very sorry, X has a meeting then that was scheduled over six months ago. Could I suggest a few alternatives?'

7 Setting up an annual orchestrated engagement of key external stakeholders, individually and in forums.

8 Refining and extending the schedule of meetings every six months so they are always set up 12 months ahead.

There is a further dimension to the creation of a DOR: a specific team meeting cycle, liberating meeting agendas and cascading the rhythm across the division!

As part of the deliberately developmental intent to enable the coachees to become more strategic, I invited them to set up a cycle of team meetings consisting of a strategic meeting, an operations meeting, a culture meeting followed by another operations meeting. If they were running half-day meetings, I suggested strategic/culture at one, and a full half-day on operations at the second. Mixing the two (i.e. strategic and operations) generally always dilutes any strategic discussion and is therefore not recommended.

The strategic meeting was designed to focus on encouraging team performance based on their charter and to instigate or adapt strategic initiatives to ensure the key strategic shifts would be achieved. The culture meeting was designed to engage on a shared value agreed during the formation of their charter, one at a time, to expedite leadership development, enhance team dynamics, and revitalise the culture. These meetings followed a very simple agenda: define the value; identify ways it is being upheld, ways it is not, new approaches that would be better; and then choose one main behaviour to stop doing and another to start doing instead. This can have a significant ripple effect on generating an accountable, values-based culture.

Most *Achievists* run operations meetings by scrolling through a list of projects and initiatives to see where they are at. They are reporting meetings, holding people to account in a collective setting rather than meetings that engage people on their thoughts and ideas. There is very little discussion except around who is doing what by when, what needs fixing, and who needs help.

The coachees were invited to lead meetings with open, liberating agendas and not the typical fixed list of items. This enables more emergent dialogue and a greater contribution by team members and is more conducive to their individual development and team performance. For instance, the operations meeting was based on the five P's of praise, progress, problems, potential, and priorities.

Praise was invited from all to recognise extraordinary efforts. Then each person volunteered their key accomplishments. The coachee would recognise their progress in a genuine, authentic way. This set up a cycle of positivity. Problems were then aired, and the coachee would facilitate collaborative problem-solving by asking questions rather than giving direction. Potential turned to new opportunities that had emerged or could arise. The final part of the meeting turned to setting priorities where the coachee was free to be more directive in order to establish and confirm clear strategic direction.

Similarly, I suggested that one-on-one meetings be based on three questions evenly spread time-wise: 'How is the work going?', 'How are you going?', and 'How is your team going?' This ensured that the management of the work was undertaken by the coachee's direct reports, and not the strategic leader, requiring their team members to exercise leadership in terms of raising and managing their own agenda. The coachee was thereby freed from operations management and could focus on strategic leadership instead.

Furthermore, the coachee invited their leaders to cascade the same series of team and one-on-one meetings with their team members immediately following their meetings (i.e. on Wednesdays). The lack of time delay ensured that everyone was singing from the same song sheet and that conversations on important strategic topics and their espoused values were also in synch and on point.

Case study examples

A common template used by coachees to set up their operating rhythms is shown in Figure 7.1. A few of the executive assistants were highly creative and used colour coding and other innovative elements to ensure consistency. Note that emails, calls, travel, and quick prep are interchangeable, and can all be covered in the 30-minute intervals. Catch-ups were arranged on an ad hoc basis by the executive assistants for people who wanted to touch base with the coachee more informally. The 8am and 10.30am time slots also proved to be effective options to meet others for a coffee on any sensitive or informal matters. Tying up loose ends at the end of the day is important to turn off a busy mind and release any stress later in the day.

Every coachee had their own version and it did take time to automate. The easiest options were the first two days. As the week went on and more people external to the division were involved, it became more challenging. However, it also became possible to arrange a day of the week to work from home as all colleagues in the division adopted the same approach.

Mondays are largely for strategic thinking and planning. Tuesdays are for team meetings where the agenda shifts fortnightly: once a month the focus is on strategic performance and corporate culture, and for the other the focus is on operational effectiveness. One-to-one meetings with direct reports also take place fortnightly, and project meetings and stakeholder meetings on Wednesdays and Thursdays respectively, take place every three weeks to accommodate all activities. Friday is set aside for catch-ups and to build goodwill by doing favours for others and renewing relationships without a specific agenda.

The coachees' experience with it

Overall, the coachees retrieved control over their own time and began to trust in emergence. They put their team first and thereby built engagement and psychological safety and certainty. Their team could rely on their support, guidance, and encouragement as a priority. The coachees also attended to their own wellbeing and found creative ways to have other meetings rearranged, simply volunteered someone else to attend instead, or declined further participation recognising that their contribution was not necessary.

They also developed courageous authenticity to decline meetings with higher-ups due to the order they had created for themselves and others. To renege after all that effort would have been irresponsible. They found more peace of mind, a personal rhythm that made life significantly easier, and developed a greater sense of trust and confidence in their own power to create their own life and effectively steward the people in their charge.

Figure 7.1 A Dynamic Operating Rhythm Template

Time	Monday	Tuesday	Wednesday	Thursday	Friday
8am	Set-up & Prep	Set-up & Prep	Set-up & Prep	Set-up & Prep	Set-up & Prep
9am	Strategic Thinking	TEAM Strat/Opns	MGMT TEAM	Stakeholder A/E/I	Catch-up Catch-up
10.30am	Emails	Calls	Travel	Quick Prep	Catch-up
11am	Strategic Planning	TEAM Cult/Opns	Project A/C/E	Stakeholder B/F/J	Catch-up Catch-up
12.30am	Calls	Travel	Quick Prep	Emails	Catch-up
1pm	WALK IN PARK	WALK IN PARK	WALK IN PARK	WALK IN PARK	WALK IN PARK
2pm	Coaching Mtg	121 Mtg B/E	Project B/D/F	Stakeholder C/G/K	Build Goodwill
3.30pm	Travel	Quick Prep	Emails	Calls	Chats
4pm	121 Mtg A/D	121 Mtg C/F	FREE	Stakeholder D/H/L	Build Goodwill
5.30pm	Tie Up Loose Ends	Tie Up Loose Ends	Tie Up Loose Ends	Tie Up Loose Ends	Tie Up Loose Ends

Setup time on Monday is proving to be very valuable . . . Feeling of being more effective and more productive. Have time to get prepared to think about things, think more strategically, taking the 90 minutes and then 30 minutes break . . . My message to my executive assistant is 'as few meetings as I need as consistently as possible'.

Implementing dynamic diary . . . Finding myself with more free time . . . Strategic, all on the same page, got work done that we didn't think we'd get done.

Not spending weekends working . . . Strategic plan with each of my directors . . . Cascading the Dynamic Operating Rhythm . . . They need to step up . . . Their senior officers need to step up . . . This will lift the whole organisation . . .

Following these practices disciplines us to till the ground and create the environment where change can happen.

I now have time to synthesise; what's my position going to be in the next meeting?

More influential in meetings? Yes, absolutely, if I'm going to be in a meeting, I'm going to be in a meeting . . . Really present, not absent. Articulating point of view on exec team. Now paying attention to the human dynamics, interesting drama playing out in front of me.

It's been noticed, a lot of priorities . . . Streamlining correspondence . . . Getting ahead of the reactive things . . . Seeing the achievement . . . I've grown . . . I've got some confidence back.

The impact of this driver on the coachees

Eleven of the twelve coachees (92%) established a Dynamic Operating Rhythm (DOR). Many applied the same discipline to their home lives in relation to dinner time, and recreational and family activities. I also suggested mindful rituals for mornings and evenings such as journaling, visualisation, and meditation which some incorporated.

By taking the time during coaching meetings to set up their DOR together, coachees felt emancipated. Implementation also required them to demonstrate integrity by saying 'no' to higher-ups graciously, and to discover how to engage more collaboratively and sensitively with others from the emergent sense of the collective. The first demanded a release of fear of those in authority and the second, the adoption of a more open mindset to embrace emergence typical of a *Catalyst*, to trust their team and hold them fully accountable to collaborate effectively in order to achieve the desired outcomes.

By adopting a DOR and a 'family-first' approach, where team meetings and one-on-ones with direct reports were given priority (i.e. were not rearranged), it was possible for coachees to become significantly more productive and effective as strategic leaders and actively expedite the performance of their teams. The additional level of accountability for each team leader was also mostly embraced. Exceptions often pointed to a team leader with a centre of gravity at *Specialist* who therefore found priority and agenda setting challenging.

The underlying principles of the driver

A consistent weekly diary supports the generation of flow, automatically adjusts the quantity of work to its allocated highway, and reduces the workload of the conscious mind. If the diary is consistent, the mind can switch to autopilot just as it does when we drive the familiar route home. If the diary is constantly changing, the mind has to use its limited amount of precious conscious energy or willpower each day just to navigate (Baumeister and Tierney, 2011). Consistency is key to optimise the valuable use of mental energy.

Consistency also automates the mind's expectations. When the mind knows that it has Monday mornings every week to undertake strategic thinking, it becomes highly creative and generative during those time periods. Somehow or other if we program the mind in advance, it becomes activated to design and deliver what is needed at the time.

The 90/30 rhythm facilitates an engagement in alpha brain waves that opens up creativity in contrast to the busy beta brain waves of 60-minute back-to-back meetings. This approach also integrates the shift from managing time to managing personal energy (Loehr and Schwartz, 2004). The 30-minute time interval for the brain to process the information exchange, interpretation, and understanding that had taken place in the preceding 90-minute time period, helps to ensure a peaceful sleep that night (Immordino-Yang et al., 2012).

The shift from meeting agenda lists to open liberating frameworks where the content is supplied by the team leaders elevates and confirms their accountability for achieving the results in the Strategic Business Charter. Rather than relying on reporting and receiving further direction, they are free to engage, inquire, collaborate, decide, and implement. Any significant strategic initiatives are more closely monitored as a special project or through the course of strategic meetings.

The nature of the shift that was activated

This driver *operationalises* the strategic shift to business outcomes, strategic initiatives, espoused values, and divisional performance. Together they create the content and the channel for everyone to be proactive based on agreed targets and standards. From an organisational perspective, the strategic scaffolding, the DOR, and liberating meeting agendas together set the frame for the organisation to consolidate a performance outcomes orientation at orange, and shift through to a values-based authentic engagement at green (Laloux, 2014). The strategic initiatives, if led as cross-boundary initiatives with a diverse cross-section of committed volunteers, also transcend organisational boundaries and free people to follow their interests enabling the emergence of teal.

Team leaders and team members all have the opportunity to elevate their centre of gravity to *Achievist*. With an investment in leadership development for them to release the shadow of the *Specialist* and *Achievist*, they have the potential to form high-performing teams.

The leaders of the strategic initiatives have the opportunity to shift to *Catalyst* due to their reliance on personal authenticity and not positional authority, engaging volunteers organically and roaming through the organisation to pull together disparate resources and diverse views. An executive coach to support the leaders of these strategic initiatives as change leaders rather than project managers, also facilitates the growth of the leader and the active engagement of people participating in the initiative.

These two drivers generate a shift in the Subtle Collective Tier where the *Catalyst* and *Synergist* have their centres of gravity. They transform the strategic operating system for the coachee's division in the organisation by incorporating and transcending the existing more standard activity-based operating system. As the coachees led the implementation of these new strategic operating frameworks for their people, their transformative leadership capacity emerged. Its ripple effect progressively led to the transformation of the culture.

Chapter 7: Key Points

1　The purposeful, values-based and outcomes-oriented Strategic Business Charter inclusive of key strategic and culture shifts and EQUIP KPIs was designed to provide the context for the emergence of high-performance teams at *Achievist* and *Catalyst* (orange and teal).

2　This offered an empowering context for the coachee's direct reports to share an inspiring purpose, uplifting values, key outcomes, renew their commitment and lead their teams in engaging and empowering ways. Their team members had the opportunity to shift from being task-driven *Specialists* to becoming proactive team players at *Achievist*.

3　The coachee is actively leading a transformation of the structure and culture of their Collective strategic context, a capability that only emerges at *Synergist*. With the appropriate attitude and intent, proven processes and reliable coaching guidance on the resulting work, they could confidently uplift their own leadership capacity to enable this.

4　Being busy and time-poor where work overtakes home life is a typical *Achievist* shadow. It leads to stress and burnout. Creating an entirely new way of viewing time, as an avenue rather than a limited resource, altered the coachees' perspective.

5　A strategic leader can take charge of their time by prioritising the week's work around a repeating cycle of the most important meetings that lead to sustainable team, divisional, and organisational performance. This reduces the workload of the conscious mind.

6　The conscious and consistent utilisation of time throughout the day has a significant impact on the quality of creative thought, collaborative intent, and courageous vulnerability that strategic leaders can demonstrate throughout a 12-hour work-day.

7 A dynamic diary rhythm orchestrating the days of the week to consistently hold the same workflows leads to psychological safety, significantly higher productivity, and an amazing boost in creativity.

8 A generative flow-state that inspires intuitive awareness and revelatory insight becomes emergent through the course of a consistent rhythm of 90-minute meetings and intervening 30-minute breaks. This rhythm results in high-quality time, higher energy levels, enhanced wellbeing, and better sleep.

9 Establishing and cascading open liberating meeting agendas for a repeating cycle of strategic, culture, and operating team meetings as well as one-on-one meetings in a Dynamic Operating Rhythm always scheduled 12–18 months in advance enables wide strategic engagement, the development of collaborative and trusting relationships, the opportunity to demonstrate stronger team leadership, and sustainable high performance.

10 The combined power of the Strategic Business Charter, Dynamic Operating Rhythm, and liberating meeting agendas leads to the emergence of an orange-green-teal organisational culture spectrum that is continuously and organically evolving.

Next Chapter

This chapter has reviewed the nature and implementation of liberating evolutionary strategic scaffolding for an organisation. The next chapter moves to the deeper holistic development of the strategic leader in relation to their own life patterns and in their interactions with others. Their expanding leadership presence is essential for them to be able to hold the emergent space for everyone to rise in their division or organisation.

8 | HOLISTIC DRIVERS 5 AND 6: HOLDING SAFE EMERGENT SPACE

DRIVER 5: Exploring Psychodynamics to Heal Shadow and Eliminate Triggers

The problem or need the driver addressed

Emotional triggers lead to personal dramas in relationship to others: managers, peers, team members, other stakeholders, and family members and friends. These dramas often contain an interpersonal power dynamic. I approached dramas ignited by emotional triggers in three steps. These steps take emotional awareness to a deeper level beyond self-awareness and self-regulation to undertake a healing process.

The first was to acknowledge that this life experience was turning up to facilitate growth. The challenge could be considered as an opportunity for growth if it was interpreted to be a uniquely customised, perfectly timed, individual learning experience. The emotional trigger was simply signalling that a personal emotional wound from the past was ready to be explored, understood, and healed.

Second, the interaction was analysed from a psychodynamic point of view to gain a greater understanding of the interpersonal power dynamic. The motives and fears that underlie human actions and behaviours are intriguing avenues of inquiry that can lead to quantum leaps in self-awareness.

The third step was to source the same dynamic in the coachee's past and process the emotional wound. When we are young and feeling threatened, our only recourse is to depend on the reptilian brain to fight, flight, freeze, or appease. As we mature, we can process earlier life dramas now hidden in our shadow yet mirrored in our life experiences. It is possible to disarm the ability of events to trigger an emotional reaction by healing past suppressed emotional wounds with our heart and mind, emotionally and cognitively. This is a spiritually oriented inner perspective of heart resonance, mindful awareness, and our innate healing capacity as human beings.

What the driver involves

The first part of the inner process was for the participants to realise that their situation was designed to facilitate personal growth. It was of their own making. *Life does not just happen to us, life happens through us*. This perspective was both scary and empowering for the participants. It meant they could mature as a leader by taking the opportunity to explore their inner subconscious to fully appreciate the nature of the event and heal the dynamic from within to prevent it happening again. This demanded that they take full accountability for their life experience, exemplifying the *Synergist* perspective that life and self are interpenetrative, congruent, or one – they permeate each other.

This interpenetrative capacity enables us to increasingly understand at a deeper more conscious level why we do the things we do, say the things we say, and make decisions in our lives. The more we can take account of personal biases and become conscious of limiting beliefs and reactive emotions, the more effective we become in creating more desirable outcomes and generating a more fulfilling life experience.

The coachees were invited to undertake a process of inquiry by reflecting, processing, and revising their thoughts, meanings, emotions, and responses to incidents. This was done from a psychotherapeutic perspective based on a psychodynamic interpretation of interpersonal power dynamics.

Based on my thousands of hours' coaching experience as a transformative holistic executive coach, I came to realise that six themes commonly reappeared as emotional dramas in people's lives. They are abandonment, betrayal, rejection, abuse, neglect, and deceit. I've since added the controlling power of rigid merciless expectations. One person is the perpetrator, another the victim, and sometimes a rescuer amongst the typical triad of roles available. They are all psychological dramas that destroy trust, confidence, and self-esteem and require significant personal courage to address and resolve.

By objectively examining the root of the dynamic within their own identity and exploring the history of that dynamic, coachees could move past the drama. An analysis of the psychodynamics of similar incidents from the recent and distant past is very revealing. Earlier incidents come to light that may have long been suppressed or avoided.

The heart and mind open and expand to appreciate the drama within the learning opportunity. By responding to a coach's questions, reflecting while walking, journaling, or talking to a friend, new insights arise. Dramas and traumas can then be transcended with heart-centred forgiveness. In this way, coachees can eliminate the manifestation of future similarly provocative, volatile events and free themselves of the continuing drama. They have healed their subconscious from within and therefore will no longer attract the same type of drama.

How the driver is implemented

The coaching process to let go of the past is a cognitive–emotional approach captured by the acronym: GRIEF (Figure 8.1). The first step is to seek out the

Figure 8.1 The GRIEF process of shadow resolution and healing

G is for Gift . . . I look forward to the gift I will receive once I complete this process . . .

R is for Resent & Regret . . . What are the things about this situation or relationship that I am mad and sad about?

I is for Inquiry . . . What were the facts of the earliest memory I have of a similar psychodynamic? *If the associated emotions have been fully expressed under R above, then it becomes possible to be objective. Otherwise return to previous step.*

E is for Empathy . . . *Imagine yourself in the shoes of each person in the original event . . . embrace each person including your younger self with love and compassion.*

F is for Forgive & Forget . . . *If you have fully navigated each of the above steps, your heart will be able to forgive all people involved in the original and similar events. You will know this is the case as you will be able to forget, and an event with a similar psychodynamic will not transpire again. You have healed yourself.*

'Gift' in the drama although it does not arrive until the end of a fully navigated GRIEF process. At this initial point in the process, it rests as a question, a request.

R stands for 'resent and regret', i.e. what am I mad and sad about? It is important to express the emotions related to the specific series of incidents, current and past. This second step of examining, exploring, and expressing one's emotions, is essential before going onto the next step. Sometimes a person simply needs to sit with the emotions and experience them on a fully embodied level until they evaporate. This is a process of surrender that works well for deeply embedded emotions.

As a coach, I invite the coachee to cognitively become aware of their emotions, to fully express them by journaling, thinking while walking, or in talking to friends or with me again at our next coaching session. It may also take time to process newly emergent emotions alone. If anything disturbing comes up that the coachee needs further help with, I refer them onto a psychotherapist. Otherwise, as a coach who has studied shadow significantly and processed and experienced her own release of shadow patterns, I feel qualified to guide and support the coachee.

I represents 'inquiry', i.e. an inquiry into the actual facts of the past situation. Often our memories are highly emotional and become distorted. However, if we have fully expressed our emotions and can stand back and look at the facts quite objectively, they no longer have the same power over us. This step is only possible if the emotional residue is fully expressed in the previous step. If the facts are not yet clear, then it's important to return to the previous step.

E is for 'empathy'. At this point, it is important to empathise with all the players in the drama, including the coachee themselves when they were young. This invites the heart to show compassion and understanding for all involved. Everyone was doing the best they could in the situation. By walking in the shoes of each person in the early drama with a wholehearted sense of love and deep concern for self and others, a person develops compassion. Activating the GRIEF process in the present drama provides the opportunity for this human capacity to be expressed.

When the people in the drama are given love and understanding, the final step transpires of its own accord: **F** stands for 'forgive and forget'. Once we've truly forgiven, we automatically forget. As we forgive ourselves and others, the gift appears and makes itself known to us. The emotional wound in the soul is healed and the slate is wiped clean. This approach is along similar lines to those developed by David Clutterbuck (2010) and Kilburg (2004). The GRIEF process is more succinct and yet still offers a deep dive into the coachee's emotional history. It is an illuminating, life-changing process.

Case study example

Managers can exercise power over others in a unilateral manner by using their positional authority. This is in direct contrast to respecting each person's individual experience and their right to be authentic and autonomous, and exercise integrity as they see it. This type of unilateral power is typical of a compliant collective at *Conformist* where people must comply with others in authority.

An independent play-to-win individual at *Achievist* is less compliant yet still controlling. They will act now and ask permission later. Peers also vie with each other in unfavourable ways to gain patronage from people who are more senior, especially their boss, to ensure they look good and are not blamed for any unsatisfactory results, and to expand their scope of work in others' territories to increase their profile. They are simply competing with others to gain attention just as we do as children. The exercise of mutual, reciprocal, authentic power begins in a values-based, empowered green organisation and becomes the norm in a liberated, collaborative, interdependent teal organisation.

The key was to realise when and how coachees had given their authentic power away in the past or allowed it to be taken away. Or how they may have taken another person's power away or allowed them to submit to them. Power is an intriguing concept. When we give our power away in one setting, we tend to take it away from another in another setting to restore our personal balance. This is how an executive can be compliant with their manager yet controlling of their team members.

Relationship power patterns repeat during our lifetime unless and until we appreciate and understand that being authentic means exercising personal power graciously yet assertively with consideration given to the interests of all and where decisions are made to optimise the highest common good. Here are a few examples drawn from a case study of a coachee navigating her experiences, beginning with one of the situations outlined above.

The immediate first challenge is my relationship with my boss whom I also have a personal relationship with as a friend; at work I'm devalued by my boss whereas personally I provide her with lots of support outside of work. It's an impossible situation . . . If I was guaranteed a pension regardless, then I'd leave now and be gone . . . I'm an easy target, too dedicated, too loyal, not enough assertiveness.

The manager was taking power away from the coachee at work by demeaning her, and the coachee was giving away power to her manager at home by supporting her. There was no mutual respect but more of a master–servant relationship. The coachee was becoming more and more powerless with each event that occurred. It turned out that the coachee had an early memory of a teaching nun who had insulted her repeatedly in private yet appeared outwardly to others to be highly supportive of her. She had found it impossible to defend or protect herself from the emotionally hurtful invective or to raise it with others. She had felt as powerless then as she did now.

> I was under suspicion . . . I was upset with myself for putting the deputy director general [DDG] in a challenging situation . . . Now I had to be extra careful about the information I provided . . . Reinforced for me that the director general [DG] won't back you . . . and the DDG was reactive and not strategic . . . He's too trusting . . . I have no protection . . . I was concerned I'd exposed X but X exposed me . . . Any vestige of reliance on X has gone . . . The decision-maker is actually me, the inventor, the creator, another shadow being exposed, I'm out on a limb, being judged as inept, and can't trust others as then my head could roll!

Relationship dynamics amongst managers, direct reports, and peers are often symbolic of family dynamics amongst parents, children, and siblings, respectively. In this scenario, of the 'parents', the DG (father-figure for the coachee) will blame rather than back his team, and the DDG (mother-figure) is reactive and complicit. 'Sibling' X has betrayed the relationship by being disloyal and suggesting that the blame lay with the coachee. Suspicion, trust, exposure, and judgement are interplayed amongst the actors in the vignette.

A sense of betrayal reoccurred in a number of different instances for the coachee at work. Through inquiry, the coachee became aware of the need to become more discerning when extending trust to another person and to become more self-reliant, self-trusting, transparent, and vulnerable in her own exercise of integrity. Her own new sense of integrity prevailed. In a later situation, the coachee advised, '*I stated the facts . . . Knight in shining armour by coming up with the solution . . . You never get thanked for it . . . But you do get remembered for it*'.

The coachees' experience with it

Work and family dynamics were transformed through the course of reflective inquiry. It is highly enlightening to understand that once a person has completed the self-work embedded in the GRIEF process, the relationship itself automatically changes without needing to say much to the other person involved. The work has been done at a much deeper energetic level with the heart and soul, dissolving the past.

Using the deep dive with the heart generates greater understanding . . . And the power is that it leads to optimal intuitive solutions.

Once we've done the relevant self-work, our life experience alters. One participant, who included amongst his aspirations to serve his family with wisdom and kindness, reflected hard and long on big disruptions in his family dynamics as well as in his partner's. Members of neither family saw much of each other as a result of the conflict. Following this inner work, however, he took charge of a significant family event, arranging the funeral of his mother-in-law while supporting all family members as best he could. He was emotionally moved and felt deeply honoured after her funeral by the words of his father-in-law:

Mother-in-law died suddenly on Mother's Day. One of the most interesting weeks of my life . . . My father-in-law said, 'Well X, this is one of your most successful projects ever'.

The impact of this driver on the coachees

This healing process has many benefits. It eliminates future dramas of the same type. Once a lesson has been learned, and the subconscious healed, it does not need to be relearned. The voices related to the drama disappear from our mind, and it gradually becomes calmer and clearer. Once the dramas are eliminated at source and splintered identities are integrated, the mind empties. We are left with the harmony of heart and peace of mind of a *Synergist*.

If there is a similar drama in the future, it does not affect us in the same way. It no longer triggers us. We have enough objectivity to clearly see the psychodynamics and act with maturity and confidence to set things right by articulating the standards, boundaries, and priorities that have been circumvented or compromised. Driver 6 expands on this.

Furthermore, by healing ourselves, we can prevent the same emotional patterns repeating in future generations. Once we are healed, we no longer need to enrol others, often the people closest to us such as our immediate family members, in our own psychodynamic dramas. They see us present and behave differently and have a new role model to copy. This type of healing also works on an energetic and biochemical level. Read Bruce Lipton's *The Biology of Belief* (2015) for more information on the science.

My mind has quietened . . . Yes . . . Space externally is also space internally in the mind . . . What do I want to explore? . . . I have a deeper yearning for greater meaning . . . Is this all there is to life? I'm doing the journals regularly to reveal my feelings, really trying to understand my life experience by bringing understanding to situations that present challenges . . . Understanding means detaching yourself from feedback. Acceptance is remaining totally cool.

The underlying principles of the driver

Thoughts are one thing, emotions quite another. While the power of the mind to select thoughts and imagine great outcomes is a key driver in shifting to later stages of conscious awareness and leadership capacity, the power of the heart is also essential to release the shadow in earlier stages of consciousness. I conceived of the GRIEF process as part of my own spiritual journey towards peace of mind and harmony of heart.

The processing of emotions is based on spiritual teachings, mindfulness stories, scientific research into energy fields (McTaggart), and the research undertaken by the HeartMath Institute. The value of it is based on my personal experience of using the process. I came to understand that the voices in my mind were vestiges of residual emotional dramas that I had suppressed sometime in the past. By witnessing the dramas and listening to the voices, interpreting the dynamic and using the GRIEF process to forgive and forget, my mind gradually emptied. While I have also meditated daily for decades now, I believe it was the heart-based GRIEF process that enabled me to arrive at the calm, clear mind of the *Synergist*.

Our depth of self-awareness continues to unfold throughout our lifetime like the layers of an onion. There are always new layers to peel away and delve more deeply within our consciousness. In my experience as a person and as a coach, we begin with illuminating and processing our own shadow, and complete this journey with regard to our relationships with our father and last of all, our mother. Then we shift to understanding and healing the collective shadow in our culture as we move into the MetAware Tier.

Any of these subterranean processes may involve what is known as a 'dark night of the soul' (Myss, 2007) where despair and grief may intermingle until they, too, are transcended with greater wisdom and compassion for the human condition. We continue to explore to gain a greater meaning of life in its fullness and emptiness, and for our own fulfilment and enlightenment. We become more gracious and a little wiser, and life becomes more graceful and a little kinder.

The nature of the shift that was activated

In power hierarchies, the more senior you are, the more positional authority you have to behave as you please to instruct and subvert others, robbing them of their power and self-esteem. The use of unilateral power, using power over people, is prevalent up to and including the *Achievist*.

However, from the later stage vantage point of the *Catalyst*, becoming more authentic, appreciating diversity, accepting others for who they are, and setting values-based standards and behavioural norms establishes the foundations for mutual power. This capacity to set standards, boundaries, and priorities in the interests of the common good with a sense of personal integrity, courageous authenticity, and mutual respect for others integrates at *Synergist*.

DRIVER 6: Sustaining Standards with Courageous Caring Conversations

The problem or need the driver addressed

All participants experienced self-doubt and/or victimhood, and some shared distressing situations right at or near the beginning of their coaching program, as soon as sufficient trust had been built. All also had concerns, some more serious than others, with their direct reports, managers, and/or their peers and some felt that their employment was at risk as a result of recurring restructures. Here are some examples of the significant emotional distress, frustration, and anxiety caused by personal doubts, inappropriate behaviour, and interpersonal power dynamics in the guise of corporate politics.

> There is a director who is a bully, texting me deprecating messages and ridiculing others . . . It started two years ago. He switches from one of two modes, either aggressive or playful at the extreme ends. He has come into my office and been particularly threatening and aggressive . . . He would say things quietly in a meeting, but very aggressively . . . This tends to happen in steering committee meetings sometimes with my direct reports. He effectively orders me to do things . . . I really didn't know what to do but now I've got some clarity and realise it's inappropriate and I'd like it to stop completely. There are no second chances here; I've had absolutely enough.

> My position is under threat. There's been a litany of allegations . . . but I have a new mortgage to do renovations . . . My choice was to resign or be sacked or confess to a reality that I didn't accept . . . could I do the latter in a way I could live with? . . . I say that I regard myself as a professional, trustworthy, caring, and compassionate person. I regret my actions and take responsibility for them and will apologise. I recommit to being that person. He said he couldn't imagine a better response and couldn't ask for anything more. Apologised same day to Y. Can't wait to get away from work . . . Feel anything I say will be misconstrued . . . Total challenge re being in the firing line . . . yet with big mortgage and desire to stay rather than take stigma of bad performance!! It's a train wreck!

These are distressing, threatening, and intimidating incidents that are sadly typical of many conventional workplaces. In each case, the coachee felt a sense of guilt, shame, injustice, and helplessness. Virtually every senior executive and strategic leader must navigate, transcend, and transmute political and behavioural dynamics to thrive and flourish in large conventional corporations (amber and orange). If they do so with integrity, they will rise above conventional norms and develop their later stage leadership capacity. Their main default, used by many as their only option to survive, is to succumb to the politics and play a manipulative win–lose game at the stage of *Achievist*.

What the driver involves

I worked with each of the participants to enable them to play an authentic, empowering, and compassionate role in the midst of their unfolding dramas and make the shift from victim to victor. The technique is related to conflict resolution but also quite different. Rather than endeavouring to find a solution or balance or resolution amongst conflicting perspectives often laced with emotion, this driver is focused specifically on expressing one's personal truth in an open, vulnerable, yet confident manner. The intention is not to reconcile points of view but to uphold principles or values that are important to the authentic self and create a very distinctive turning point in the future behaviour of oneself and/or another person.

Up to and including the *Achievist*, there is a high level of tolerance of other people's inappropriate behaviour. There is a preference to look the other way, only see and even honour the good, and focus on what needs to be done to the exclusion of how. People at earlier stages are more timid, more compliant, and more exacting of themselves. They accept others' weaknesses as they have their own and accept others' misuse of authoritative power due to fear and the dire consequences of speaking out. PRIDE, the #metoo and #blacklivesmatter movements are examples of social shifts from victim to victor.

Bullying is often underestimated by the way it creeps up on a person. It can be very surreptitious at the start. It is like the proverbial frog in boiling water. If only the worst event took place in an isolated way, most executives would challenge it, condemn it or distance themselves immediately. A frog that leaps into boiling water immediately leaps out. However, bullying often begins at barely perceptible levels and then increases insidiously one small notch at a time. A person is aware that something is amiss but cannot quite put their finger on it. Humour is often an initial response but over time their self-esteem weakens, and they realise that the situation is far worse than they ever could have imagined. Without support or help, they continue to suffer as a victim. The frog, in slowly heating water, is cooked alive.

It is one thing to set standards, boundaries, and priorities; it is another to defend them. It is one thing to have someone else protect you; it is another to stand up for yourself, to stand your own ground, and quite another again to potentially put yourself in harm's way to defend or protect someone else when your values have been disrespected. These ways of demonstrating leadership and courageous integrity are embodied at *Synergist*. When there is a leader present in a room who has demonstrated this leadership capacity without a qualm in the moment, everyone feels psychologically safe, respected, and empowered when they are present.

How the driver is implemented

The technique developed during the course of the coaching program as it was being employed with each participant. It was called a Courageous Caring Conversation (CCC) and was made up of three parts: the Truth, the Implications, and the turning Point: TIP. The Truth is a full and gracious articulation of the situation. It is designed to set the person free. The Implications are designed to engender greater shared awareness of the longer-term ripple effect of the situation on relationships, reputation, culture, and performance. The Point is designed to reset the situation, to create a turning point where the previous behaviour is no longer possible or will be met with serious consequences.

The conversation requires 'prethought', by way of scripting, to really ascertain the underlying truth and its implications and to fully consider the optimal way forward. It requires great courage and great care to *hold* the conversation rather than just have it, by holding unconditional positive regard for the self-esteem of the other person. It is a CCC, a mindful, heartfelt intervention.

Furthermore, there is a pause between each of **T**, **I**, and **P**. This provides space for the other person to comment and engage. While this does not change the points to be made that follow, it does enable greater empathy and understanding. The pause is limited to 20 seconds, as research shows that it is very challenging for most people to hold this period of silence. The more practice a person has, the more they develop this capacity to be a moral and ethical leader of culture as they evolve to *Synergist*.

It is not easy to hold Courageous Caring Conversations. There is risk involved, and often high risk related to continuation of employment, loss of reputation, or risk of being ostracised in the future. I shared my personal experience with coachees the first time I held what I now realise was such a conversation. My heart beat quickened, my throat went dry, my knees shook, and my hands felt clammy. I was in dire fear of the repercussions of my authentic exercise of courageous integrity.

My memorable event of standing my ground at great risk to my own livelihood was during the global financial crisis when I worked as a freelance consultant. I was also a solo parent with very little in the bank account and no other immediate support. I was only a few months in on a fabulous transformation assignment that was going exceedingly well when the CEO asked if he could meet the coaches of his direct reports. I had made all the arrangements and simply did not think it was a good idea. It probably would have constituted 'best practice' but I felt that the executives concerned would lose trust in the confidentiality of the coaching relationship if their coaches had one-on-one meetings with their CEO.

So I held my ground and advised the CEO in what was a rather terse meeting between us late in the day that I just didn't think it was appropriate. I felt all the above physical sensations all the while hearing a voice in my head saying: 'Stupid, stupid, what do you think you're doing?' However, I felt it was important to protect the integrity of the coaching arrangements to support the overall transformation. I went home that evening thinking that I would probably be fired the next day, that I had really taken the wrong route in line with my conscience rather than taking care of my family responsibilities.

The next day at work I discovered that somehow or other word had got out. There was a buzz in the air. Apparently I was the first person to have ever stood up to the CEO. It didn't matter over what, all that mattered was that I had spoken up and survived. Walls do have ears – well at least, people could hear through thin walls. To my surprise, the CEO continued to collaborate with me as usual. We went back to our old dynamic that grew to become one of the most trusted partnerships I ever experienced while leading an organisational transformation. Someone in my team actually told me when I needed to be in a meeting so that everyone could feel safe. This was quite an eye-opener to me at the time.

I advised coachees that once they had held four Courageous Caring Conversations, their neurotransmitters would be rewired, and they would no longer feel the fear of conveying the truth to another. They will have learnt to do so with kindness and candour. I describe it in relation to your turn to bat in baseball. If you can hit the ball and make it safe to base 1, you're on your way. 'Making it safe' means nothing too untoward happens as a consequence and in fact the respect others have of you rises. Hold a second CCC and make it to base 2 with all relationships still intact, and you're halfway. Hold two more CCCs and make it back to home-base, and your brain is rewired. Holding a CCC then becomes part of your normal everyday repertoire.

The CCC can also be escalated. It is essential to intervene immediately if the same unacceptable behaviour continues. When escalating, it is valuable to hold the CCC a second time with others present, the people who are being affected, and invite their perspectives too. This can lead to broader awareness of your concerns and why it is important to you and others. The next escalation point is to brave the CCC in an external environment with other stakeholders present. A gracious but honest revelation will have a profound ripple effect on the interpersonal dynamic going forward as everyone concerned will develop and renew their own perspective. Respectful openness, with a good shot of authentic humility, can generate significant goodwill and mutual understanding.

Case study examples

This driver was the most common ongoing intervention across all the coaching programs. It wasn't an easy exercise because it required truth-telling, courage, and clarity beyond an emotional lens to be effective. We collaborated on scripting Courageous Caring Conversations during the coaching session. I found that it takes some practice before a coachee is able to discern their own clarity and truth due to the cloud cover of emotions.

Also, most coachees, including senior executives, have a need to have the inappropriate behaviour affirmed as inappropriate. They are concerned not to misconstrue a situation due to the perception of high risks at stake. Here are two examples from the case studies – one behavioural, the other performance-related.

TRUTH

We work in a respectful workplace. The email you sent X regarding . . . is in breach of this.

[Pause]

IMPLICATIONS

If everyone wrote emails like this, we would end up with a toxic culture. Everyone would be casting blame on others and we wouldn't be able to work well together, not even enjoy our work or rely on each other to overcome challenges. No matter what has happened you cannot send emails like that.

[Pause]

POINT

I would like all your emails to be respectful in future. I would like you to attend the respectful workplace training program. If I do find it happens a second time, it'll be a disciplinary issue and will go on your record. You'll also need to apologise to X and Y today.

TRUTH

In the last three years, IT has become more sophisticated. This is because the business of IT has moved from a technical model to a services model, and therefore new skills became essential. It doesn't seem that you were able to keep up with the pace of change. Three months ago, things came to a head, and we both knew things couldn't continue as they were. Since that time, you've been away and not available and not visible. Business-wise, we've needed to contract-in commercial acumen and engagement capability to cover what would otherwise have been your role.

[Pause]

IMPLICATIONS

I know this must be tough for you. It seems you've been withdrawing, disengaging, not happy and just not really here any more.

[Pause]

POINT

I'm sorry to see us in the situation, but we can't ignore it. The decision I must make at this point is to say that we need to move to weekly performance management. This will involve a weekly meeting you will have with your new manager, on specific deliverables every week. You've been here a long time, we've known each other for a long time. If you'd like to open up any other avenue for discussion, if there's an alternative you'd like me to consider, or a different role you'd like to explore, then please come and talk to me when you've had a chance to think about it. I want to help.

The coachees' experience with it

The frequency with which this intervention came up signifies the value of it to the coachees. The frequency with which this intervention came up, signifies the value of it to the coachees. Finding one's authentic voice and being able to assert oneself confidently and graciously is a significant challenge given the power and patronage structures in conventional organisations. In the following situation, the coachee has decided to take unilateral action to ensure a significant restructuring initiative succeeds across their division and needs to communicate this effectively to their manager while maintaining their relationship.

> *TRUTH*
>
> *From what I've seen to date relative to my experience of these sorts of initiatives, the restructure's off track and not being managed well. I believe X [the change project manager] is out of her depth.*
>
> *[Pause]*
>
> *IMPLICATIONS*
>
> *I'm afraid this is not painting a positive picture of you, of our leadership team, and ultimately for all the [external stakeholders] we serve and must take account of and honour in this major transformational process. We stand the risk of losing their support not just now, but as we go forward with our new strategic intentions.*
>
> *[Pause]*
>
> *POINT*
>
> *I believe strongly that we need to take a different approach. I've already begun re-engineering the restructure in my division and its working much better. I'm going to advise the Regional Directors to take a similar approach and let X know. She doesn't really understand the implications of how a restructure affects people to be able to influence others to do things differently.*

Taking charge, even of one's own division when major new strategic initiatives are inappropriately rolled out from the top, takes initiative and courage. However, to not do so would be to be complicit with the inappropriateness of the initiative. This complicity begets distrust and even disrespect. It is essential to speak up and out if a strategic leader is to maintain respectful standards of conduct in all of their relationships with others.

Many CCCs resolved what had been implacable situations.

> *My boss' behaviour has changed and this has coalesced into the team, and across other teams. I ended up having open conversations with my boss, at her*

> insistence. She accused me of failing to be a team player! I said: 'That's not fair. You're treating me very badly'. And then she immediately apologised. First time ever! She's switched.

The impact of this driver on the coachees

This driver led to much greater authenticity and vulnerability across conversations generally. Even when accused of an error or miscall, coachees found words to express themselves assertively. Some gave voice to the fact that their way of leading had changed, their relationships with colleagues had changed, and how others perceived them had also changed.

> Felt healthier, wealth of experience at X, I wasn't associated with the bad guys any more . . . it's made me a wiser person and I'm doing more exciting work. I seem to have more credibility than I used to.

> We've had conversations for a while now, there are places I've gone to as a leader, that I wouldn't have gone. I wouldn't be having conversations that I needed to have with my team, things that I would've been blind to in the past . . . Ability to have conversations . . . Leadership is a lot of things, that's one of them.

> The things that I've been working on, me tuning into me, has really allowed me not to baulk at these situations. I can have an open conversation with any one of my team members, team members have been in tears because they are learning things that are fundamental to who they are, gaining in self-awareness . . . It allows me to help others become more authentic, authenticity breeds authenticity . . . Me growing is causing or generating their growth! . . . because I'm empowering the team to grow.

The underlying principles of the driver

People behave inappropriately from a lack of self or other awareness, their own personal sense of helplessness and victimhood, or inability to find the resources within themselves to resolve a situation with greater maturity. To communicate authentically and assertively showing a breadth of understanding and commitment to higher values or principles that support self-esteem and endorse respect of others, is both challenging and immeasurably rewarding.

'The truth will set you free'. We uncover the truth by delving deep, we explore the implications by thinking broadly, and we then venture forth on the path to transformation by insisting on a change. By holding the other person in high regard and speaking with compassion, there is less embarrassment and more authentic vulnerability. Others admire the honesty and respect the candour. Most importantly, they feel that they can trust a person who is both courageous and caring when speaking up.

The nature of the shift that was activated

The self that is activated in Courageous Caring Conversations is the Subtle Self in the Collective Tier. While the conversation is often unilateral, it speaks to the broader culture and what is acceptable and what is not. Speaking the truth and setting boundaries, limits, or standards with conviction does require significant heartfelt, mindful presence that becomes fully embodied at *Synergist*. The journey of holding Courageous Caring Conversations is in and of itself self-validating as the world around a person tips more in their direction. One of the most common and one of the most significant drivers is finding one's own voice in alignment with one's values and principles, through the course of graciously and sincerely holding Courageous Caring Conversations.

Chapter 8: Key Points

1 The shadow of our identity held in our subconscious is reflected in the emotional dramas and traumas of our life experiences.
2 We can illuminate shadow by acknowledging our emotional triggers as custom-designed personal growth learning opportunities.
3 Most interpersonal emotional triggers relate to an interpersonal power dynamic that began in our childhood: either the act or threat of abandonment, betrayal, rejection, abuse, neglect, deceit, or merciless rigidity.
4 By opening one's heart and mind to earlier events of the same dynamic using the GRIEF process, it is possible to integrate disparate identities and heal emotional wounds, leading to a clear, calm, and peaceful mind and a more open, warm, and harmonious heart.
5 This healing process eliminates the same type of psychodynamic drama from appearing in our lives as the wounds are no longer in our subconscious to attract the event, silences the voices associated with those dramas as they have been heard, understood, and integrated in our identity, and inhibits the same emotional pattern perpetuating in future generations.
6 Taking a stand to expose and stop inappropriate and sometimes threatening and intimidating behaviour is essential to stand your ground in the context of corporate politics. Setting and consistently holding mutually respectful standards, boundaries, and priorities is embodied at *Synergist*. Only then do people feel psychologically safe, respected, and empowered in the workplace.
7 The proven StageSHIFT approach is the scripting, rehearsal, and delivery of a unilateral or collaborative Courageous Caring Conversation undertaken in three steps – TIP: the Truth, the Implications, and the turning Point.
8 A Courageous Caring Conversation is something a person 'holds' rather than 'has', holding the self-esteem of the other persons involved in their mind and heart as the conversation takes place. This ensures that relationships remain intact and mutual respect can grow.

9 Holding Courageous Caring Conversations generates psychological safety, mutual respect, trust, and confidence in the workplace. They are essential to shift an organisation's culture to green and teal where people feel empowered to speak up and share unconventional, new ideas, and feel supported in their personal development when they do react emotionally or need to express themselves in vulnerable ways.

10 Courageous Caring Conversations highlight inappropriate behaviour as soon as possible after it has taken place. They must be repeated if they are not attended to or the situation repeats. They can then be escalated with others present, internal and external to the organisation, if needed.

Next Chapter

This chapter has reviewed the nature of a compassionate and empowering response to emotional triggers, traumas, and dramas in coachees' lives at work and at home. Instead of self-regulation, the focus is on eliminating the subconscious source of any emotional triggers and standing one's ground to ensure mutual respect, trust, and confidence are consciously built in the workplace. The next chapter moves into strategic coaching once more in relation to purposeful presentations and building collaborative intent with external stakeholders.

STRATEGIC DRIVERS 7 AND 8: LEADING WIDE COLLABORATION

DRIVER 7: Articulating a Unique and Inspiring Living Signature Presentation

The problem or need the driver addressed

Another focus of attention was creating presentations. Most of the participants were invited to present at external and internal conferences, award ceremonies, work farewell events, or at special family events where they wanted to say something of value. Over the coaching period, the type of presentation they created came to be known as a Compelling Signature Presentation.

It was to be 'compelling' because it covered an important topic of intrinsic human value, something that could make a difference in the lives of others, or something that moved people to change their way of thinking or behaving. It was also a 'signature presentation' as it needed to be something that was of unique importance to the participant, something that had had a significant impact on their life or career, such as a breakthrough moment of truth, an insightful revelation into why things were not working and what needed to shift, or the potential realisation of an extraordinary aspiration that they could share with others.

What the driver involves

Rather than be descriptive of events or clinically business-like, a Compelling Signature Presentation is intended to be authentic, developmental, transforming, and inspiring for others. The intent of the coaching intervention was to invite the participants to articulate the genuine, wise, and compassionate authoritative voice of the *Synergist* within, with a view to transforming the perspective of the audience. The coaching process evolved into the 12 P's:

INSPIRE
1 Problem: What is the issue, challenge, or dilemma you are concerned with?
2 Paradigms: What is the paradigm shift you are speaking to?

3 Perspective: What are the worldviews globally? What examples can you give?

4 Positioning: How will you frame your topic? What is the strategic context?

INFLUENCE

5 Passion: Why are you passionate about this? Why is it so important to you?

6 Parable: How did this revelation unfold in your life experience?

7 Principles: What universal principles support your position?

8 Point: What is your main point and a key memorable phase that captures it?

TRANSFORM

9 People: Who is your audience? What's important to them?

10 Promise: What will happen if the audience follows your advice?

11 Proof: What evidence do you have to support your claims?

12 Pitch: What would you like your audience to do?

Of course, you will also need many vivid pictures, poignant visuals, and memorable symbols to support your key messages. A 13th P is your stage presence. This will be evident from many of the above elements and you can expand your presence with physical stance, an energetic, enthusiastic delivery, and measured resonant tone of voice.

How the driver is implemented

By inviting the coachee to respond to all of these questions, they developed a profound understanding of a perspective on their life or work that was extremely personal and poignant for them. Often, revelations emerged from childhood and their chosen path in life. They found themselves engaged in an inquiry that was personal yet universal, something that interconnected their life with their vocation where they were drawn to clarifying the type of significant difference they could make in the world at large or in their own community.

The benchmark was to leave a legacy or celebrate a personal aspirational commitment through the powerful presence of their voice and clear articulation of their aspirational and inspiring message. The nature of the presentation was adapted in many ways to accommodate all types of speaking engagements, business or personal, small and large. It was designed to be a living document, a presentation that evolved with each outing, so that it became richer, more eloquent, and more evocative each time.

Case study examples

We're being invited to present the evidence. Another huge opportunity is the wealth of information available to the public, so it is our role to present information clearly and responsibly to the government and the community, taking the role of a non-partisan arbiter in the interests of a healthy and vibrant environment that sustains and enriches life in New South Wales.

Phone call out of the blue, re conference presentation . . . This year Sydney . . . Industry only . . . Presenting at this conference in October. Promise quantifiable value to be created, very aspirational to lift your passenger voluntary conversion from 65% to at least 85%.

Congratulated 60 people who were graduating with their Diplomas. And then I was invited to present at a Forum . . . 1,000 people in the auditorium . . . Fantastic presentation with video clips of people almost being hit by trains . . . The need for every single person to be vigilant, follow the rules, take personal accountability . . . don't assume trains will stop, always be alert . . . Conference next year. Inviting submissions from presenters now.

Speaking can be a bit of a struggle, 35 on Friday, 150 next week . . . Once in the groove, speaking from the heart . . . Very passionate . . . So exciting . . . Envisaging what is going to be happening in 10 years' time today . . . I've been advised that I was the top speaker at the conference.

Colleague left after 15 years and I gave his farewell speech. 100 people came, 30 current and 70 alumnae . . . It was a bit of a reunion . . . including some top people . . . I received a fabulous response to my speech.

At the University of Wollongong there was a mixture of graduates . . . I asked myself what would I tell my kids? . . . If I was graduating today, what would it be really good for me to know and understand? This changed knowing how to answer it. This time I added more. Found from me, a totally different perspective.

The coachees' experience with it

Ability to articulate in a succinct way that really hit the spot.

Could tell stories and was able to articulate things from the heart.

Getting airtime and being known, now understand the importance of getting your message out there.

The impact of this driver on the coachees

The coachees were encouraged by the power of their own thinking and the eloquence of a few carefully chosen words to symbolise their key message.

The underlying principles of the driver

Presenting with passion from the heart is an uncommon capacity. It requires significant thought and reflection to really discern, appreciate, and share an appropriate context and authentic message with a specific audience. The focus on presentation was not about skills, but on content and presence, on generating a shift for the audience in their minds and hearts.

The nature of the shift that was activated

Becoming attuned to personal values is part of the journey as a *Catalyst* in terms of clarifying and integrating your own identity. Finding your unique voice to influence people as a visionary, to honour another person with grace and compassion, or to advise future generations on how to best navigate life in the years ahead are all substantial challenges that blossom at *Synergist*.

It was also intriguing to note that once a participant had embarked on developing their Compelling Signature Presentation, new speaking engagement opportunities arose. The rich and revelatory coaching conversations led to inspiring presentations that received laudatory feedback. This lifted the confidence of the participants and their commitment to creating a better future through the scope of their work and sphere of influence. Their sense of self expanded as a result of their whole-hearted commitment to their life's potential contribution while appreciating others who had gone before and would come after.

DRIVER 8: Collaborating Widely with Stakeholders to Generate Synergy

The problem or need the driver addressed

The eighth driver focused on proactive engagement with stakeholders, first internally and then externally. One of the keys to leadership is to lead with passion and conviction, to be proactive and engage others in your purpose and vision with a view to co-creating the future together.

This way of working across an organisation is quite distinct from the more traditional approach of seeking permission from more senior executives to proceed with a proposed initiative. I called this 'working in the orange light zone'. I suggested to coachees that they not ever ask for permission to do anything but to engage, engage, engage everyone in the thinking, relating, creating, and doing of it.

Many of the coachees were also responsible for community engagement. Yet most of it was reactive in the light of media issues or responding to requests to present or update interested stakeholders. Shifting their perspective to proactive engagement in the form of a campaign to inspire a movement around their Compelling Signature Presentation so as to unite and enlighten everyone concerned, was an exciting and inspiring new strategic initiative for most.

Wish to lead state engagement at national level.

Need to reframe role to take account of the customer experience, community viewpoints and implications, and stakeholder challenges rather than just project deadlines.

We need to build confidence that the public health system provides effective advice support and treatment to improve the health and wellbeing of NSW community.

Seeking to make the industry more accountable.

Public opinion is at stake . . . We need to work with this proactively not passively . . . We need to operate openly and transparently to build trust and confidence in us as leaders.

What the driver involves

This driver involved creating a list of stakeholders and estimating the nature of the relationship on a scale of 1–5, where 1 was Connected, 3 was Cooperating, and 5 was Collaborating. I later added the 0 option of Conflicted! The coachee was also asked to gauge the strategic significance of the relationship – A crucial, B important, and C helpful. The third element was to assess the ideal nature of each relationship. These three elements constituted a very simple way of mapping stakeholders, identifying the gaps as opportunities and then initiating a stakeholder engagement strategy to either foster, build, or maintain relationships.

At a more advanced level, this driver was used to create a quarterly engagement map over a period of three years leading into industry forums and conferences, integrating celebratory weeks such as Science Week, while taking account of elections, relevant national and international events. The frequency of engagement was carefully considered, and the nature of engagement shifted to and from presentations and workshops to share needed information and facilitate genuine participation.

How the driver is implemented

Initially engagement, talking, simply became the first option. For instance, when a coachee did face a crisis with a UK contractor missing deadlines, he explored the source of the problems they were experiencing. He discovered that critical internal business issues were the cause of under-performance.

Rather than negotiate or blame the contractor, the coachee boarded a plane to London once a quarter to collaborate, 'perform triage', resolve the financial issue, and placed one of his own team members there for six-week stints. In other words, he collaborated directly with the supplier, invested support and funds to resolve the underlying causes, increased engagement, and enabled everything to be brought back into order to meet the overall project deliverables on time. He operated as a *Synergist* generating win–win–win collaborative, eco-centric solutions and outcomes.

My approach is successful, meeting every timeframe to the day. Tear down the transactional framework, getting away from the contract to the relationship. It's unheard of to hit deadlines like this as consistently as this. Met every single deliverable on time every time, 15 June for X, 17 August for Y, and with really strong partnership relationships with suppliers and stakeholders . . . Our key supplier relationship has evolved into a real partnership.

More advanced implementation involved setting up a spreadsheet of monthly place-based engagements to ensure state and national coverage. Executive assistants who had previously been occupied with changing meeting schedules became responsible for proactively setting up a meeting and workshop-oriented engagement schedule 6–18 months in advance.

Case study examples

Coachees took full responsibility for proactive engagement in their communities, their corporate reputation, and ensuring that people were aware of key concerns.

> Our relationship with the media is synergistic, mutually respectful and creating a whimsical sense of delight for all the people involved . . . we're celebrating the amazing legacy that will transform the transport experience for people in NSW.

> We are valued partners with an enviable corporate reputation with all stakeholders across the community . . . there is a clear community understanding of environmental sustainability.

> Active community participation is helping to shape the decisions with government.

> Greater community awareness around the issues and understanding of the facts in a cultural context is helping longer-term sustainability.

The coachees' experience with it

The coachees who had mastered the previous drivers were most adept at orchestrating internal and external stakeholder capacity. Most of the coachees proactively engaged more and more stakeholders, reflecting their increasing capacity to embrace diversity and conflict and lead a broader representation of political, supplier, and community interests for the longer-term benefit of the whole.

> I'm becoming really good with the collaborative stuff, finding the intersections, common ground . . . building trusted relationships.

> If [our strategy] is accepted by all our major stakeholders . . . Now we've got to do it . . . Need to get a lot of people involved . . . New sense of commitment and dedication to the bigger picture, and the possibility and challenge of really realising an aspirational purpose.

The engagement was primary – the highway – and the content of whatever was emerging as the most important next strategic challenge became the focus of everyone's attention. The frequency of meetings and authentic engagement fostered the development of mutual understanding and built strong partnerships amongst diverse, widely spread, and often conflicting stakeholders.

The impact of this driver on the coachees

These components engender later stage leadership capacity. The collaborative co-creation of sustainable synergistic solutions that all could design, support, and commit to is a hallmark of the collective orientation of a *Synergist's* leadership capacity.

The underlying principles of the driver

Wide stakeholder engagement is highly externally-facing and demands a discerning yet collaborative perspective that embraces diverse and conflicting views that may have become deeply embedded over time. The power of their vision and intent as an inspiring strategic leader leading the co-creation of the future, together with the emergence of intuitive and embodied guidance, is thought to activate a cosmically attuned evolving collective.

The nature of the shift that was activated

By leading these types of collaborative engagements, internally and externally, the participant could lead the development of a new emergent collective, first at *Catalyst* and consolidating at *Synergist*. While *Catalysts* are able to consciously adjust their communications and behaviour to engage proactively in the orange light zone, the *Synergist* becomes the green light. They are able to engage with unconscious competence in collaborative inquiry to better understand other stakeholders and advance their mutual understanding of each other's passions and concerns to develop an enduring accord of interests and aspirations that shapes ongoing endeavours.

Synergists are able to hold the space for diverse and disconnected stakeholders to become able to release their anxieties and trust in the process of dialogue to realise mutually beneficial outcomes. Coaching in building an orchestrated stakeholder engagement campaign and relationship development map led to greater internal cohesion, flourishing partnerships, and systemic strategic solutions for wider communities. This reflected the participants' intentions:

Chapter 9: Key Points

1 A Compelling Signature Presentation is intended to be authentic, developmental, transforming, and inspiring for others to learn new insights or take new actions.

2 There are 12 P's in a Compelling Signature Presentation that are designed to inspire, influence, and transform the audience to see the world in a new way.

3 The first four P's designed to inspire are: Problem, Paradigms, Perspective, and Positioning.

4 The second set of four P's designed to influence are: Passion, Parable, Principles, and Point.

5 The third and final set of four P's designed to transform are focused on: People, the Promise, Proof, and your Pitch.

6 The Compelling Signature Presentation was designed to be customisable to meet the needs of all audiences, a unique living document that was personally poignant and universally significant, that would be enhanced and enriched with each outing so that it became increasingly eloquent and evocative each time.

7 The preparation of a Compelling Signature Presentation in and of itself seemed to attract invitations and opportunities to present at conferences, work events, and personal occasions. The coachees' sense of self expanded as their influence broadened and inspired many others.

8 Internal stakeholder engagement involves 'working in the orange light zone' where wide engagement replaced ever asking for permission to move forward; the purpose was to invite, listen to, and bring together the diversity of views to collaborate on shared aspirations that were important to all.

9 Proactive stakeholder engagement was a strategic process that involved mapping current and desired relationships to ensure that the engagement activities were relevant to foster, build, and maintain critical and important relationships, and lead a co-creative collective.

10 Stakeholder engagement became a planned activity over a 3- to 5-year time horizon to engage diverse stakeholders individually, in small groups, in plenary forums, and across the community to celebrate memorable accomplishments or participate actively in national or global annual events (e.g. Science Week and Women's Day), to generate social evolution.

Next Chapter

This chapter has reviewed Drivers 7 and 8 related to building an inspiring presence while engaging widely with external stakeholders across the business and broader communities. The final chapter highlighting the factors that appeared to lead to the rapid transformation to *Catalyst* and *Synergist* outlines the often-repeated beliefs of the later stage coach to activate attitudinal shifts in perception.

10 THE ATTITUDINAL SHIFTS IN PERCEPTION AND PERSPECTIVE

In reviewing the empirical data further, there were a number of phrases that seemed to come up again and again, without conscious intent on my part, that I then shared with the coachees during our coaching meetings. These shifts in the perception of self and others introduced to all of the coachees are outlined in this chapter.

They reflect memes common to later stage thinking that are not present at earlier stages. I discovered these beliefs, phrases, and points of view when reviewing the dynamics and patterns in my own life and through being in the privileged position of listening to the life stories of hundreds of executives. They highlight aspects of a *Synergist* perspective that are in direct contrast to how an *Achievist* might think about events and situations. These new memes support the integration of the holistic self at *Synergist*.

SELF-WORK FOSTERS EVOLUTION
 1 Masterpiece in progress
 2 Recurring life events
 3 From self-conscious to the conscious self
 4 We can transform relationships individually
 5 Life is a miracle

EMOTIONS FOSTER EVOLUTION
 6 Emotional judgements of others
 7 Emotional triggers are opportunities
 8 Emotional traumas and dramas
 9 Talents admired in others
10 Communications that resonate

ENGAGEMENT FOSTERS EVOLUTION
11 Everyone is doing their best
12 Feeling seen, heard, and understood
13 The orange light zone
14 Everyone is a cousin
15 Engagement involves thought generation

FAMILIES FOSTER EVOLUTION
16 Strengths distinguish families
17 Families include opposites
18 Wounds travel generations
19 Early childhood is critical
20 Parents are later stage shadow work

Self-Work Fosters Evolution

1. Masterpiece in progress

Seeing everyone as not just a work-in-progress, but as a work of art, a master-piece-in-progress, provides us with a shot of humility and a sense of wonder of our own unique personal life journey. We all evolve in different stages at varying paces with individual aspirations, challenges, and dilemmas to realise, resolve, and dissolve.

We are very fortunate if we are given the opportunity to do this work consciously by trusting others who have the hindsight or insight to guide and light our way. As a masterpiece-in-progress, we are an evolving cosmic mystery where life is a miracle, and everything becomes meaningful.

2. Recurring life events

When we review our personal biography, we often see recurring patterns. These are immensely important to understand. The patterns and themes of recurring life events can be explored by undertaking a highly informative if emotionally painful Life Review of the highs and lows in our life experience. Often the most provocative situations when we realise in hindsight that we have been at fault, are our greatest sources of healing, wisdom, and compassion.

Sometimes patterns in life are the result of beliefs inherited from parents and teachers who influenced us at an early age. They become automated voices in our heads that we are not consciously aware of, until we look into our repeating life experiences and explore our underlying beliefs. For instance, 'money doesn't grow on trees' is something I heard many times growing up. Finding my way to consistent abundance became a lifelong journey for me.

3. From self-conscious to the conscious self

The conscious self is always ready to emerge from a feeling of being self-conscious, shy, or the universally pervasive 'not good enough'. By switching our attention from our own preoccupations of what we think of ourselves or how we might be perceived by others, to being of service to others, we can shift our inner perspective to the conscious self. The shift from being self-conscious to being the conscious self is activated by switching from being nervous to being of service. This activates vulnerability and reciprocity at *Catalyst*.

4. We can transform relationships unilaterally

If we're having a troubling time in a relationship, we can do much to change it fundamentally by exploring our own shadow in relation to it, activating healing and transforming our attitude to the other person. Doing this work of emotional processing and resetting your intentions in a heartfelt and mindful way, will transform your relationship with another person unilaterally, even if it is only you doing this type of work. It will fundamentally alter your relationship with the other person for the benefit of both.

5. Life is a miracle

Albert Einstein suggested that there are two ways to view life: one as though nothing is a miracle, and the other as though everything is a miracle. When life is seen as a miracle, everything that comes to our attention is meaningful, and everything that flows from our intention is miraculous. The fact that we can develop the conscious awareness to develop ourselves is to do a great service for all of humanity.

Emotions Foster Evolution

6. Emotional judgements of others

All emotionally laced judgements and criticism of others relate to qualities hidden in oneself. They draw our attention to serve our evolution. For instance, to disparage someone for being too verbose, insensitive, or controlling, suggests that the particular quality is latent within us.

This is in contrast to discerning judgements, where you simply perceive that a person could enhance their self-expression with greater self-awareness if they approached the situation in a more sensitive, respectful way. If your judgement is objective and it is not resonating within you emotionally, bringing up feelings of distaste, then the quality of character is not indicative of you.

7. Emotional triggers are opportunities

Being emotionally triggered indicates that an emotional wound is ready to heal and therefore is to be embraced rather than avoided or ignored in order for healing to take place. When triggered, the conventional practice is self-regulation, physiologically and emotionally such as through heart-based smooth rhythmic breathing. This is very valuable in the situation.

However, to avert emotional triggers re-occurring, it is important to explore the nature and source of what was triggered. This is an invitation to do the shadow work that is required to integrate a part of self that was harmed when young, and the experience suppressed at a time when it was too challenging to process.

8. Emotional traumas and dramas

Extreme turbulence in the form of disorientating, frustrating, and stressful events appears to arise after a situation has been ignored or suppressed for some time. It is the ultimate wake-up call to our own authenticity and what we are prepared to tolerate from others. We can 'go along to get along' for only so long until suppressed emotions accumulate and then explode in the form of a personal, situational, or existential crisis. Discovering what has been ignored over time leads to new insightful solutions and a form of transcendence and healing.

9. Talents admired in others

Strengths and characteristics that we ardently admire in others are also latent within ourselves. These are sometimes called the golden shadow or hidden halo within oneself. In other words, what is emotionally perceived as a talent in another is indeed latent within oneself. Being drawn to these qualities suggests that it is a good time to invest in developing them in oneself, as they will support our evolutionary journey going forward and equip us with the capabilities we need to realise our goals and aspirations.

10. Communications that resonate

All expressions by others that resonate with a person are also designed to foster our self-awareness or indicate opportunities to enhance our self-expression. These communications can come from anyone – even children say the most astounding things that can wake up our self-awareness in very direct ways.

Engagement Fosters Evolution

11. Everyone is doing their best

Everyone is always doing the best they can within their own level of awareness and is therefore deserving of respect, empathy, and understanding on their journey in life, rather than criticism or ridicule as is the conventional norm. One-upmanship is typical of *Achievists* in their competitive perspective. Being seen to be better than another and looking good are *Specialist* concerns. A more compassionate and understanding attitude on the evolving nature of human beings where everyone is doing their best evolves at *Synergist*.

12. Feeling seen, heard, and understood

To feel good and develop self-esteem at conventional stages, everyone needs to feel seen, heard, and understood. To be seen, we must be acknowledged with eye contact – the avoidance of eye contact can be highly distressing at early stages of development. To be heard, is to give people time and attention to express themselves, genuinely and authentically, while we listen openly without giving thought to what we might say next or how the situation is the same or different for us. Indeed, the best response for people to feel heard, is to ask them an open question that enables them to explore their situation or remarks further. To get ready for your own response signifies the self-preoccupation up to and including the *Achievist*.

For people to feel that they are understood, they must feel empathy, concern, understanding, and/or compassion from the person who is listening. Heartfelt acknowledgement that the situation they have been describing is challenging, joyful, momentous, or miraculous is to share in their experience of life. To invite them to share their feelings further, or to explain the events that led up the situation, or what this means for them in the future, is to participate in a genuine dialogue with them. Then they will feel understood and, provided there is no other surrounding negative activity, they will learn to trust you. Taking this time to be present with people enables leaders to authentically engage with others and open up to their feelings, aspirations, and vision.

13. The orange light zone

To become truly empowered, it is essential to operate in what I call the orange light zone. In this zone, we do not ever ask for permission – that would invite a red or green light. Instead, we express ourselves and engage with others in order to lead a dialogue, explore views, and generate possibilities. Most executives are trained to respect hierarchical levels of authority and approval requirements by asking for permission. This is highly disempowering. Much better to engage, engage, and engage, until you build shared momentum to realising mutually desired outcomes.

14. Everyone is a cousin

There are always dynamics in the workplace that can lead to inappropriate behaviour. It may be akin to sibling rivalry, romantic entanglements, either giving away your authority to people in parental type roles or controlling others in reporting roles. Rather, it is a very useful power-equalising and gender-neutral strategy to think of everyone as your cousin. A cousin is someone who cares but is not intimately involved with our concerns and issues. Cousins are also part of your interconnected family network. They must therefore be respected and honoured, can be asked for help and support, and they all talk to each other so you know word will get around. Talking to everyone as a cousin keeps many psychodynamics and romantic illusions at bay.

15. Engagement involves thought generation

For everyone's minds and hearts to be engaged, they must participate actively in inquiry and dialogue. Without the invitation and freedom to personally generate thoughts and feelings, ideas and suggestions, they are not engaged. However, once their minds and hearts are engaged, constructive dialogue can lead to mutual understanding and a shared vision. This is immensely more empowering than strategies of buy-in or entrainment. These strategies often involve a statement of this is how it is – ask any questions but things aren't going to change. Much better to gain a wide engagement of perspectives on how things appear to be to facilitate mutual shared understanding and invite a collaboration on how best to move forward.

Family Dynamics Foster Evolution

16. Strengths distinguish families

Abiding strengths also play out in future generations, and over time enhance and distinguish a family's identity. You will often see how a family dominates politics, for instance, or that all the members of a family are in professional occupations, or they all run successful businesses. These families have learned to optimise their family histories and tacit learning over generations to facilitate effectiveness in their chosen domain. This is also true of qualities of character and types of talents.

17. Families include opposites

Opposites within families are designed to illuminate the contrast. You may have one sibling who is wealthy and another who is perpetually broke. You may have one sibling who is highly educated and another who refused to advance their education. One may love design and fashion, and the other prefers wearing staples year in and year out. They have the potential to become more balanced and integrated through mutual awareness of the distinctive differences, celebrate each person's uniqueness, learn to respect each other's choices, and offer mutual support and assistance so that everyone enjoys the benefits of desirable advantages in life.

18. Wounds travel generations

Emotional wounds continue to play out in family dynamics in future generations. I have seen this so many times in my own life and find it revelatory when executives also share stories of their history in relation to current dilemmas. Therefore, when we heal an emotional wound of our own, we are inhibiting its perpetuation in our children.

Family issues can follow us throughout our lives and some seem just too large to engage with in collaboration with each other. Shadow work can be undertaken very effectively on an individual basis in order to resolve situations energetically and bring a sense of peace even if the relationships themselves are not restored. They may have outlived their usefulness.

19. Early childhood is critical

When I have taken the time to explore a person's history when they appear to be stalled in their development, I have often found that an ongoing lack of love in one's early childhood has also been present. I cannot speak to cause and effect, only coincidence. However, it aligns with the need for babies to experience love, to be held and nurtured, for them to have the wherewithall to live.

20. Parents are later stage shadow work

I have found that the shadow work we undertake on our personal father and mother, generally in that order, seems to be left to last as we consolidate at *Synergist* and potentially lean into the next stage of development. It is often the most invasive and deeply challenging, as many of our resentments and regrets, and emotional trials and tribulations, relate to what we perceive our parents did or didn't do for us.

Chapter 10: Key Points

1 This chapter sets out a series of memes, encapsulated beliefs, phrases, or ways of seeing life that serve to enable and expedite the shifts to *Catalyst* and *Synergist*.

2 They endorse the value of a later stage executive coach who is mindfully present and aware of their distinctive perspective and the ways that it can shift and expand wiser and more compassionate thinking amongst others.

3 The personal evolutionary process was highlighted in terms of the continuing cultivation of self while seeing life as a miracle and mystery, as well as a movie and mirror through the earlier chapters in this part of the book.

4 The patterns and themes of recurring life events can be explored by undertaking a highly informative if emotionally painful Life Review of the highs and lows in our life experience.

5 It also emphasises the value of emotions and how they play a critical signalling role in our lives in relation to our own personally unique yet universal evolution to enjoy greater peace of mind and harmony of heart. Exploration of any emotionally geared engagements will guide us to our own inner work and help us to integrate our identity.

6 To navigate shadow and heal soul wounds, it is especially important to excavate the meaning to be found within triggers, traumas, and dramas. This type of work remains within the coaching repertoire provided we are working with robust individuals and the nature of the events are disorientating rather than distressing.

7 Our relationships and interactions with others are critically important. This is especially so in the evolution within the Collective Quadrants to *Catalyst* and *Synergist* where giving attention to our social setting and

mutual interactions and aspirations prevails over our individual endeavours that principally benefit our self-interest.

8 Positive engagement with colleagues, friends, and family members based on open inquiry, deep listening, and positive regard within a power-mutual, gender-neutral, and expectation-free zone will enable wide collaborative engagement that yields strong emergent outcomes that benefit everyone.

9 Families, in particular, are the origin of most emotional dilemmas and quagmires we find ourselves in. They can follow us throughout our lives and some seem just too large to engage on together. Then it is recommended to do the shadow work individually on self in order to resolve situations energetically and bring a sense of peace even if the relationships themselves are not reinstated.

10 Overall, every experience in life, every element of self-expression, everything that gains our attention are all custom-designed to propel our cultivation of the whole or our holistic self. With every new insight, understanding, and revelation, we gain in wisdom and compassion which we can then extend to others.

Next Part

This concludes Part II, the Drivers of Later Stage Transformation. These drivers were taken from a thematic analysis of the content of the transformative coaching conversations. Part III moves from the analysis of data to a more conceptual exploration and emergent interpretation of why the eight strategic and holistic drivers were so effective in generating later stage development so quickly.

PART 3

The Dynamics of Later Stage Transformation

The eight drivers responsible for enabling and accelerating later stage transformation were highly instructive. They were the explanatory variables that led to the unprecedented coaching outcomes. However, I wanted to explore why they were so significantly instrumental in the later stage transformation to *Synergist*. This I believed could foster further research beyond a positivist approach.

The dynamics of later stage development arose from reflections on these drivers. By exploring the underlying factors of stage development as a dynamic process, I sought to better understand the interplay and implications of the drivers involved, and the nature of the coaching approach in the transformative process.

In particular, I was keen to gain a deeper appreciation of the dynamics underlying the shift to *Synergist,* given that the coaching was inspired by the need for this level of leadership capacity to transcend the interconnected complexities, disruption, and wicked problems of our VUCA (volatile, uncertain, complex, and ambiguous) world. This part of the book is thus more of a discovery process in terms of meaning-making. It is based on a deeper interpretation of the systemic nature of the dynamics at play and intuitive insight into the transformative process beyond the analytical approach that served well to distil the drivers of development.

Chapter 11: The 2-Step Square Dance of Vertical Development

Chapter 12: Generating and Holding Safe Expansive Space

Chapter 13: Correlation with Human Faculties and Energy Fields

Chapter 14: Linking Coaching Effectiveness to Stage Development

Chapter 15: Transformative StageSHIFT™ Executive Coaching

11 THE 2-STEP SQUARE DANCE OF VERTICAL DEVELOPMENT

This chapter investigates the eight drivers in the light of the AQAL Framework introduced in Chapter 1. It highlights the significance of the different quadrants in relation to the pathway of later stage development, and the inner and outer zones of development within the Individual and Collective dimensions of O'Fallon's STAGES model. This explains the latent value within the StageSHIFT Matrix of working intimately with both our inner and outer worlds to expedite later stage vertical development.

The Evolution of Individual Identity

The four quadrants are commonly referred to as the upper-left, upper-right, lower-left, and lower-right quadrants (Figure 11.1). While the upper-right quadrant termed Behaviour has been commonly addressed in talent and developmental capability and competency frameworks, the other three are less commonly represented as composite factors in human development.

The upper-left quadrant of Individual Identity, a person's internal operating structure and system of beliefs in the form of mindset, psychology and thought patterns, values and attitudes, was given significant prominence in the StageSHIFT approach to holistic leadership development.

Ken Wilber (2000) embraced constructive developmental psychology in terms of the congruent levels of perspective or holarchic stages of vertical development identified in ego, cognitive, moral, values, and faith development from various researchers, encompassing the evolution of worldviews and consciousness itself. It was realised that this quadrant was a fundamental source of transformative change beyond a more symptomatic focus on individual behavioural change to address capability gaps in the upper-right quadrant.

The focus on identity is also the realm of the development of authentic leadership capacity, exploring who we are relative to others. This stretches the understanding and identification of the Self beyond what we do at *Achievist*, to how we choose to define ourselves, how we feel when interacting with others, and who we aspire to become as we reinvent ourselves in the journey from *Catalyst* to *Synergist*.

This includes identifying our purpose, values, principles, and aspirations, while reflecting on the virtues of our character and the ripple effect we have in

Figure 11.1 Adapted AQAL model (Wilber, 2000)

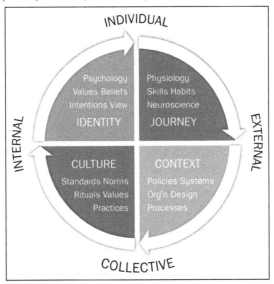

the world around us. This is necessarily accomplished in the Subtle Collective, as it is only by exploring our inner selves in relation to our life experiences and thereby gaining a better understanding of others and our interactions with others, that we can refine and cultivate our own character.

In constructive developmental psychology, our identity is continuously evolving. As we become aware of blind-spots, latent talents, and reactive life patterns, we can re-engineer ourselves at the source of our identity. This ongoing evolutionary process involves cultivating the self, healing shadow, and embodying spirit or our higher self, in order to become all that we aspire to be. These elements were at the heart of holistic leadership development.

To start with, the transformative coaching involved setting aspirational intent and developing awareness of the importance of positive self-expression, positive psychology, neuroscience, and the value of heart-based practices such as kindness and gratitude. Coachees learned to witness and uplift their self-expression, i.e. their thoughts, words, tone, and behaviours, to become more positive, enthusiastic, and optimistic, as well as kinder and more caring and considerate of others. This was followed by shadow resolution and graciously asserting and defending important standards, boundaries and priorities based on mutual outcomes and universal principles.

The Evolution of the Collective Context

The transformative pathway included a strong focus on the lower-right quadrant of Context, the Exterior of the Collective. In an organisation, Context is made up of the policies, systems, processes, and protocols that form the architectural infrastructure of our lives at work. We work within this Context; it becomes our container. As discussed in Chapter 1, contexts also evolve from the informality of new ventures (red), to the formal hierarchy of the industrial age (amber), high-performance teams generating profits (orange), empowered communities with a triple bottom line (green), and the organic holacracy of the digital age (teal).

The different levels of the Collective have been beautifully documented by Laloux in his book, *Reinventing Organizations* (2014), building on the earlier work of Beck and Cowan in *Spiral Dynamics* (1996). Laloux describes the systems and cultures that predominate in evolving organisations from red to amber, orange, green, and onto the new emergence of teal enterprises.

A red organisation has a short-term focus with a survival instinct. The founder, gang leader, or mafia boss rules by fear, as would an *Opportunist*. The amber organisation reflects the top-down command-control system that typifies many institutions and traditional governmental organisations similar to the stage of the *Conformist*.

The orange enterprise thrives in capitalism where businesses typically focus on results, profits, and continuing, consistent growth for shareholders, similar to the *Achievist*. The green organisation adopts conscious capitalism values and balances the three P's comprising people, planet, and profit outcomes. It actively builds a values-based culture that empowers people and engages all stakeholders rather than only shareholders to build more lasting sustainable value that contributes to the wellbeing of society as well as shared prosperity. This reflects the stage of *Catalyst*.

This spiral of organisational development evolves to teal, an evolutionary purpose-led organisation that facilitates self-management and ongoing development across wide networks of interdependent peers. It is described as a complex adaptive living system that trusts in the intrinsic evolutionary impulse within committed individuals who innovate, collaborate, and continuously evolve. There is respect for the whole self and a commitment to serve the needs of the whole arising within and around them. Trust is key to engender individual, mutual, and collective accountability to generate more sustainable, equitable, and healthy outcomes for people, the planet, and all of life. This organisational capacity reflects the leadership capacity of the *Synergist*.

From an organisational operating perspective, I have found that this evolution of collective enterprise can be visualised in relation to types of transport, and their strengths and limitations. For instance, a new enterprise is like a boat sailing out on the waters. All directions are possible based on the captain's command. A large hierarchical organisation is the rail transport system where trains travel only on certain lines, stop only at certain stations, and meet schedules down to the minute (!). They are rule-based and designed to be as efficient as possible.

A customer-centric, results-based organisation reflects the road transport system. It is designed to be more effective and much more flexible. Cars, buses, and trucks can travel on multiple roads and highways, individually or in groups, where everyone is headed to the same destination but can take different routes. The key is to arrive having used the least resources to maximise the specific outcomes sought. An empowered team-based organisation takes us to the air

Figure 11.2 A transport analogy of organisational evolution

RED	AMBER	ORANGE	GREEN	TEAL
Opportunistic	Conformist	Achievist	Catalyst	Synergist
Entrepreneurial Enterprise	Hierarchical Organisation	Empowered Chaotic Matrix	Shared Direction Shared Values	Integrated Ecosystem

transport system. Armed with shared vision and values, clear business goals based on a balanced set of outcomes, planes take people far and wide with all the resources on board to accomplish far-reaching aspirations that are impossible on the ground.

Teal is an imagined galactic system in space where people fly together in spaceships to accomplish a particular mission as it arises, and then return to the mothership hub to discover their next endeavour in potentially differently assorted groups relative to what is needed and unfolding. It is an organic, emergent system to sustain the wellbeing and flourishing of all (see Figure 11.2).

As they evolve, these contexts are more purposeful, more empowering, more liberating, and more engaging of the whole person and their own developmental trajectory. Collaborating with peers becomes a principal governance mechanism in contrast to top-down control or financial incentives. People unite as part of a network and organic emergence of the whole in response to evolutionary demands and challenges to protect and sustain people, life, and our planet Earth.

Driver 3, the Purposeful Strategic Scaffolding (PSS), set the scene for the articulation of aspirational outcomes. Driver 4, the Dynamic Operating Rhythm (DOR), operationalised the implementation of this agenda in a liberating and empowering way. Having an entirely new approach and operating structure that empowered the team to trust each other and to work more organically together as needed while having a robust meeting cycle to take stock, verify progress, and overcome challenges, lifted their engagement, productivity, creativity, collaboration, and performance. A number of executives were absolutely delighted with the significant rise in people engagement ratings in their division. Their new operating structure and rhythm offered them the opportunity to work at a more strategic level in the business, to become the more strategic leader they aspired to be.

Drivers 3 and 4 combined to transcend and transform the collective through aspirational content and elevated systems and structures of accountability and engagement. Both interventions reflect the systemic collective consulting perspective of a later stage transformative *Synergist* with a proven track record in organisation transformation. This consulting orientation is in contrast to the inclination of most developmental coaches who tend to focus on the individual –

their productivity, their creativity, their authenticity, their development, and their performance.

Another way of viewing the co-creation of the PSS and the DOR is as the construction of an expansive playing field with new rules on how to play the game. No longer was the coachee executive or their people contained by a set of tasks and objectives (tasks with deadlines); instead, they could really come out to play on a much more expansive elevated plane. They could take more decisions on why, who, what, how, where, and when, and unleash their creativity and productivity in emergence with their shared intent. The expansive playing field created a much larger yet defined safe and secure supportive space for experimentation, collaboration, implementation, trust and energy to flow into and through. It proved to be an exciting and liberating way for their people to work!

By enabling each coachee to transform the environmental context of their workplace in empowering and liberating ways, they were able to transcend the typical turmoil found in most corporations. They could rise above the noise, hold their direct reports accountable for the performance of their divisions or teams, and genuinely take a strategic stewardship leadership perspective befitting their role. Many strategic leaders, as were the coachees, are stuck with operational minutiae due to the lack of a strategic performance framework that transcends and transforms the obsolete amber and orange collectives.

In fact, if the old Concrete Collective is not transcended through the course of coaching or consulting in organisational development in this lower-right quadrant, I suggest that the vertical growth of strategic leaders becomes stalled at *Catalyst*, as it is today. The tyranny of office politics and conflicting interpersonal dynamics simply continues if there is no strategic scaffolding containing a safe expansive holding space where trust replaces fear. People need an empowering and liberating framework or container within which to grow, thrive, create, collaborate, and flourish.

The Pathway through the Quadrants

On initial reflection, I realised that the eight drivers formed a pathway through the four quadrants of the Integral AQAL Model of All Quadrants, All Levels (Wilber, 2000). While these levels represent the stages of development, the four quadrants represent the four fields of human experience: the Internal and External worlds of the Individual and the Collective. Given that the evolution to *Synergist* is the culmination of the Collective Self in the Subtle Tier, it seemed highly appropriate that all four quadrants were involved in the transformative process.

By creating the strategic scaffolding in the lower-right quadrant of the Collective Context involving policies, frameworks, systems, and processes, and cultivating their Individual Identity in the upper-left quadrant with reference to

Figure 11.3 The pathway through the quadrants of the adapted AQAL model

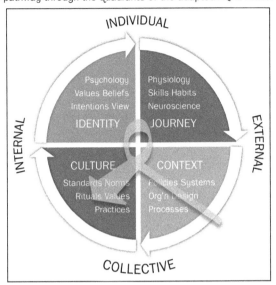

psychology, worldview, values, and beliefs, the coachees confidently embarked on their Hero's Journey in the upper-right quadrant, the external expression and manifestation of their life as an individual person. This includes our physiology or physical body, the components of our neurology, biology and chemistry, and the multiple complex interconnected intricate systems that support and enable our life. It also includes our skills, habits, and behaviours, and how we go about living our life through our self-expression, i.e. what we say, what we do, what we focus on, and what we give our attention to.

Undertaking this journey as the strategic leader holding the expansive space engineered by the new more liberating organisational context made significantly more challenging demands on the coachees. It was now up to them to model the type of values-based, respectful behaviour that mature adults demonstrate in a win-win-win paradigm. The shift from competitive behaviour to collaborative thinking is a quantum leap in organisational behaviour.

This transformative approach then manifests in the lower-left quadrant representing the Culture in the Collective. It is based on the values and memes through which people coordinate, cooperate, and collaborate together in the light of their individual capacity and the collective context they occupy. The Culture is understood with reference to the shared perception and alignment with higher-order values and principles, rituals and practices, standards and beliefs that become encoded as a living reality within a particular collective. The Culture is often seen as the outcome of the other quadrants, the interplay of identity, leadership, and organisational context based on historic influences, current policies, and future aspirations.

The source of transformative change emerged through the lower-right and upper-left quadrants. This is in contrast to many coaching and leadership development approaches that focus on changing behaviours in the upper-right quadrant as the main leverage for change, or even by imposing values congruence in the lower-left quadrant, without realising that genuine engagement demands a much deeper and broader understanding of identity.

It also had implications further along the coaching process that I had not anticipated. Those coachees who did the most work on co-creating Purposeful Strategic Scaffolding (PSS) with their people, and proudly showed me their A3 big-picture, one-page strategic framework on completion, also ended up with more free time to invest in internal and external stakeholder engagement. The empowering team performance framework effectively delegated full responsibility to their team leaders to take charge and realise the agreed outcomes.

The PSS opened up the opportunity for their team members to step up into leading the teams to accomplish annual performance goals (of their own making). They felt free to make decisions and take actions without continuous recourse to their executive leaders. The executives, and particularly those that did this well, were freed to move into the more expansive *Synergist* perspective and take greater responsibility for the broader outer collective.

The Inner and Outer Zones of Leadership

As I continued to study with Terri O'Fallon, it dawned on me that there was also a type of symmetry between the items in the 'From Within' Intrapersonal column and those in the 'With Others', the Interpersonal column of leadership transformation (Figure 11.4). For instance, manifesting the intent of evolutionary personal aspirations identified from within, demanded the exercise of

Figure 11.4 The StageSHIFT Executive Coaching Matrix

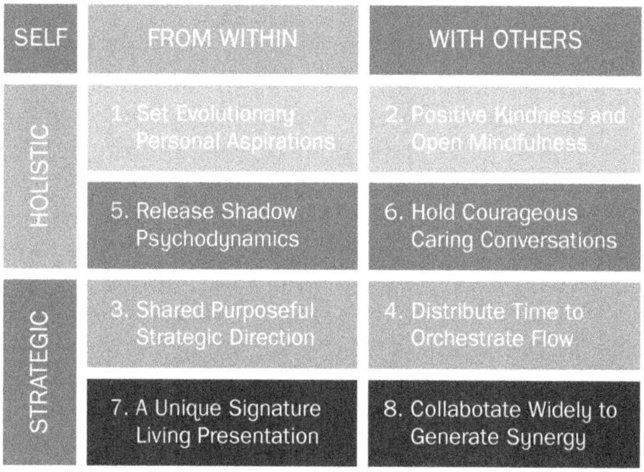

SELF	FROM WITHIN	WITH OTHERS
HOLISTIC	1. Set Evolutionary Personal Aspirations	2. Positive Kindness and Open Mindfulness
	5. Release Shadow Psychodynamics	6. Hold Courageous Caring Conversations
STRATEGIC	3. Shared Purposeful Strategic Direction	4. Distribute Time to Orchestrate Flow
	7. A Unique Signature Living Presentation	8. Collabotate Widely to Generate Synergy

positive, open mindfulness with others in the world, while engaging in purposeful strategic direction identified from within, demanded an approach to time distribution that orchestrated collaboration with others. There was both inspiration and application, an Inner and Outer Zone of awareness and engagement.

This reflects O'Fallon's (2011) sequence of stage development through the Inner and Outer Zones of each Tier, first identified by Cook-Greuter as a 2-step process of individuation followed by a stage of integration. The individuation stage of, for instance, *Catalyst*, takes place in Inner Zones of the Collective Quadrants in the Subtle Tier, while the integration stage shift to *Synergist*, takes place in the Outer Zones of the Collective Quadrants in the Subtle Tier.

The stage shift coaching did involve both the individual, holistic development, and the collective, strategic development. The intrapersonal drivers related to work within the inner self in the context of the organisation and the community to activate the *Catalyst*, while the interpersonal drivers related to outer engagement in the organisation and community invited the *Synergist* to become fully present and manifest.

It seems that while inner self-awareness and outer self-expression were manifest in the Individual Quadrants of the Subtle Tier, they were informed from the later stage perspective of the Collective Quadrants in the Subtle Tier. In other words, they were informed by the inter-systemic perspective of an eco-systemic worldview and not based on the ego-centric perception of the *Achievist's* worldview.

In conclusion, it would appear that the eight drivers of development were effective because they included both the Holistic Self and the Strategic Collective, as well as the blend between the Inner Self and Collective Awareness, and Outer Self-Expression and Collective Engagement with others. The synthesis of individual and collective, internal and external, inner and outer dynamics of development, from the coach's transpersonal perspective, each played an interweaving role in accelerating the later stage transformation to *Synergist* (Figure 11.5)

The Broad Spectrum Stage Shift

It is clear from the work of theorists that a person's stage of development includes a spectrum of developmental stages. We each have a centre of gravity or a primary stage that we are most comfortable operating in. We have a secondary stage that could be the next or prior stage depending on where our developmental focus is. If, for instance, our primary stage is at *Achievist*, as was the case for most of the executives in the case study, our secondary stage could be *Specialist*, the previous stage, or *Catalyst*, the stage after.

This would seem to depend on the extent to which we are completely comfortable at *Achievist*, the extent to which we have released elements of our operating mode at *Specialist*, and the extent to which we have the organisational, management, or other support, such as with an executive coach, to extend beyond our current comfort zone to the next stage, in this case, the *Catalyst*.

Figure 11.5 The Inner and Outer Zones of the Eight Drivers

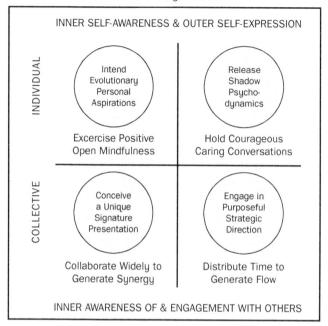

We generally also have a leading edge and a trailing edge that fit around our primary and secondary operating modes. Furthermore, we may have peak experiences that peer into stages beyond our own normal range of operating modes, and shadow crashes reminiscent of events when we were young that drop us back down to earlier stages so we can process these past experiences in order to rebuild our character foundations to better support later stages of development.

However, for the most part, you could say we operate across four stages simultaneously to cover both Individual and Collective Quadrants: a trailing edge, a secondary stage, a primary stage, and a leading edge. The primary and secondary stages, as suggested above, are generally neighbouring stages but each could be a later stage than the other. This depends on the degree of growth we are currently experiencing across our spectrum of stages. The participants in the research study were mostly selected based on their primary stage at *Achiever* and secondary stage at *Specialist*, with a very light leading edge at *Catalyst*.

The curious thing was that while they all shifted a full stage after an average of eight coaching sessions in a single year, mostly from *Achiever* to *Catalyst*, their *Achiever* profile barely altered. This is significant in developmental terms. It seems that our primary stage is sustained as a strong secondary stage even when we shift to the next stage. Thus, while our primary stage shifts, we retain our previous primary operating mode as a very strong secondary stage.

In the case of a shift from *Achievist* to *Catalyst*, their leading edge at *Catalyst* grew significantly (+24% to 36% of their profile) to become their new primary mode or centre of gravity, and their familiar *Achievist* mode was retained as a strong secondary mode. It barely changed (−6%). This was similar to the release of their trailing edge at *Conformist* (from 7% to 1% of their profile). The more significant change was the substantial release of what had been their secondary operating mode at *Specialist* (from 29% down to just 9%).

The same progressive shift took place for five of the executives who moved through to *Synergist*. It was only at this point that their previous secondary stage of *Achievist* was largely released to make way for their increasingly stronger *Synergist* perspective. Their previous primary mode at *Catalyst* turned to secondary. These progressions can be seen in Figure 11.6. The *Achievist* and *Synergist* are shown in **bold** as they are both integrating stages where a person demonstrates confidence and self-assurance in contrast to the stages of individuation where a person is discovering new, unfamiliar territory.

Therefore, in terms of the dynamics of later stage development, it is not a question of a linear step-by-step process as in a staircase, but a Broad Spectrum Stage Shift. Development seems to be accelerated when we focus on expanding a person's leading edge to cultivate their emerging new self (i.e. *Catalyst*), while releasing their secondary stage and trailing edge by healing their shadow (i.e. at *Specialist*). This proved to be a highly effective and efficient transformative combination. The coachees' previous primary stage was automatically transcended yet included, and only gave way to become a trailing edge when the new primary integrating stage at *Synergist* became their new default.

While the aggregate shifts in stages support the above argument, there were also the exceptions who shifted from *Achiever* to *Synergist* in the one year. They catapulted the developmental process by gaining rapid familiarity with their new emergent self at *Catalyst* and demonstrating the outer engagement capacity of the *Synergist*. The intention of the coaching program was not the shift to *Catalyst*, but to navigate the shift from *Achiever* to *Synergist* through the stage of *Catalyst*. The individuation phase of *Catalyst* was essential to enable the executive to embark on their journey but it was not a place where they could stabilise. *Catalyst* is really a form of limbo as a person becomes acquainted with the new terrain. I described individuation as setting up tent in a new territory and integration as buying a house to settle in once a person was familiar with the new territory. We had our eyes on the longer-term outcome of *Synergist* and settling down to stay for a while.

Figure 11.6 The broad spectrum stage shift

Spectrum	Trailing Edge	Secondary	Primary	Leading Edge
Year 0	Conformist	*Specialist*	**Achiever**	*Catalyst*
Year 1	*Specialist*	**Achiever**	*Catalyst*	Synergist
Year 4	Achiever	*Catalyst*	**Synergist**	*Constructivist*

Chapter 11: Key Points

1. Coaching in Identity and the Organisational Context is significantly more transformative than focusing on shifts in behaviour or gains in capabilities and competencies.

2. Coaching the coachee in how to transcend and transform conventional Concrete operating systems based on authority, bureaucracy, and shareholders, to engineer a more empowering, caring, and liberating workplace focused on stakeholder outcomes was significant.

3. This created the expansive space for the coachee to grow and develop to later stages and also, just as importantly, enabled the people they were responsible for leading to grow to at least the *Achievist* stage of development and become accountable for short- and medium-term performance outcomes.

4. Coaching the coachee to reframe their life experiences as learning interventions, interpret the psychodynamics of confronting situations and take accountability for the interpenetrative nature of life and self in a holistic sense, was also highly empowering and transformative.

5. Both the strategic and holistic coaching involved inner and outer development in terms of inner self-awareness and outer self-expression, as well as inner social awareness and outer engagement with others.

6. Most people operate across a spectrum of stages including a primary and secondary stage, with a leading and trailing edge.

7. Giving attention to traversing the shift from *Achievist* all the way to *Synergist* as a single journey was transformative.

8. Giving attention to developing a person's leading edge while releasing their trailing edge and secondary stage was transformative.

9. Attention given to the development of awareness and aspirations combined with attention to the enactment and engagement of new personal understandings in the outer world was transformative.

Next Chapter

The next chapter focuses on the responsibility of leaders to generate a psychologically safe space for others.

12 GENERATING AND HOLDING SAFE EXPANSIVE SPACE

On further reflection, I began to explore the dynamics of the four holistic drivers for self as a systemic interaction, and similarly, in relation to the four strategic drivers for the collective. In terms of the holistic self, I realised that the four key elements exerted simultaneously had the capacity to create a psychologically safe, secure, and supportive space around one's self.

Psychological safety, defined by the absence of any threat of punishment for making a mistake, was the key feature that distinguished the highest performing teams from others in Google's two-year research project called Aristotle (Delizonna, 2017). I sought to explore the concept that a leader at *Synergist* was responsible for, not a broad set of responsibilities, but for holding a psychologically safe, secure, and supportive space for the people in their care and in their community to grow and develop, innovate and collaborate, thrive and flourish.

The Cycle for Self-Transformation

The four holistic drivers reminded me of the process: 'waking up, showing up, cleaning up and growing up', which are part of the integral conversation related to vertical learning. It seems to me that the evolutionary developmental process captured in the cultivation of the holistic and strategic self, reflects this process with an ever-widening ripple effect. These first four key elements are shown as propellers in Figure 12.1 to symbolise the interweaving momentum they can create as a unified centrifugal force for development.

In terms of the holistic self, Driver 1 involved the Aspirational Leadership Brand Declaration (ALBD), a way of 'waking up' to one's **Spirit** or spiritual purpose or consciousness. It was a pivotal turning point that activated the personal cultivation of themselves as the leader they wished to be. These aspirations were uplifted during the course of coaching conversations and were often returned to by the executives as they reflected on their journey in hindsight. Many refined their aspirations over time giving conscious intention to who they chose to become. It could be said that the level of aspiration suggested a transpersonal reach.

Figure 12.1 The propellers creating space for the holistic self

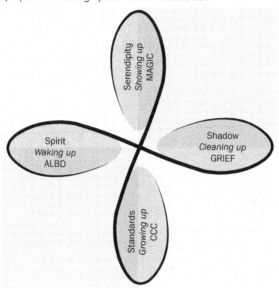

Setting this aspirational intent creates the suspended space that attracts the very blessings and lessons designed to cultivate the higher self. In this way, we become receptive, open to understanding life experiences as magical gifts and learning opportunities. Rather than operating as an *Achievist* – if you want it, go get it – we experiment with operating as an *Alchemist* partnering with the universe or cosmos. We set the intention and are open to gratefully receiving, enjoying, and learning whatever is needed for our self-actualisation.

The new way of looking at their life as having a ripple effect on others was at the heart of the second holistic driver, Driver 2: how they were invited to 'show up'. They were invited to monitor and lift their self-expression in positive, kind, and consciously mindful ways to facilitate their own growth and that of others.

It demands that our effect in the world is gracious and loving, mindful and inspiring. This relates to 'showing up' as our highest or best self, divinely guided to be for others everything we can be, and to do 'no harm'. This does take discipline, such as using positive language at all times and making special efforts to be kind, mindful, constructive, and caring when engaging with others. Engagement with the acronym MAGIC: Mastery, Abundance, Gratitude, Imagination, and Celebration, attracts the miracle of **Serendipity**.

Once we understand transference, we can also turn critical judgement into self-awareness and compassionate understanding for self and others. This also takes time and a conscious process to work through and discover in oneself, source in the past and let go of. In this way, we are not only adjusting our self-expression but also enhancing our self-awareness to integrate what we have otherwise been projecting onto others. If you spot it, you've got it!

The coachees' new-found appreciation for taking a primary focus on supporting, empowering, and encouraging people rather than focusing on task, uplifted their view of and engagement with others. I still recall one of the coachees' most profound realisation was that their role was all about the people, not the work. This reflection of reciprocity and their growing awareness of their own impact or ripple effect on others, something that becomes a priority at *Catalyst*, encouraged their vertical development.

The third holistic driver, Driver 5, entailed 'cleaning up'. It was designed to understand and heal the psychodynamics of their relationships with others, to clean up their shadow. Set in the context of relationship, this too was an essential inner driver to navigate the integration of disparate, wounded selves on the journey to *Synergist*. It involved the GRIEF process: we invite the Gift from past wounds that have been triggered, express what we Resent and Regret (mad and sad about), Inquire into the facts (subsequent objective clarity), Empathise with all actors including ourselves when young, and Forgive and Forget. The power of forgiveness is central to A Course in Miracles.

Seeing life experiences as learning opportunities to illuminate **Shadow** in the cultivation of the whole self, brought an entirely new dimension to the interpretation and framing of dramatic and traumatic events. These were often deeply emotional heart-wrenching experiences for which executives could find resolution and healing. Shifting beyond self-regulation to understanding the source of drama and actively embarking on the process of eliminating emotional wounds proved to be highly liberating.

This is a cognitive, emotional, and spiritual healing process that transcends self-regulation. Self-regulation, while useful in the moment to avoid hurting or harming others, is still a form of emotional suppression. Attention needs to be given to integrating the wound found in our shadow, triggered because it is ready to be healed. Once the integration process is fully completed, we are no longer triggered, as the wounds that were triggered in the past have been healed. It is not possible to be emotionally triggered if wounds are healed. This leads to peace of mind at *Synergist* as we empty of voices within us seeking to be heard and healed. This also prepares us for surrender of the ego in the shift to the MetAware Tier.

The fourth holistic driver, Driver 6, holding Courageous Caring Conversations (CCCs), guards the emergent space. This type of conversation protect the surrounding space from all negativity, criticism, judgement, and anything other than goodwill. It requires both personal courage and reverent care for others as we express ourselves to ensure that everyone is held to the agreed mutually respectful **Standards** needed to hold a safe, secure, and sacred space for all.

This has the effect of generating trust. It is a way of 'growing up'. It was most effective in enacting the values and principles that were becoming more and more important to their growing authenticity and increasing responsibility for their organisational culture. To hold CCCs was literally to 'grow up'. By being prepared to stand their ground on principle rather than look the other way, the executives grew in their appreciation of the bigger truth and implications that play out in human psychodynamics. By increasing their capacity to stand their ground and hold the co-creative emergent space around them, everyone involved felt more safe and secure.

When extended to others (i.e. you defend others' self-esteem by whistleblowing whenever anything inappropriate or disrespectful is said or expressed through gesture or behaviour) in a polite, respectful, and gracious way, then others feel safe in your presence too. This leadership capacity is the courage to express yourself courageously with care in order to hold respectful standards of behaviour and conscious boundaries for respectful engagement. The intervention can take the form of a direct question: 'What did you mean by that?' The full TIP approach – Truth, Implications, Point, described earlier in Chapter 8 – enables others to learn from your more expansive perspective, and is therefore more impactful.

I recall two critical moments that relate to this. The first moment was when a member of the senior executive team of an organisation where I was leading a strategic culture transformation asked me: 'What do you actually do Antoinette?' I found the question a little odd. I had been collaborating with the CEO, executive team, and senior leaders for some time, so what I did was relatively evident. I felt that I was being asked a deeper question. My response was: 'I'm holding space for people'. At the time, I was bewildered. What sort of answer was that! Now I realise that I was indeed holding the space for people to be safe and develop.

A second time, I caught a few phrases in passing when someone in my team was defending me. They said something along the lines of: 'She's brought respect back to the People and Culture function. We're on the strategic agenda now. We're presenting to the CEO and executive team. She's the one who brings us in. And I feel safe to speak up when Antoinette's around. I didn't use to'. For me, this was also quite profound. Could something as simple as psychological safety be so extraordinarily powerful?

These four holistic drivers of development, associated with Spirit, Serendipity, Shadow, and Standards, were focused on the executives' reformulation of their identity by design and then using discipline to rise above the norms and demonstrate this new self to others. This is a design, development, and cultivation process that invites and nurtures one's new holistic self to wake up, show up, clean up, and grow up.

The outcome of these four propellers is the creation of safe, secure, supportive, and sacred emergent space around the self and inclusive of others, shown as a circle in Figure 12.2 to illustrate the dynamics at play. They set up a very large expansive, virtually unlimited space within which to be and become more. A phrase I often coined for myself during my own transformative journey was: 'I surround myself with sacred space and walk the world with ease and grace'.

The Aspirational Leadership Brand Declaration sends out an outgoing signal to the universe to invite this new holistic self to come into being. In response, the universe sends in incoming blessings and lessons that are joyously, wholeheartedly, and mindfully integrated into the self. The dramatics of incoming drama that affects others in their immediate care but not the

Figure 12.2 The expansive space held by the *Synergist*

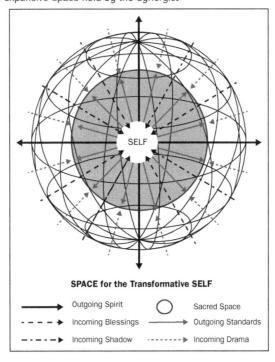

SPACE for the Transformative SELF

⟶ Outgoing Spirit		◯ Sacred Space	
- - - ➤ Incoming Blessings		⟶ Outgoing Standards	
— · — · ➤ Incoming Shadow		· · · · · ➤ Incoming Drama	

leader, are dispelled by Courageous Caring Conversations, and later dealt with at a deeper level through coaching conversations during one-on-one meetings. This ensures that everyone held within that psychologically safe, secure, and supportive space is also welcomed to wake up, show up, clean up, and grow up.

Expansive Space around the *Synergist*

The expansive space around the *Synergist* is in contrast to the *Achievist's* space-holding capacity. The *Achievist* is still largely focused on task, individual performance, and sometimes team leadership – even divisional and organisational leadership for those in more senior roles with greater responsibilities.

However, the *Achievist* cannot hold space *per se* as their perspective is transactional, not transformative. They are not yet entertaining the self-esteem and growth of the individual human being as a *Catalyst* begins to do and a *Synergist* sees as integral to their life purpose. An individual competitor in the Subtle Tier working their way around the bureaucratic *Conformist* Concrete Collective to achieve success is not interested so much in how others fare, unless it is being measured and reported.

Figure 12.3 The contrasting expansive space held by the *Synergist*

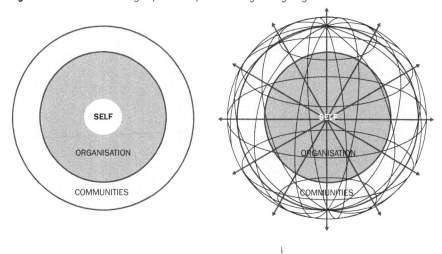

This is in direct contrast to the maturity of a collective collaborator who has transcended and transformed the collective systems to support and encourage others. This is their *raison d'être*. The discrepancy is evident in the two diagrams depicted in Figure 12.3. Regardless of their level of responsibilities, an *Achievist* directs people rather than holds space. Thus, the role of a person seen in a hierarchical format or as a single circular space. However, the organisational leader at *Synergist* is attuned to the interactive systemic dynamics of a more expansive space replete with multiple levels. Their leadership presence is significantly more expansive. They are the organisation. They are the Interpenetrative Self.

Engagement Cycle for the Inner Collective

Given that the *Synergist* is the culmination of development for an individual in the Subtle Tier by way of their leadership of the collective, it seems essential that four of the eight drivers were focused on uplifting and transforming the collective. They were focused on the lower-right quadrant of Context, re-engineering the structures, systems, processes, and policies that made up each executive's collective. This had the impact of expanding the playing field for each executive, generating a much larger open space to provide the stage for their exponentially increasing leadership capacity.

Let's explore the inner collective, the people within the organisation led by the executive, and peers and colleagues with whom they were engaged to realise their division's purposeful strategic outcomes. This space is held by the executive as described above, to enable the work of the division to be done in an organic, emergent, intuitive, deliberately developmental way, highly respectful of each person's individual journey.

The first strategic driver, Driver 3, the Transformative Strategic Agenda (TSA), invited each executive to set a shared aspirational purpose, uplifting values, strategic outcomes, and articulated strategic shifts in performance and culture to generate more sustainable, equitable outcomes and evolve to a more empowering, liberating culture. Developing the draft content to enable the executive to give voice to their highest meaningful aspirations in a business framework, and the empowering processes for the active engagement of all involved, formed part of the coaching conversations.

The TSA provided cascading strategic scaffolding, a business framework with a large open space for emergent engagement, shared understanding and agreement, so that all teams reporting in to the executive had an appropriate context within which to become high-performing *Achievist*-oriented teams focused on the realisation of agreed goals, results, and outcomes.

The second, Driver 4, the Dynamic Operating Rhythm (DOR), orchestrated the engagement of all people involved in contributing to the Transformative Strategic Agenda including team members, peers, other colleagues, and external stakeholders. Again, it was an open, expansive, invigorating framework. It did this by both structuring time to generate flow, and adopting Liberating Meeting Agendas (LMAs) to encourage and indeed demand authentic engagement. The DOR offered a new system for collaborative engagement that aggregated existing position descriptions and gave priority to 'family first' rather than adhering to the top-down command-control system.

It also seems highly valuable to better understand the dynamics that underpin the strategic drivers that related more specifically to external outcomes and the processes within that space that would enable effective communication, navigation, mutual understanding, cooperation, and collaboration. It is lit up by four other propellers that operate in that space to effectively co-create the world we choose to live in. Instead of working on the dynamics of the self, we are working with the dynamics of the inter-systemic reality that we see and perceive, co-create and generate.

Let's extend and expand the theme of 'waking up, showing up, cleaning up, and growing up' for the self to the collective. In the inner collective of the organisation, we have: lifting up, setting up, speaking up and stepping up. Driver 3, the transformative Strategy involved "lifting up" intentions, while Driver 4, the Synchrony of the DOR was a process of "setting up" operations. Driver 7, the Compelling Signature Presentation (CSP) offered "speaking up" to share important thoughts and insights while Driver 8, Synergy through Orchestrated Stakeholder Engagement (OSE), expanded the opportunity for "stepping up", engaging all voices to develop mutual understanding and take inspired action. Together they transcend the concrete collective of position descriptions and conventional cultural operating norms, to evolve into a more equitable, empowering, and liberating organisational context in the Subtle Collective serving evolutionary aspirational intent. A new collective operating system is generated.

The new strategic scaffolding engineered by the four propellers holds the open expansive space for their endeavours. By engaging in this work, each coachee was engaged in their outer world with the need and know-how to

Figure 12.4 The propellers creating space in the inner collective

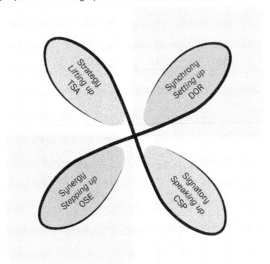

demonstrate their newly developing leadership capacity. Not only would they attract personal drama, trauma, blessings, and intuitive guidance to proceed effectively on realising their personal aspirations (ALBD), but their noble purposeful goals were also now in play in the collective energy field through all people they engaged and encountered along the way. The strategic scaffolding provided the expansive space for personal growth and mutual accomplishment.

One of the defining elements of the TSA was the identification of Key Strategic Shifts (KSS) in performance *and* culture, selected carefully and sequentially over a period of 3–5 years to enable the achievement of transformative outcomes. Accountability for the KSS added a transformative dimension to the organisational architectural context to transform the culture.

In tune with Kotter's (2012) secondary networked organisation of work transposed on the hierarchy, the KSS were led by 'champions' who had a vested interest in their success. Team members were drawn from across divisions by way of open invitation to circumnavigate silos and bring together a set of eight or so committed people with aspirational intent and developmental readiness. This structural component of self-managing evolutionary teams paved the way for a green and later teal organisation (Laloux, 2014) to emerge in the future.

The Dynamic Operating System (DOR) also transposed the organisational architecture a level higher. It set up an orchestrated approach to facilitate emergent flow and release the generative energy available from the highly taxing work of navigating individual standards, boundaries, and priorities, to the opportunity to contribute in a mutually encouraging and empowering way. The safe and secure space held by the executive enabled this to occur.

A final essential element in the renewal of the operating system were the LMAs. In operations meetings, what had previously been traditional agendas identifying lists of items to report progress on, the meeting structure opened up voluntary engagement around four key items: Praise, Progress, Problems, and Priorities, as described in more detail above. In one-on-one meetings, lists were also scrapped to invite voluntary engagement on the work, the person and their people: performance, development, and dynamics. They therefore took on the nature of coaching meetings.

The monthly cycle of strategic and culture meetings was also an innovation for most executives. By holding their people at the higher level of strategic outcomes and the psychodynamics implicit in values-based development, their attention was sustained on the bigger picture and their personal evolution as individuals, team members, and contributors. In previous transformative programs I have led, the inclusion of a values-based or open transformative leadership program for the top 10% of senior leaders had always formed part of the strategic intervention to support and provide time and process to facilitate transformative development to later stages.

I suspect that the implementation and consolidation of this collective operating system was sufficient to enable executives to integrate at *Synergist*. This would seem to be the case given that 17% of executives in the research study shifted from *Achievist* to *Synergist* in the one year after just eight 90-minute coaching sessions. Furthermore, only a few of the executives fully implemented the two final drivers, 7 and 8, to generate a wider collective transformation. This suggests that these two final drivers served to expand lateral learning at *Synergist* to incorporate the shared generation of even broader equitable and sustainable community outcomes.

Figure 12.5 The expansive space held in the inner collective

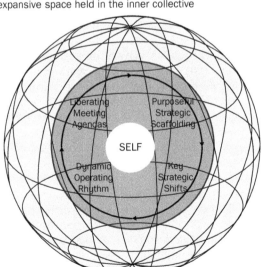

Engagement Cycle for the Outer Collective

This green/teal evolutionary approach to organisational design was further expanded by Drivers 7 and 8. These were not fully exploited by most executives in the first year but were actively implemented by those who evolved the most. Driver 7, the third collective driver, involved developing a Inspiring Signature Presentation (ISP) that articulated their most profound and aspirational purposeful intentions into form (i.e. speaking up). It was to be their **Signatory** legacy.

The depth and breadth of inquiry during coaching conversations contributed to the development of their expansive *Synergist* perspective. Rather than presenting facts based on logic, they articulated purpose based on aspirations. They became passionate advocates about the co-creation of a more equitable and sustainable future in their area of responsibility. Their heartfelt presence, balancing and integrating all perspectives with perfect and imperfect **Symmetry**, was designed to inspire others.

Driver 8, Orchestrated Stakeholder Collaboration (OSC), provided the avenue for **Synergy**. Generating wide proactive engagement on their ISP is needed to build momentum for others to consider, engage in, and adopt their heartfelt aspirations (i.e. stepping up). The sense of this type of orchestrated engagement seemed to more closely resemble the breadth and depth of engagement that cements a grassroots movement, than a typical business negotiation.

It was designed to bring people together, to share in their own highest aspirations and gain a mutual understanding of the emotional concerns and conflicting interests that mattered to the diverse stakeholders. The level of engagement was extremely wide, suggestive of social evolution at *Alchemist*. It seems to me, on later reflection, that the highest aspirations together with the

Figure 12.6 The combined power of the individual and collective propellers

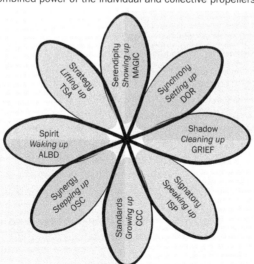

Synthesis of genuine mutual understanding amongst people enable them to collectively forge a new and better world.

Drivers 7 and 8 invited each coachee to turn their attention to the outer collective of stakeholders and interested or impacted members of the wider community. This work only became possible when Drivers 3 and 4 had been effectively activated, implemented, and had become normalised as the automated internal operating system. Only then did the executive have the time and energy – and emerging *Synergist* perspective – to effectively embark on even broader longer-term concerns that necessarily would involve working constructively and courageously with conflict and even distress.

Driver 7 invited the executive to develop their ideas and thoughts around their aspirations in respect of longer-term outcomes with a view to bringing together wider stakeholder and community participation and build shared momentum towards realising these extraordinary goals. The exploration of the 12 P's to articulate a **Signatory** ISP involved speaking up! While Vision begins at *Achievist*, and Values become genuinely important at *Catalyst*, the expression of one's own Voice with Inspiring Leadership Presence culminates at *Synergist*.

It was most interesting that as the executives embarked on this work, opportunities to present came their way. The energy of the universe is activated with personal intent that is aligned with the cosmic evolutionary impulse to bridge disharmony and create a more equitable, sustainable world. This is a transpersonal belief system that I acknowledge is not tested or believed by many, yet it was effective. Giving voice to heartfelt intent is a significant challenge yet honours the person's intrinsic desire to make the most of their life to leave a legacy that is purposeful and meaningful to them.

The expression of their authentic, courageous, aspirational, transformative Voice in the outer world was optimised with the development of Orchestrated Stakeholder Collaboration (OSC). Similar to the Dynamic Operating Rhythm within the organisation, this was a strategic initiative to engage, listen to, and open the minds of all stakeholders and community members in a concerted way to generate **Synergy**. Various modes were used, including online communications, creation of videos, and setting up and facilitating an iterative series of workshops and presentations at plenary conference forums to encourage mutual understanding and collaborative endeavours.

This was virtually an unsurmountable challenge at first, but with clear aspirations, the developing leadership capacity to invite and inform, engage and enact, transformative change gradually transpired. Individual transactional interests were transcended by shared transformative outcomes. Conflict was able to be embraced, open minds and warm hearts were encouraged by giving respectful and gracious attention to all parties, and a new **Synthesis** of transformative possibilities emerged.

The propellers generating propulsion in the outer collective invite the *Synergist* to speak up and light up others, and whole communities to meet up and rise up to co-create a better world for all to live in today and for future generations to enjoy tomorrow. The **Signature** ISP would be the most beneficent

Figure 12.7 The expansive space held in the outer collective

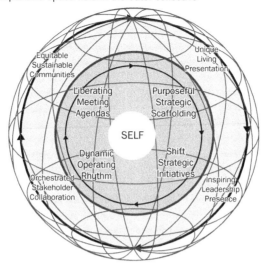

legacy each coachee could contemplate contributing to the world. The equanimity and **Symmetry** of their aspirational leadership commitment would inspire others. Orchestrating wide stakeholder engagement across all interested parties would lead to a **Synergy** of aspirational intent to generate a **Synthesis** of equitable sustainable communities. Rather than divided, people would be united.

The Expansive Sphere of Transformation

All in all, the eight drivers were not simply separate contributing factors. They generated a set of inter-systemic dynamics that was held by the executive leader in what the integral community refers to as a 'we-space'. This changes the usual picture from which we view organisations whereby the self is included and subsumed within the larger collective.

Synergist leadership holds this larger collective, both the inner and outer collective, through their later stage human capacity to perceive and influence inter-systemic complex adaptive realities, navigate wicked problems, and embrace humanity with wisdom and compassion. Instead of being subsumed by the whole, the *Synergist* leader energises and liberates it through the strategic holistic drivers of vertical development.

The integration of receptivity, activity, and reciprocity leads to the interpenetrative self at *Synergist*, interpenetrative with the dynamics of self, interconnected invariably and simultaneously with life. At *Synergist*, who we are is how we are and why we are, in addition to what and where we are. In this sphere of expansive space interconnecting within self, others, and with source (universe,

Figure 12.8 The expansive sphere of holistic transformation

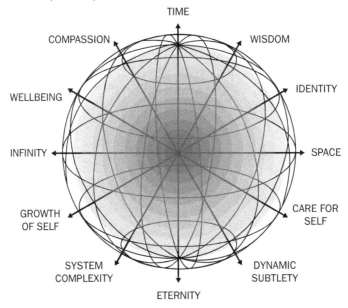

cosmos), we are holding the collective dynamic so that everyone can thrive and flourish within it. This sphere captures the holistic development of the Self.

Indeed, it sets up a refreshing understanding of the interconnected dynamics and outcomes of later stage leadership development on an evolving continuum of emergence and expansion. Time and space become two critical dimensions in the sphere of development leading to infinity and eternity respectively. This continuum of forever time and unlimited space transforms through the stages of development. Figure 12.8 depicts the expansive sphere of holistic transformation.

Complex meaning-making in relation to inter-systemic complexity has the power to generate wisdom. Subtle sense-making in relation to interpersonal psychodynamics and the personal healing processes involved, has the power to generate compassion. The development of wisdom and compassion are central to holding spacetime to enable all to be encouraged, upheld, and active contributors to the co-creation of a new transformative reality.

While growth of self is intrinsic to constructive developmental psychology, the recalibration of identity through the stages, care for Self is the feminine counterpart that is intrinsic to one's sense of wellbeing in the world. By incorporating the open heart to heal and integrate shadow and thereby generate a calm and clear mind, our sense of wellbeing is interconnected with our transforming identity. This congruence is mutually reinforcing in relation to our life experience and soul evolution. The sphere of stage leadership development incorporates each of these avenues as progressively attainable outcomes on the pathway of transformation.

The sphere of stage development incorporates interconnected transformative elements: the continuum of time and space, the transformation of identity and enhancement of wellbeing through personal growth and self-care, and an expanding meaning-making capacity in relation to systemic complexities and the subtleties of psychodynamics to develop wisdom and compassion.

Chapter 12: Key Points

1   The four drivers of holistic leadership development create a safe, secure, sacred, and emergent space that is transformative for the self. They lead to the generation of psychologically safe, secure, and supportive space for the people led by the leader.

2   The vertical development process of 'waking up, showing up, cleaning up, and growing up' is reflected in the four holistic drivers in relation to Spirit, Serendipity, Shadow, and Standards.

3   The *Synergist* as organisational leader is better depicted as the holder of space that surrounds them, and even includes space beyond the organisation to embrace community interests, than the holder of specific strategic responsibilities.

4   The first two drivers of strategic leadership development create an aspirational liberating operating system that is transformative for all within it.

5   The vertical development process was enhanced by 'lifting up, setting up, speaking up and stepping up' reflected in the strategic drivers: Strategy, Synchrony, Signatory and Synergy. The vertical development process was further enriched by 'speaking up, lighting up, meeting up, and rising up' based on the final two strategic drivers, each in two parts in relation to Signatory, Symmetry, Synergy, and Synthesis.

6   The second set of two drivers of strategic leadership development create an aspirational liberating operating system that is transformative for all involved and affected by it.

7   Viewing the Self as holding the Collective rather than being subsumed within it was transformative.

8   The expansive sphere of holistic leadership development integrates time and space, system complexity and dynamic subtlety, the growth of self and care for self, leading to infinity, eternity, a new identity, wellbeing, wisdom, and compassion.

Next Chapter

The next chapter dives more deeply into the nature of holistic leadership development across the spectrum of stages. It offers a new, insightful, and perhaps revelatory view of stage development.

13 CORRELATION WITH HUMAN FACULTIES AND ENERGY FIELDS

The stages of leadership development in relation to increasing awareness and evolving consciousness has always intrigued me. In this chapter I bring together the theory of stage development with my experience of my personal journey, and what now amounts to over 3,500 individual coaching hours intentionally focused on vertical stage development from *Achievist* to *Synergist* with over 250 senior executives.

I offer you an interconnected picture of the stages of development, our human faculties and the energy fields of our life experience. This provides a coherent underlying framework to inform and support the navigation of the holistic Spectrum Stage Shift.

The Human Faculties of Our Self-Expression

Based on my life experience and wide reading on the nature of being human, especially eastern philosophies around the chakra system (Ten Hoopen and Trompenaars, 2011), it seemed to me that different human faculties come into fullness at each stage of development (Figure 13.1). Over time, I developed a model of the broad Spectrum Stage Shift that illuminated this holistic evolution.

Impulsive responses and the creation of lifelong habits begins in the Concrete Tier. By the time we arrive at *Conformist*, we have formed an ego, a persona, a set of beliefs, and a personality that fits into the world we occupy. It is largely constructed by our reactions and responses to external events and we remain submissive to external conditions, but it nevertheless forms a reference point to understanding a sense of the individual albeit dependent self.

This self then develops in the Subtle Tier with a new sense of independence. At *Specialist* we exercise our personal will to learn, develop our skills and expertise, gain in knowledge, and begin to exercise self-discipline to meet our commitments and deliver on our responsibilities. This will is extended as an *Achiever* when we strive for results and to meet the needs of customers. 'If it is to be, it is up to me', becomes our philosophy of life. We use our will to do as much as we can to fulfil our goals as well as our heart's desires. The heart comes alive as we start to appreciate our feelings and what we want out of life. Our understanding of life is largely task-oriented and transactional – do the work and the results will follow – yet we have an appreciation of what feels good and what doesn't.

As our heart opens up to our inner world at *Catalyst*, we can tune into our intuition. Now we begin to understand what feels right within us in a subjective sense and we tap into this new sense of knowing to better navigate our life. Only with an open heart is our intuition available to us. Perhaps this is why it was once called female intuition given its connection with the heart and the feminine nature of nurturing. As we appreciate the openness of our heart to all of our experiences, joys and sorrows, pain and good fortune, and lead our life more intuitively, we realise the immense power of our heart to give attention to our sense of being in the world. The loving nature of the heart resonates in the present and is the basis on which we develop presence.

The mind is central for the *Synergist*. This mind is not the intellect, our analytical, conceptual, or systemic agility, but the place where intention and attention reside. The mind is a reservoir of voices from the past that beckon our attention, a consciousness that works like a GPS to bring us the precise learning experiences and blessings that will support our aspirations and endeavours, and an imagination that is boundless, colourful, and vibrant, full of infinite and abundant possibilities for our life. As the heart heals past pain, the associated voices disappear and the mind empties to become clear and calm, open and trusting, to lead a more enriching, purposeful, and meaningful life. At this point, we also integrate our masculine (*Achievist*) and feminine (*Catalyst*) qualities to enjoy both and become gynandrous.

From there ensues the transpersonal self, anchored as a spiritual being having a human existence. We move into the MetAware Tier, gracefully following embodied guidance that is beyond thought yet trusting in the goodness of life in partnership with the universe. By following our guidance rather than rationalising or questioning it, we become instruments of the divine universe on Earth and become attuned to our spirit at *Alchemist*. This is followed by an understanding of the soul, our holistic being together with all life, the universe as a whole, at the subsequent stages, *Ironist* and *Holist*.

By integrating these dimensions into the concept of progressively transposing our way of being or operating through the integration stages, our understanding of evolution becomes more tangible. Given the process of individuation and integration, it becomes patent that we shift from an anchoring point in our

Figure 13.1 The human faculties correlated to the stages of development

fear	work	play	grow	flow	calm	care	free	love	joy
Opportunist	Conformist	Specialist	Achievist	Catalyst	Synergist	Construct	Alchemist	Ironist	Holist
IMPULSE	EGO	WILL	HEART	INTUITION	MIND	GUIDANCE	SPIRIT	LIGHT	SOUL

ego at *Conformist*, a stage of integration, to our heart at *Achievist*, the next stage of integration, to our mind at *Synergist*, the following stage of integration, and onto our spirit at *Alchemist*. These are all anchoring points, holding spaces, consolidation modes, where we feel comfortable and confident. They represent the presence of yin.

The in-between stages are trajectories, energetic movements, active, the yang. Our will, intuition, and guidance enable us to individuate into the next person perspective at *Specialist*, *Catalyst*, and *Constructivist*. The system is holarchic, so while we continue to draw on our earlier human faculties, we give precedence to the insights and revelations in our emerging human faculties as we realise the increasing transformative magnitude of our personal power at later stages.

The Energy Fields of Our Life Experience

A further dimension to our evolution through the stages relates to our life experience. It had come to my attention that our life experience transforms as we traverse the stages of human evolution. That life experience is made up of the quality of the space or energy field that surrounds us at different stages of consciousness. These are illustrated in Figure 13.2 below.

The Reactive Patterns that we appreciate from Horney's (1950) work on the ego relates to the early stages when our ego is still being formed. Horney's understanding of neurosis in relation to human growth and the sabotaging power of emotional Reactive Patterns was based on developing strategies to cope with insecurities during childhood. These are the fight, flight, freeze, or appease options of the amygdala within the reptilian brain and extended to wiring in the limbic brain when feeling physically or emotionally threatened.

In corporate speak, we move against the person in opposition (aggression), away from the person with resignation (withdrawal), or towards the person in appeasement (compliance). Each strategy is a reactive one designed to protect ourselves. It is based on our past life experiences. This creates a lot of frustration and feelings of inadequacy within us, which makes life a struggle. Until we explore understand and heal the past, we remain subject to Reactive Patterns.

Another energy field that gained in popularity was Fritz's (1984) concept of creative tension that arose in the gap between current reality and a future

Figure 13.2 The changing energy fields of our life experience

REACTIVE PATTERNS		CREATIVE STRETCH		EMERGENT FUTURE		EASE & GRACE		BLISSFUL WONDER	
fear	work	play	grow	flow	calm	care	free	love	joy
Opportunist	Conformist	Specialist	Achievist	Catalyst	Synergist	Construct	Alchemist	Ironist	Holist
IMPULSE	EGO	WILL	HEART	INTUITION	MIND	GUIDANCE	SPIRIT	LIGHT	SOUL
Struggling		Striving		Thriving		Flourishing		Surrender	

vision, later endorsed by Senge (1990). This energy was articulated as an active pursuit of our goals and dreams, so they become closer to becoming reality and clearer in our mind. We must produce the desire and discipline to do all we can to achieve them. I prefer to call this energy field Creative Stretch to give it a positive ambience. It is particularly relevant to the striving nature of the *Specialist* and *Achievist* as they focus on continuously improving their craft or delivering results respectively. They are preoccupied with working towards and creating the future they want.

A level beyond striving is thriving. I really admire Scharmer's (2018) articulation of Theory U. He refers to the generative social field, a type of holding space, which reflects the experience of a person living in the present as it emerges. It is a collective space that draws on our capacity to listen into and sense from within the generative field for something new to emerge. It is representative of the space navigated at the collective stages of *Catalyst* and *Synergist*.

In Scharmer's words, with the courage of an open will, the compassion of an open heart, and the curiosity of an open mind, we can connect into source, the universe, through a process he calls 'presencing'. It is interesting to note that he also draws on the open will, open heart, and open mind to bring this energy field or container for emergence into being. By suspending past patterns and voices of judgement, criticism, and fear, we can co-create with vision and intention drawing from the whole. Based on Scharmer's description of this energy field as 'the future as it emerges', I term this the Emergent Future. We become receptive to a greater cosmic unfolding harnessing our intuition.

From thriving, we move to flourishing. Not only are we at one with co-emergence, we are also blossoming into our fuller potential. A number of spiritual and new-age authors such as Eckhart Tolle in *The Power of Now* (1997) and Michael Bernard Beckwith in *Spiritual Liberation* (2009), talk of this field of energy as one of Ease and Grace. It comes into our life experience when we are fully integrated at *Synergist* and reach into the transpersonal MetAware Tier realising that all of life is constructed as we expand our perspective to the evolutionary *Alchemist*.

The consequent energy field is based on Joseph Campbell's (2004) famous pronouncement to 'follow your bliss' in the sense of following our sense of awe and wonder in attunement with the universe. By following our bliss, we begin to live the life that manifests from within our own being, where open windows and doors appear for us in ways we could not possibly imagine to live a more wonderful and inspiring life. To emphasise the incoming appreciation of oneness, I called this energy field Blissful Wonder, a state of surrender to all that is.

The Figure-8 Holistic Energy Operating System

The Figure-8 Holistic Energy Operating System is a conceptual framework to bring all of the above ideas together. The Figure-8 is adopted to depict the centre of gravity or anchoring point for each integration stage. Its natural curves

Figure 13.3 The Figure-8 Holistic Energy Operating System

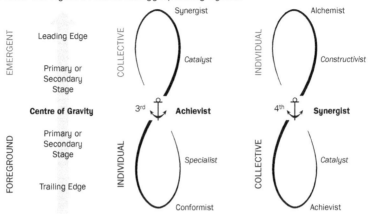

are reminiscent of the spiral depicting a sense of movement from one integration stage to the next through an individuation process. The full spectrum of neighbouring stages that each person's profile is a composite of, forms part of each Figure-8. And, of course, it is the symbol of infinity suggesting an infinitely unfolding embrace of humanity, life, the cosmos, and the universe.

Figure 13.3 is an illustration of two Figure-8's, exemplifying the Figure-8 Spectrum Stage Shift. The central point is the centre of gravity which shifts from one stage of integration to the next, i.e. from Achievist to Synergist. This could be a primary or secondary stage. I define the centre of gravity as either the primary or secondary stage, whichever is the latest integration stage of development. This means that any one person's spectrum of stages falls on a single Figure-8. To transform their identity to the next stage of integration involves the transformative shift from the previous integration stage. In this case, based on the research study, x.5 then diminishes as the new trailing edge.

The Spectrum Stage Shifts transform from being anchored at *Opportunist*, to *Conformist*, to *Achievist*, to *Synergist*, and onto *Alchemist*. This is reflected in the transformative shifts from impulse, to ego, to heart, to mind, and onto spirit. Each stage forms part of a holarchy including all elements and aspects that have been previously integrated.

The loops in the Figure-8 represent the Energy Fields of our life experience. I suggest that 80% of our life experience is composed of the Energy Fields surrounding our anchoring point. There are always peak experiences and shadow crashes to take account of, but in my experience, life continues along similar lines unless and until we consciously and actively re-engineer our identity and perspective. Figure 13.4 illustrates this concept.

For instance, when anchored in the ego at *Conformist*, our life experience is largely composed of Reactive Patterns and Creative Stretch, subject to the past and focused on the future. We struggle and strive. Following a Spectrum Stage Shift to anchor in the heart at *Achievist*, our life experience is largely made up of Creative Stretch and the Emergent Future where we begin to embrace

Figure 13.4 The life experiences around our Central Stage of Integration

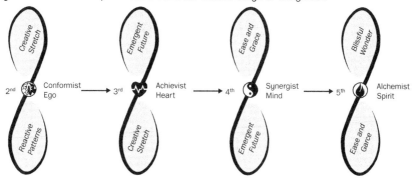

The Figure-8 Holistic Energy Operating System Spectrum Stage Shifts

the present. We're striving and thriving. Anchored in the mind at *Synergist*, having let go of most of our egoic struggles, our life experience upgrades once again to largely incorporate the Emergent Future and the pathway of Ease and Grace. We're thriving and flourishing. When anchored in the spirit at *Alchemist*, we flourish and surrender in Blissful Wonder.

The individuation stages fall on either side, as do the associated human faculties. For instance, when anchored in the heart at *Achievist*, the will of the *Specialist* precedes this stage, indicated by the driving and striving of Creative Stretch. When the heart opens to later stages of consciousness, the heart opens to become aware of and listen to intuition which guides the *Catalyst*, the succeeding stage, to lean into the Emergent Future where the person begins to thrive. New opportunities in the form of lessons and blessings arrive to inform our self-expression and self-awareness. The heart also has the power to heal the shadows held within the *Specialist* and preceding *stages* and is thus freed from the past to ultimately fully transform into a *Synergist* anchored in a calm, clear, and open mind.

Figure 13.5 All preceding and succeeding stages surrounding Stages of Integration

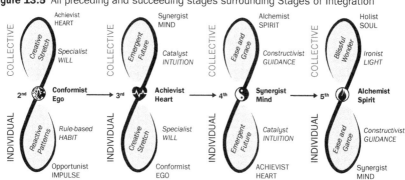

The Figure-8 Holistic Energy Operating System Spectrum Stage Shifts

Figure 13.5 provides a full explication of the stages, associated human faculties and surrounding energy fields displayed within Figure-8 Holistic Energy Operating Systems. The Spectrum Stage Shifts occur when transforming from one Figure-8 centred around a mature person perspective to the next mature person perspective.

This conceptual framework sheds light on the nature of evolutionary transformations, both cognitively and visually. It helps to reset the commonly held notion that vertical development is a linear step by step process. Vertical development can be seen and understood as a migration or transposition of the Holistic Energy Operating System by way of Spectrum Stage Shifts. It follows that to ignite vertical development from *Achievist* to *Synergist*, it is essential to realise and reify a new operating system anchored in the subsequent integration mode.

The coachees found that the conceptual framework added substance and simplicity to what were otherwise theoretical terms representing increasingly expanded levels of consciousness. The Holistic Energy Operating System Spectrum Stage Shift offered a visual, coherent, and comprehensive model of transformative leadership development.

Cultivating Self, Healing Shadow, and Embodying Spirit

In the shift from *Achievist* to *Synergist*, an open heart was key. It was important to shift effectively into the mode of *Catalyst* in order to build reciprocity, inner awareness, and the emergent capacity of a listening heart to hear one's inner intuition. Further, once all splintered parts of ourselves have been integrated and our emotional wounds healed with our hearts, their voices disappear within our inner world and the integration of the *Synergist* becomes embodied. One of its key indicators is the emergence of a calm, clear, open mind no longer subject to emotional triggers or reactive patterns. By connecting these human faculties to the stages of development, the research participants were better able to appreciate the holistic nature of their transformative journey from *Achievist* to *Synergist*.

This diagrammatic conceptual portrayal transcends emotional intelligence (EQ) (Goleman, 1995), self-regulation, and social awareness with the application of spiritual intelligence in terms of shadow healing and the nature of psychodynamics found within relationship dramas. The processes employed to work through these situations are deeper and therefore more transformative than conventional approaches to applying EQ. The healing power of the heart is fundamental to feeling fully in charge of one's life and developing the capacity to build authentic relationships and learning to trust rather than control others as *Achievists* are prone to do.

Until the Reactive Patterns are understood and resolved, they continue to prevail and diminish, if not prevent, a person from shifting into the broader and deeper expanses of consciousness. Just like a rubber band, our life expe-

Figure 13.6 The Holistic Energy Operating System as a whole

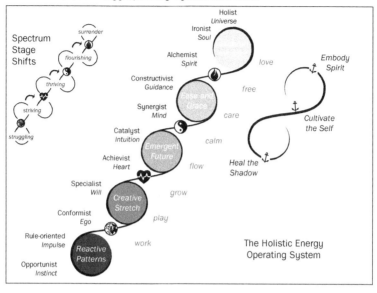

rience continues to repeat iterative patterns that sabotage our efforts until we give them proper attention from our inner being. Just as a large tree with a multitude of branches reaching up into the sky needs a deeply embedded root system to flourish, a person can only evolve to higher stages of consciousness by developing correspondingly ever deeper self-awareness into their inner world.

This led to an appreciation of the importance of holistic leadership development in relation to cultivating the self, healing shadow, and embodying spirit, as shown in Figure 13.6. In addition to my own personal life experience, there is tentative evidence that these later stages of development integrate the capacity for more complex meaning-making with a greater sense of wellbeing. This lends the evolution of stage development to give as much attention to the notion of eudaimonia, leading the good life as Aristotle said, the dharma, offering holistic psychological health in terms of meaning, growth, and wellbeing.

The four-letter names for the stages – from fear to work, play to grow, flow into calm, care and free, love and joy – were based on personal experience and witnessing of others embodying the fundamental nature of the Spectrum Stage Shifts. The synergy realised by consciously working with shadow, self, and spirit systematically underpinned the four holistic drivers in terms of developing deeper self-awareness and uplifting one's self-expression. The realisation of this conceptual model led to the development of my own signature statement:

The higher our self-expression and the deeper our self-awareness, the richer our life experience and the greater our soul evolution.

Chapter 13: Key Points

1 The human faculties can be correlated with each of the stages of development based on an understanding of their core values, motives, intentions, and capabilities.

2 The energy fields of our life experience can be situated between the integrated stages of development to provide a sense of how life transforms as our self-expression evolves through the stages of development.

3 Together, stages, human faculties, and energy fields, combined with a focus on the anchoring capacity of stages of integration, leads to the concept of a Figure-8 Holistic Energy Operating System along a spectrum of stages in our personal evolution.

4 Coachees found the depiction of the Holistic Energy Operating System highly informative and instructive in terms of gaining a deeper understanding into their life's journey and experience.

5 Navigating the Holistic Spectrum Stage Shift from *Achievist* to *Synergist* requires three complementary strategies: healing shadow, cultivating the self, and embodying spirit.

6 My Signature Statement: *The higher our self-expression and the deeper our self-awareness, the richer our life experience and the greater our soul evolution.*

Next Chapter

The next chapter turns to the transformative coaching approach and distinguishes it from the standard typology of skills-based, performance, and developmental coaching. It offers the progression of stage development as a measurable outcome for coaching effectiveness.

14 LINKING COACHING EFFECTIVENESS TO STAGE DEVELOPMENT

One of the key emergent themes in executive coaching is the objective measure of its effectiveness beyond general indications that it is one of the most effective interventions in learning and development today. The most common executive coaching typology concerns three different types of coaching: skills coaching, performance coaching, and developmental coaching (Cox et al., 2014). The latter is also sometimes called personal coaching (Ives, 2008) or evolutionary coaching (Barrett, 2014).

This set of three has been extended by Hawkins and Smith (2013) to include transformational coaching and Stelter (2014) also offers a new form of executive coaching he calls third-generation coaching that focuses more specifically on clarifying the meaning of one's life experience. The interesting thing is that these four main types of executive coaching – skills-based, performance, developmental, and what I will call transformative coaching to include both transformational and third-generational coaching – also align with the stages of vertical development. Navigating a shift to the relevant stage could therefore be an effective objective measure of coaching effectiveness.

Current Assessments of Coaching Effectiveness

Executive coaching has been positively correlated with a range of capabilities and outcomes, although most are more indicative of lateral learning rather than vertical development. Examples are improved individual performance, goal accomplishment, confidence, self-efficacy, communications, resilience, leadership, managerial flexibility, conflict-resolution, professional relationships, self-awareness, self-regulation, work satisfaction, workplace wellbeing, balance between personal and professional lives, time management, organisational commitment, and performance. These outcomes relate more to being a high-performing *Achievist* than realising the developmental outcomes at *Catalyst* and particularly *Synergist*.

Jones et al. (2016) undertook a meta-analysis of the impact and moderating influences of executive coaching. A total of 17 research studies met their strict criteria for executive coaching at the workplace. They covered many industry sectors across seven countries involving 2,267 coachees, 67% (1,527) of whom were in senior management roles. Jones et al. suggested an executive coaching evaluation framework based on Kirkpatrick's (1967) model for training evaluation, adapted by Kraiger's outcomes approach (Kraiger et al., 1993).

This resulted in four criteria: affective outcomes (e.g. self-awareness and self-efficacy), cognitive outcomes (e.g. problem-solving and new knowledge), skill-based outcomes (e.g. leadership and technical skills), and results related to individual and organisational performance. Their key finding was that coaching did have a positive effect on all outcomes, especially affective and skill-based outcomes beyond new knowledge and enhanced skills, and a significant beneficial impact on individual performance.

Athanasopoulou and Dopson (2018) carried out the most extensive systematic review of executive coaching outcome studies published in peer-reviewed scholarly journals to date. They identified eight coachee outcomes that have been consistently assessed and positively impacted in executive coaching studies along the lines of Jones' framework.

Four criteria fell within intrapersonal skills: overcoming regressive behaviours, embracing life changes, self-regulation, and developing new and improved skills; two within interpersonal skills: leadership and relationships; and two focused on the workplace: building a productive and nurturing work environment and experiencing enhanced workplace wellbeing. These three types of criteria still fall short of a vertical developmental evaluative framework. Leadership skills contained within the category of interpersonal skills are more aligned with the team leadership capabilities of an *Achievist* than with the inspiring, visionary stewardship of an organisational leader at *Synergist*.

Athanasopoulou and Dopson also identified a range of coaching interventions as moderating influences. They included cognitive-behavioural, positive psychology, solution-focused, emotional intelligence, systems-oriented approach, psychodynamics, developmental coaching, coaching in context, transformative coaching, the three principles psychology approach, and process consultation coaching. The diverse blend of coaching interventions speaks to the breadth of expertise in the coaching profession and the inclusion of psychodynamics, suggesting that the coach's therapeutic role may be more prevalent than previously considered.

One of the most in-depth studies in executive coaching was undertaken by Wasylyshyn et al. (2006). They studied the effectiveness of executive coaching with 28 participants over a period of eight years. Coaching meetings followed a typical structure including an update on work issues and challenges, coaching in behavioural interpretations, insights and guidance, a review of previous assignments and setting new assignments, concluding with a recap/wrap-up. In line with experiential learning (Kolb, 1984), the intervening period was regarded as an important time to apply learning, experiment, and discover strategies that work.

'The primary objective [was] to expand the participant's versatility for handling a broad range of business and/or management situations in a more emotionally, interpersonally smart manner' (Wasylyshyn et al., 2006: 70) and thereby groom them for the top 30 leadership roles in the organisation. Each coach undertook significant assessment, feedback, and development planning activities with the participants, including 8–10 stakeholder appraisals by interview, an extensive face-to-face 360 process, 8–10 two-hour monthly coaching meetings followed by a coachee presentation on their learning outcomes after a 12-month period, and a further coach follow-up four months later. From a practitioner's perspective, this program would reach towards the intensive end of the spectrum of executive coaching interventions.

Ninety-five per cent of participants self-reported 'learning sustainability' and 'behavioural change' as either medium or high, and 70% advanced their careers. They measured behaviour change based on the Rohm and Haas leadership competency model which focused on developing self-awareness, interacting effectively with others, organisational stewardship, and developing a broader view of the world including curiosity, complexity, and cultural sensitivity.

The outcomes tabled were more effective leadership, improved interpersonal skills engaging a more diverse group of people, increased employee commitment and productivity, more effective performance management of others, and a positive impact on the company's bottom line by negotiating better in high-stress situations (Wasylyshyn et al., 2006). These behavioural and performance outcomes cross incrementally into *Catalyst*, while organisational stewardship is typically a *Synergist* capability as shown in Figure 14.1.

Figure 14.1 The assessment of coaching effectiveness

Stage	Intrapersonal Skills	Interpersonal Skills	Organisation | Outcomes
Specialist	Professional growth		
Achievist	Individual performance Self-efficacy Time management Goal accomplishment Increased productivity	More effective leadership Conflict-resolution Improved professional relationships Improved resilience Behavioural change Interacting effectively with others More effective performance management Improved negotiation in high stress situations	Satisfaction with managers and colleagues Work satisfaction Organisational commitment and performance Improved workplace wellbeing Career advancement Increased employee commitment Positive impact on company's bottom line
Catalyst	Self-awareness Learning sustainability	Greater managerial flexibility Curiosity, complexity and cultural sensitivity	Balance between personal and professional lives
Synergist			Organisational stewardship

Skills-based and Performance Coaching

Skills-based coaching focuses on improving specific activities such as sales, negotiation, listening, and presentation skills (Grant and Cavanagh, 2004). It has a behavioural-improvement bias and is generally short term in nature and focused on role modelling, rehearsal, and feedback. This is highly relevant to an executive whose primary operating stage is at *Specialist*, as they are then focused on continuous improvement, perfecting their skills and capabilities, and developing their expertise in practice. Skills coaching is more commonly undertaken by junior managers rather than senior executives.

Performance coaching is focused on goal achievement. It is designed to enable an executive to meet the demands of their role, overcome anything that can derail them, and optimise their performance. Performance coaching is highly process-oriented. It is focused on planning and implementing specific tasks to achieve workplace goals. Grant (2006: 153) advises: '[C]oaching is essentially about helping individuals regulate and direct their interpersonal and intrapersonal resources to better attain their goals'. This involves clarifying goals, developing action plans, overcoming obstacles, monitoring performance against desired results, and then adjusting and adapting strategies to improve performance (Grant and Cavanagh, 2004).

Whitmore's (1992) GROW process designed to maximise a person's performance consists of Goal, Reality, Options, and Way forward. It is the quintessential performance coaching acronym. Performance coaching is highly action-oriented, strengths-based, and solutions-focused to resolve how the coachee can best accomplish their goals. The focus is on enhancing the coachee's self-motivation, strategies, and discipline to become increasingly productive and effective.

Performance coaching facilitates achievement, which is clearly highly appropriate to stage development to the *Achievist*. Whereas the *Specialist* focuses on tasks, the *Achievist* looks to results. The *Specialist* casts their eyes downward to accomplish and improve their work, while the *Achievist* casts their eyes outwards to ensure customer needs are met. The *Specialist* is also more of an individual player, whereas the *Achievist* enjoys working within a team environment.

If a *Specialist* needs to deliver against deadlines, meet customer expectations, use resources efficiently, and contribute as part of a team, they will benefit from performance coaching. This gives them the opportunity to consider the larger context of their role and ensure that their efforts are directed towards setting priorities and maximising results. The creativity to suggest new ideas, the agility to consider multiple options, and the emotional awareness to build relationships with colleagues are all developed as part of performance coaching to expand an executive's capacity to become a high-performing *Achievist*.

Based on positive psychology, Kauffman (2006: 220–221) argues that coaches 'shift attention away from pathology and pain and direct it toward a clear-eyed concentration on strength, vision, and dreams … from what causes and drives pain to what energises and pulls people forward … [P]ositive psychology theory and research will provide the scientific legs upon which the field of coaching can firmly stand'. This is clearly an important paradigm within performance coaching where the primary focus is on the achievement of goals in the future. It is an entirely forward-looking process rather than an inward-looking process that is highly appropriate to the shift from *Specialist* to *Achievist*. While a *Specialist* can tend towards negativity and adopt a fixed mindset (Dweck, 2008), an *Achievist* embraces the positive paradigm of a growth mindset.

One of the essential elements of positive psychology is to focus and build on the coachee's strengths in service of the greater good, a worthwhile purpose, rather than correct for weaknesses (Seligman, 2007). The strengths-based approach of positive psychology (Fredrickson, 2010; Seligman, 2011), a solutions-based focus (Stober and Grant, 2006) intended to reframe, resolve, and overcome problems rather than simply analyse them, and the emotional intelligence to become more self-aware and self-regulate (Goleman, 1995) all make a contribution to enhance effective performance. By focusing on creating a better future rather than salvaging the past, the coach stimulates access to a person's intellectual and psychological resources (Kauffman, 2006). Positive psychology also makes a substantial contribution to intentionally fostering wellbeing and building good relationships with others by drawing on the latest research findings in neuroscience (Doidge, 2010) and emotional intelligence (Goleman, 1995). It has been shown to have many health benefits, a positive impact on interpersonal relationships, and to be a powerful route to a purposeful and happy life (Seligman, 2011).

Developmental Coaching

As the inner game of coaching (Gallwey, 1999) gained in influence, developmental coaching emerged. Developmental coaching invites greater personal engagement on the self of the coachee, at the level of their identity. The focus shifts from the process-oriented approach to maximise outer performance in the short to medium term, to the more intimate person-centric humanistic orientation of self-actualisation (Maslow, 1962). The purpose of developmental coaching is to help an executive realise their inner latent potential in order to make a greater contribution in the organisation over the longer term. Developmental coaching is highly relevant to building the authentic leadership capacity of high potential, high-performing executives shifting into the following collective stage of *Catalyst*.

This type of executive coaching turns to the coachee's personal purpose, values, aspirations, thoughts, and feelings so they become more productive and effective in alignment with their core identity (Grant, 2003), and therefore experience a greater sense of professional satisfaction and personal wellbeing (Grant and Cavanagh, 2004). The coaching conversation embraces concerns and challenges beyond performance in the role itself such as work/life balance, career progression, values alignment, and political dynamics. It takes a broader, more holistic view, often dealing with more intimate, personal, and professional questions. This can involve the creation of a personal reflective space.

Bachkirova (2011: 4) defined this type of development as 'a combination of changes in the organism manifested in a sustained increased capacity to engage with and influence the environment and to look after internal needs and aspirations'. A 'sustained increased *capacity*' is in contrast to the development of *capabilities*. The phrase denotes an inner generative source rather than simply outwardly observable behavioural change. Cox et al. (2014: 214–215) also endorsed the importance of building inner capacity in contrast to outer capabilities. They suggested that 'inherent in developmental coaching is an assumption of movement from where the client is now to where he or she wants to be … helping clients to expand their outlook and attitude as individuals as they work through their life experiences'.

This increasingly vulnerable and intimate personal conversation is well supported by the humanistic foundations of Rogerian (Rogers, 1961) person-centric counselling. It is marked by the warmth and unconditional positive regard by the coach for the coachee and an assumption of the coachee's inner resourcefulness to discover their own solutions. The coachee is perceived as both the source and director of change on the basis of their inherent growth potential (Stober and Grant, 2006). This humanistic orientation is at its zenith in developmental coaching. While executive coaching is differentiated from the other forms of coaching (e.g. life coaching) due to its workplace context, these boundaries become more permeable in developmental coaching. Coaching on life's challenges and concerns through open inquiry is often integrated into executive coaching programs because of their client-centricity.

The coaching relationship becomes more egalitarian in developmental coaching as the sense of the coachee's journey becomes more important than the destination (i.e. desired goals). There are no right answers as the coachee explores their own identity and psyche following the famed invocation by the erudite philosopher Socrates to 'Know thyself', inscribed at the forecourt of the Temple of Apollo at Delphi. Peltier (2001: 2) embraced the psychology of coaching in his definition of executive coaching: 'Someone from outside an organisation uses psychological skills to help a person develop into a more effective leader. These skills are applied to specific present moment work problems in a way that enables this person to incorporate them into his or her permanent management or leadership repertoire'. There is a clear shift from the performance coaching focus on doing and achieving, to the developmental coaching focus on learning and becoming.

The nature of developmental coaching has led to a significant wave of attention to questioning techniques where open questions rather than leading questions have become increasingly regarded as best practice (Katie and Mitchell, 2002). Leading questions invite reflexive inquiry along a specific pathway, whereas open questions follow the thread of the coachee's own exploration (Askeland, 2009). 'Inquiry is more than a technique: It brings to life, from deep within us, an innate aspect of our being. When practiced for a while, inquiry takes on its own life within you. It appears whenever thoughts appear, as their balance and mate' (Katie and Mitchell, 2002: 8).

Thus, coaching is often referred to as the art of asking powerful questions to enable the coachee to generate new ideas and suggestions, invite reflection, raise awareness, and inspire commitment to new actions and attitudes (Askeland, 2009; Ives, 2008). It has also expanded the realm of coaching techniques including space for reflection, awareness and context orientated approaches such as ontological, psychodynamics, narrative and systems coaching.

'Developmental coaching refers to coaching aimed at enhancing the individual's ability to meet current and future challenges more effectively via the development of increasingly complex understanding of the self, others and the systems in which the person is involved' (Grant et al., 2010: 126). This reference to more complex meaning-making is ignited at *Catalyst*. 'What is topical in developmental coaching is not the organisation per se but, rather, the way executive and coach make sense of, or construe, the organisation and their relationship to the organisation' (Laske, 1999: 142). Making sense of the organisation and their relationship to it, and its members, also reflects the *Catalyst's* curiosity in engaging others across the organisation and building reciprocal peer-based relationships.

Developmental coaching invites more subtle meaning-making agility at *Catalyst*. The executive embarks on an inner journey of exploration to realise their own intrinsic unique potential. A person operating primarily at this stage honours authenticity, diversity, and reciprocity in relationships. They begin to perceive gaps between the espousal and demonstration of those values (Torbert et al., 2004). Mutual respect, appropriate boundaries, and personal standards of behaviour come into view and under consideration to cultivate discipline amongst colleagues and stakeholders. It also embraces Csikszentmihalyi's (1990) elucidation of the high-performance state of 'flow' that emerges from the sense of being vitally engaged in a meaningful, purposeful life.

Transformative Coaching

A number of theorists extend executive coaching to include transformational coaching (Cox et al., 2014; Hawkins and Smith, 2013). It is concerned with enabling the coachee to shift levels and transition to a new and higher level of functioning. 'Transformational coaching enables coachees to create fundamental shifts in their capacity to change their habitual ways of doing things in their work and their lives. This is achieved through transforming their ways of thinking, feeling and behaving in relation to specific situations they find problematic. It is our contention that this transformation is delivered through focusing on the shift that needs to happen live in the coaching space so that a sustained change takes place beyond the coaching session' (Cox et al., 2014: 227).

Bachkirova (2014) also argued that transformational coaching is deliberately intended to ignite and sustain an upward shift in leadership capacity in relation to a specific leadership development framework (Joiner and Josephs, 2007; Laske, 1999). These developmental frameworks are often underpinned by the stages of leadership development in developmental psychology (Cook-Greuter, 1999; Loevinger, 1966; O'Fallon, 2011). Hawkins and Smith (2013) regard this type of coaching as an urgent and important calling for coaches to enable leaders to overcome the challenge of rapid change in the world today. Cavanagh (2004) concurred. He invited coaches to better support and accelerate the opportunity for people to take a bigger and more systemic perspective on themselves and the world.

Given that the progressive shifts from skills, performance, and developmental coaching correlated with the shifts in stage development from *Specialist* to *Achievist* and *Catalyst*, this fourth type of executive coaching is by extension associated with the next stage known as *Synergist*. Kegan (1982) termed this level the Self-Transforming Mind; Torbert, an equally prominent theorist in developmental psychology, also now describes this action-logic, his term for stage, as Transforming (Torbert et al., 2004). Cook-Greuter (2000) describes the *Synergist's* new way of seeing as perceiving a more holistic view of reality, an interconnected systemic whole rather than an aggregate of separate, well-defined parts or elements.

Furthermore, the eminent sociologist Mezirow's concept of 'transformative learning' also denotes a quantum shift in awareness. 'Transformative learning is metacognitive reasoning … [that] emphasises insight into the source, structure, and history of a frame of reference, as well as judging its relevance, appropriateness, and consequences' (Mezirow, 2003: 61). It reflects a deeper and broader systemic perception of the underlying structure giving rise to the dynamics and therefore the capacity to transform that structure. On a personal level, this can involve a deep and fundamental revision to beliefs, principles, habits of mind, and feelings, creating a shift in perception that expands our self-awareness and sense of possibilities. This ignites paradigmatic transformation (Mezirow, 2003).

In transformative coaching there is thus a sense of reinvention. With reinvention comes both a new identity and the surrender of a previous identity, just as a butterfly emerges from a cocoon. Wahl et al. (2013: 23–24) explain: 'Letting go is often a fertile area for coaches and is one of the most profound ideas to come from Eastern thinking … Few things are more frightening than truly "reinventing" oneself as reinvention requires a letting go of "who you were" to become "who you wish to be". The ability to consciously choose who to be is the pinnacle of living a masterful and purposeful life – precisely because the risk of letting go seems so high'. Transformative coaching therefore helps the coachee to release pain and suffering from the past as well as generate a new paradigm of a flourishing sustainable future.

While 'transformational' indicates a major substantial change, 'transformative' means having the power to continually transform. The definition of transformative is where something, such as an event or experience, inspires or causes a shift in viewpoint. Given that 'transformational' is also often thought of in connection with leadership (i.e. 'transformational leadership', reflecting an *Achievist's* leadership capacity), I prefer to use the term 'transformative coaching' rather than 'transformational coaching' to indicate the fourth type of coaching that leads to the coachee having the power to transform themselves – at the level of the transforming mind of the self at *Synergist*.

While transformational coaching could refer to a transformation from one stage to the next at all stages, transformative coaching infers the development of the capacity of the self-transforming mind at *Synergist*, also described as the transforming action-logic by Torbert. Transformative coaching operates most effectively in the liminal space of a coachee's growth edge, the edge of their meaning-making ability (Berger, 2004), the space between knowing and not knowing yet seeking to understand whatever is arising in a more expansive integrated way.

New interpretations from a later stage of development generate new choices, new approaches, new attitudes, and new intentions, and the birth of a new self or identity. This can set up a high degree of uncertainty and ambiguity, of inner conflict and lack of direction, of bewilderment and confusion, a sense of being on a journey without a prescribed destination. Navigating this journey requires hope and optimism, confidence, and inspiration as a coachee finds it puzzling to make sense of their lives.

Berger (2004) recommends that the transformative coach play an important role helping the coachee to find their edge, stand with them on the precipice as they look out into the future, and help them build firm new ground to stand on. This sense of having an experienced travelling companion supports the coachee to take the leap into the discovery of their inner self despite the discomfort of not knowing, to embrace the emergence of new possibilities as they learn to understand the nature of trust in contrast to a previous reliance on certainty and control.

Other emergent coaching concepts allude to the type of coaching rather than its transformative agenda of coaching. For instance, Stelter's (2014) third-generation coaching approach is distinctively collaborative, and Myers and Bachkirova's (2018) dialogic coaching mode within their empirical process-based model of executive coaching concerns a true partnership between coach and coachee that embraces deep reflection and the co-creative emergence of new insights and revelations. This mutual involvement of coach and coachee on the coachee's concerns, challenges, experiences, and journey, is in direct contrast to the preceding type of coaching, developmental coaching, which is an exclusive person-centric inquiry into the coachee's insights and revelations.

Bachkirova and Borrington (2018) recommend applying adult development theory to the selection of the coach by the coachee. They argue that the self and stage of the coach makes the most fundamental difference when coaching *Synergists* and beyond, notwithstanding their coaching approach. Indeed, they, and others such as Berger (2012) and Wycherley and Cox (2008), recommend that the coach be at a later stage than the coachee in any coaching situation if the coachee is to develop beyond their current mindset or worldview.

Transformative coaching sets the scene for greater emergence as articulated in third-generation coaching. The coach and coachee become dialogic partners. 'They take part in the shared production of meaning and knowledge and in the collaborative, reflective process of development, learning and transformation, and this is fundamental for third generation coaching. The coach is seen as a "generous listener" who attempts to expand on the coachee's dialogic contributions' (Stelter, 2014: 57–58).

The later stage executive coach holds the space for a deep dialogue, seeking meaning not just answers. They hold the space to cultivate awareness of the patterns between the interconnections of beliefs, intention, and expression that may have consciously or subconsciously led to the creation of experiences since being shaped into events and to revise those beliefs, intentions, and expressions in greater alignment with universal values and higher principles. From my experience, I suggest the later stage executive coach adopting transformative coaching needs to have their centre of gravity at a mature Synergist. Unless they have largely integrated the 4th person perspective it would be challenging to guide another on the journey.

This type of collaborative meaning-making ensures quality and progress in conversations, relationships, or situations. The role of the coach changes from being neutral and not knowing, and consciously avoiding providing advice or input, to being a fellow human being where there is a genuine dialogue between coach and coachee. All in all, there is a synergy in transformative coaching for all stakeholders in the conversation, with a primary focus on the individual coachee sharing their story followed by a collaborative narrative to look behind, beneath, and beyond the life event shared for the benefit of mutual meaning-making and leadership development of the coachee.

Stage Outcomes of Coaching Effectiveness

In conclusion, the focus and style of each type of executive coaching in the extended typology – skills, performance, developmental, and transformative coaching – are directly correlated with the capabilities that emerge at the progressive stages of leadership development: the *Specialist, Achievist, Catalyst,* and *Synergist.*

For each type of coaching, key elements shift. The coaching paradigm shifts from rehearsal and practice in skills coaching, to the process and the application of positive psychology in performance coaching, to person-centric humanistic inquiry in developmental coaching, and onto holistic emergence and systemic synergy in transformative coaching. The primary success factor also transforms along the coaching typology from learning, to clearly agreed goals, to the integrity of the coaching relationship, and onto mutual meaning-making of existential questions.

The transformation also seems to be holarchic in scope. For instance, the integrity of the coaching relationship is still present, but the focus on mutual meaning-making transforms the relationship from asymmetrical to becoming increasingly symmetrical. Similarly, the leadership outcomes expand in holarchic fashion along the stages of development from *Specialist*, to *Achievist*, to *Catalyst* and *Synergist*. These stages reflect the progression of popular leadership models from the transformational leader at *Achievist*, the authentic leader at *Catalyst*, and the quantum leader at *Synergist*. Figure 14.2 provides a summary of coaching dimensions relative to the coaching typology and associated coaching outcomes in relation to the stages of development.

Figure 14.2 Coaching outcomes in terms of stage transformations

COACHING TYPOLOGY	SKILLS-BASED COACHING	PERFORMANCE COACHING	DEVELOPMENTAL COACHING	TRANSFORMATIVE COACHING
Coach as...	INSTRUCTOR	MOTIVATOR	FACILITATOR	COLLABORATOR
Coaching Paradigm	Informed, Practice makes Perfect!	Positive Psychology Process Centric	Humanistic Inquiry Person Centric	Holistic Emergence Systemic Synergy
Primary Success Factor	Ability to Teach & Learn	Clarity of Agreed Goals	The Coaching Relationship	Mutual Meaning-Making
Coaching Relationship	Transactional Transfer	Mutual Accountability	Professional Trust	Dialogic Partnership
Coaching Models & Techniques	Rehearsal & Feedback	Cognitive Behavioural	Narrative Story Complex Systems	Psychodynamics Collective Identity
Typical Duration of Session/Program	30–60 Minutes 3–12 Weeks	30–60 Minutes 3–6 Months	60–90 Minutes 6–12 Months	90–120 Minutes 12–24 Months
Leadership Outcomes	Thought Leadership Best Practice	Transformational Agile Leadership	Authentic Adaptive Leadership	Quantum Visionary Leadership
Stage Outcome	SPECIALIST	ACHIEVIST	CATALYST	SYNERGIST

Objective measurement, such as stage leadership assessment, would enable executive coaching to optimise the objective outcomes of executive coaching. More reliable and relevant conclusions could be drawn from outcome-based research studies into coaching effectiveness in the future, relative to the type of executive coaching employed.

From the above discussion it seems clear that performance coaching is only effective for an executive moving towards becoming a high-performing *Achievist*. Performance coaching cannot facilitate the journey to *Catalyst*. This requires developmental coaching. To shift to *Catalyst*, it's important to facilitate the coachee undertaking an inquiry into their inner world of thoughts, beliefs, values, feelings, motives, and concerns.

Furthermore, developmental coaching cannot offer sufficient guidance to enable the shift to the uncommonly held stage of *Synergist*. Given the need to integrate shadow and transcend and transform the collective while setting aspirational intent, transformative coaching with a later stage executive coach is essential.

Navigating these issues is much more effective by collaborating with and drawing on the inner resources and insights of an executive coach who has already traversed the journey. While each journey is unique, the signals, pitfalls, obstacles, and landmines can be similar. Transformative coaching is therefore recommended with a coach at *Synergist* or later.

Multifaceted Role of the Transformative Coach

A review of Kolb's learning cycle illuminates the intervention that takes place in transformative coaching (Figure 14.3). It describes learning as a process of perceiving and processing data drawn from reflective observation, *watching*; abstract conceptualisation, *thinking*; active experimentation, *doing*; and concrete experience, *feeling*. He presents the contrast between accommodation and assimilation as did Piaget and Kegan. When we accommodate new data in a more complex way of making meaning from it, we learn vertically. When we assimilate new data in our current way of making sense of the world, we learn horizontally.

In developmental coaching, the coachee is dependent on their own way of making meaning. An open question may lead them to new ways of interpreting the situation, but this would depend on the stage of the coach too. If the coach is able to offer open questions that create a quest for a different dynamic inter-systemic interpretation, this can conceivably lead to vertical development. To shift to *Synergist* requires a coach already at this stage to hold the space for the deeper inquiry. The person-centricity of developmental coaching frowns upon asking leading questions or the coach participating actively in sharing new insights.

In transformative coaching, both coach and coachee collaborate on meaning-making. The coach intervenes at the stage of abstract conceptualisation, *thinking*, to explore alternative more empowering explanations. If the coach is at a later integrated stage, they are in a privileged situation to offer leading questions as well as insightful revelations that, when considered and explored by

Figure 14.3 Transformative coaching in Kolb's learning cycle

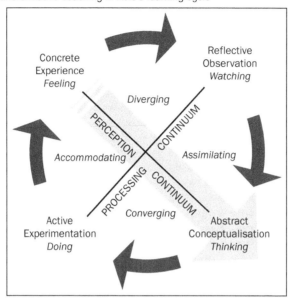

the coachee, leads to their own experimentation in the workplace. This would have the effect of inducing and expanding vertical learning.

This type of partnering by a coach that creates the space for co-creative intuitive emergent collaboration, is a capability that manifests at the stage of *Synergist*. At this stage, a person has integrated and consolidated an entirely new identity that is self-validating. Their peace of mind enables a profound transformative level of listening. 'A coach must have highly developed listening skills – listening for meaning, for the story, for the commitment in the story, for the values in the story, for the emotion, for the somatic messages, and, of course, for what is not being said. Such a tall order can only be achieved from a state of "being" that is evolved and quiet. The less noise inside the coach, the better the listening' (Stroul and Wahl, 2013: 7). This quiet, calm 'state of being' emerges at *Synergist*.

The embrace of shadow and focus on collective expansiveness in an organisational sense expands the role of coaching into a multifaceted role as shown in Figure 14.4. The role of a transformative coach includes that of a:

- Coach, as part of a mutual partnering relationship;
- Companion, in the journey of our shared humanity;
- Counsellor, understanding psychology, e.g. transference, shadow;
- Consultant, bringing in subject matter expertise;
- Guide, offering insights and guidance from a later stage perspective; and
- Mentor, sharing the benefit of your corporate experience as appropriate.

Figure 14.4 Multifaceted role of a transformative coach

The higher order of transformative coaching suggests that transference, projections, and introjections are also more commonplace. Therefore, I highly recommend that the coaching profession also moves towards mandatory supervision. Later stage coaches who have the capacity to generate and sustain a more expansive container that embraces increasing diversity, subtlety, complexity, shadow, and light are ideal coaching supervisors.

Chapter 14: Key Points

1   Executive coaching has been positively correlated to a range of coaching outcomes in terms of capabilities and capacities such as confidence and resilience.
2   The standard coaching typology is composed of skills-based coaching, performance coaching, and developmental coaching. It has recently been extended to transformational coaching and third-generation coaching, referred to as transformative coaching here.
3   Skills-based coaching is strongly related to the lateral development of *Specialist* expertise and skills to demonstrate new capabilities such as presentation and negotiation skills.
4   Performance coaching is strongly related to vertical development as an *Achievist* typified by the GROW coaching process, with the need for clear agreed goals, a feedback mechanism for accountability, and the application of positive psychology.

5   Developmental coaching is strongly related to vertical development to *Catalyst* with a focus on a person's inner world, growing authenticity, and elements beyond performance to the person such as work/life balance, and the dynamics of relationships.

6   The primary success factors of developmental coaching are the nature of the coaching relationship: its person-centric, humanistic inquiry with clean, open questions into story and narrative so that the coachee can draw on their own inner resources to find new avenues and solutions to their challenges and opportunities.

7   Transformative coaching is strongly related to vertical development to *Synergist* through the course of a more symmetrical dialogical partnership between coach and coachee still focused on the coachee but with shared insight and revelations. The later stage perspective of the coach is employed to hold a more expansive emergent space to allow new meaning to emerge and transform self, life, relationships, and systems.

8   The role of a transformative coach is multifaceted, including coach, consultant, counsellor, companion, mentor, and guide to partner the coachee in the full realisation of their potential as a transformative inspiring, visionary leader at *Synergist*.

Next Chapter

The final chapter reaches a few important conclusions on the leadership effectiveness of the *Synergist*, the outcomes of the StageSHIFT coaching program, and the value that vertical stage development can contribute to the efficacy and effectiveness of executive coaching and advanced leadership programs.

15 TRANSFORMATIVE STAGESHIFT™ EXECUTIVE COACHING

It is eminently possible if not entirely probable for transformative StageSHIFT executive coaching to enable high-performing *Achievists* to become reforming *Catalysts* within a year and transforming *Synergists* within one to three years. Over the four-year time period the research took place, the Average Aggregate Post-conventional Profile (*Catalyst+*) of the 12 participants shifted from 12% to 46% and, for three, onto 88%, in the years 0, 1, and 4.

By setting aspirational intent, incorporating a strategic focus on the collective, and adopting a holistic approach to personal development, transformative coaching with a later stage executive coach is highly effective and extraordinarily efficient. The potential to transform into expansive synergistic leaders is latent, inhibited by obsolete organisational structures and norms, just lying in wait to be released.

The Presence and Capacity of the *Synergist*

The *Synergist* can be distinguished on three main counts: their flourishing global perspective that enables them to see through wicked problems, an inner integrated identity that blesses the person with peace of mind and harmony of heart, and the transformative leadership capacity to lead and sustain a synergistic, orchestrated movement of people to generate health, wellbeing, goodwill, and abundance for all (Figure 15.1).

A FLOURISHING GLOBAL PERSPECTIVE

- Inter-systemic perspective – causation is circular, relational, and systemic
- Complex adaptive system is in constant flux – change in one element has a ripple effect on the whole
- Organisational and industry context, digital disruption
- Capitalise on interconnections across divisions, regions, cultures, and nations

- Transcend sophisticated, ambiguous, and complex challenges during uncertain, volatile times in sustainable, synergistic ways
- Late fourth person perspective sees multiple generations of families, organisations, and cultures over time
- Can take perspective on contradictions, paradoxes, polarities, and paradigms to forge unifying pathways

AN INNER INTEGRATED IDENTITY

- Interpenetrative self and life – projections, transference, and psychodynamics
- Reconciliation of combative forces and conflicting voices of disparate identities is resolved and healed within
- Understand and appreciate conflict; uplift and advocate
- Intention and attention on wide aspirational congruence, universal principles, and ethical standards that serve mutually beneficial long-term sustainable outcomes
- Common humanity – breadth and depth of fears, goals, needs and desires, shame and guilt, dreams and hopes
- Discerning and self-validating in the moment
- Tuned into and trust in their personal cosmic GPS through intuition and embodied guidance

Figure 15.1 The distinctive leadership capacity of a *Synergist*

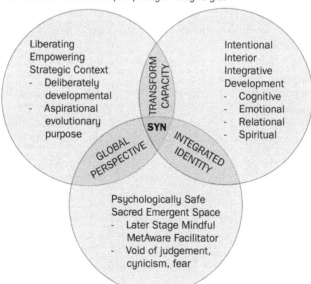

TRANSFORMATIVE LEADERSHIP CAPACITY

- Self is not authoring; self is transforming in the immediate context; self is instrumental to cosmic evolution
- While implicit frames limit one's choices, explicit frames offer choice – can zoom in and out adroitly
- Principles, integrity, and courage to lead transformation – makes long-term synergistic decisions serving social, economic, and environmental sustainability
- Personal authentic power combined with positional authority and community responsibility
- Invests in transformative development for all – trusts in distributed leadership and organic emergence
- Inter-independence operating freely yet synergistically and compassionately with *all* others

Coachee Career Outcomes and Reflections

Many of the coachees realised astonishing outcomes beyond highly effective performance outcomes. One won the National Industry Award for their contribution to the sector. Another received an industry award for the most outstanding infrastructure project of the year. A third was assessed as the most effective futuristic speaker in their industry. A fourth received a State Honours Award for their contribution to the public sector. Many were promoted and one realised three promotions to more strategic roles in increasingly larger organisations over a period of five years. They all thrived and flourished despite continuous restructuring.

Here are their reflections on their perception of the outcomes of the coaching:

The coach guided me in a strategic sense and gave good advice yet didn't tell me how to do my job. I involved everyone, listened to everybody and people felt that they were important and their contribution was valued. I tried to do the things a Synergist would do and be seen to do. My coach has been a blessing in my life.

Seeing the person in terms of strengths … When people feel seen, they respond. Wasn't doing this 6–12 months ago.

I seem to have a new presence, mana, spiritual heart energy that radiates; I'm more balanced, understanding, empathetic of others; more credible, trustworthy, believable, visionary; I'm more articulate, I explain what it is they are creating; I've become more compassionate, I look into the soul and understand others better.

Less pushing, more patience; less striving, more appreciation; less holding onto things, more letting go to trust in others.

I feel healthier, it's made me a wiser person, and I'm doing more exciting work. I seem to have more credibility than I used to.

Now surfing the chaos ... Starting to get it, a very different person from what I used to be ... Confident, relaxed, calm, and self-assured ... Giving up control, giving up striving, surrender is a key thing to progress. There are no limits to what a man can do as long as he doesn't mind not getting the credit, rejoicing in someone else getting the credit ... Much more effective ... Restructure and empowering others means that you have done this for yourself, new architecture internally, and empowered them so they can do this for others ... No fear ... Life is completely taken care of ... New way of being.

I'm valuing my life in terms of soul evolution ... I'm becoming a more holistic version of myself.

I can't believe I got simple answers to vexing questions that I hadn't previously considered. Random thoughts ... Selling one of our properties is scary because we haven't done it before. That was on 25 June. A day later on 26 June I developed a 15-point plan to sell all of my properties while sitting on the train.

It's quite pleasant and gratifying to see barriers fall away around me – people who were previously antagonistic or insular to IT are now happy to collaborate – things just falling into place. It feels that I'm hardly doing anything, yet I'm watching good and right triumph over bad. In particular, I'm finding the less there is of me and the more there is of God, the more powerful the outcomes. I guess you would say that I'm in increasing harmony with the universe. How strange that much of executive training is all about increasing and doing more, but I'm finding humility and doing less – servant leadership – brings about the most powerful outcomes.

I still feel energised and still believe in the possibility of positive change. I have a sense of faith in the future and have a different conception of how I want life and work to be. If it hadn't been for the coaching, I don't think I'd have the same understanding of future possibilities.

The Transformative StageSHIFT™ Coaching Model

Transformative coaching with a later stage coach who had already navigated *Synergist* territory was, in my view, an essential dimension of the coaching program.

To liberate later stage post-conventional development, the research outcomes suggest that a more balanced egalitarian symmetrical approach to the roles of the coachee and later stage coach is highly effective. This enables the mutual emergent collaborative process to generate paradigmatic insights and revelations, especially from the uplifting space held by the later stage coach for the coachee and from their later stage broader perspective. The coaching incorporates aspects of consulting and counselling, mentoring and guidance, extending the repertoire of the coach to the organisational, psycho-dynamic, and spiritual fields of evolution.

In distilling the transformative coaching that took place in the research study and led to the transformative outcomes to *Catalyst* and *Synergist*, it seems that there were four key elements (Figure 15.2). First, it was intention-ally transformative or deliberately vertical to these later stages. Three key interweaving elements that manifested this intention were its aspirational intent, shadow resolution, and collective stewardship.

Secondly, it was coachee-focused. All coaching conversations took place in response to the coachee's inquiry, challenges, or opportunities that lay ahead to expedite their commitment to vertical leadership growth. In addition to compas-sionate regard, the coach was often described as 'uplifting', and praised by the coachees for her 'relentless positivity and radical reframing'. These terms indi-cate the value of the later stage perspective during a coaching conversation.

Thirdly, the emergence of the coaching conversation was presence-led. The late stage of the coach offered an expansive presence and the open and leading questions of the coach offered perplexity, inquiry, and wonder. The mutual reflec-tive inquiry invited generative listening and shared meaning-making to explore the facts and implications, and excavate the underlying psychodynamics to arrive at the source of situations. The uplifting cumulative momentum engendered by the egalitarian coaching partnership generated a rich emergent co-creative spacetime that led to the development of *Synergist* leadership capacity.

Figure 15.2 The StageSHIFT Transformative Coaching Model

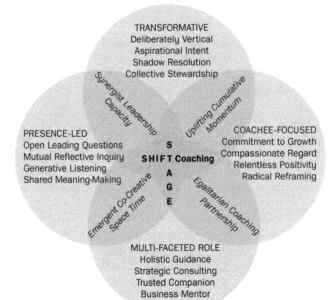

The executive coaching program involved an average of eight 90-minute monthly coaching sessions over the course of 12 months. This appeared to be sufficient to enable the transformative shift from *Achievist* to *Catalyst* and, for two plus a third starting out at *Catalyst*, onto *Synergist*. A further year or so of less intensive executive coaching appears to enable participants to continue their leadership journeys and consolidate at *Synergist*.

Distinctive Features of StageSHIFT Coaching

In addition to the nature of transformative coaching, two particular aspects within the strategic holistic coaching content are especially noteworthy.

From a strategic coaching perspective, it is essential to re-engineer the collective context so that it is empowering and liberating not only for the coachee, but for all the people they lead. Otherwise they are stuck in an amber or orange organisational context that inhibits their leadership development. They are trapped by the operational minutiae that their people can easily and effectively manage provided they are empowered and trusted to do so.

This is evident from O'Fallon's structure of development through the Tiers. Even when a person has realised the authentic leadership capacity of a *Catalyst*, this capacity has not yet manifested in the outer world. It is apparent within their inner world and is demonstrated when their outer world conflicts with this new sense of self.

However, this capacity is not yet transformative as the Outer Zone of the Conformist still prevails. This is illustrated in Figure 15.3. The new Subtle Collective is built by and through the perspective and presence of a *Synergist*. Undertaking this work as a coachee with the coaching, consulting and mentoring guidance of a *Synergist* executive coach, is highly liberating and transformative.

Figure 15.3 Transformations in the Subtle Tier

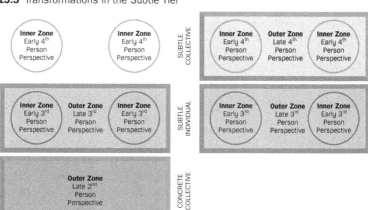

The third distinguishing feature, in addition to transformative coaching and strategic collective organisational development, is the holistic development of the coachee in a deeply personal way. It was highly effective to integrate the power of the heart, mind, and spirit to facilitate the healing and mindful endeavours that sprung from aspirational intent.

The dual focus on the window of evolution and shadow resolution beyond emotional regulation was significant. The current preoccupation with mindfulness has the potential to omit the transformative healing power of the heart that has been proven to lead to the emergence of a calm, clear, open mind. In other words, we are not looking to the right source to realise the profound shift to a continuing state of mindful awareness.

While mindfulness can be construed as a process, it is also an outcome. It is the natural outcome of heart-based forgiveness and healing, emotional embodiment and compassion. The heart enables the shadows from the past to be healed so that disparate identities within the self can be integrated for the self to become more whole. Only then can we step through the window of evolution unfettered.

If we omit this work on and in self, we remain stalled on the *Achievist's* Figure-8 Operating System. Our heart may not be sufficiently open to take us into the later maturity of this spectrum of development. We become stalled by focusing on short-term performance, remaining constantly busy so there is no time to think about anything more momentous while moving perilously ever closer to burn-out.

To embark on the Hero's Journey into post-conventional waters and understand life from an inner rather than an outer perspective is a massive paradigm shift. This was activated by taking the heart-mind-spirit holistic approach to self, with a view to understanding and embracing the ego while learning from each and every life experience as having something new to teach us. It's a question of meaning-making from a *Synergist's* or later perspective to advance our awareness of self and understanding of life as interconnected.

Without shadow resolution with an open heart, it is impossible to transform to later stages of development as we will constantly be brought back to past reactive patterns indicative of painful experiences in early childhood. While these past experiences are suppressed within us, no matter how effective we are at regulating our outer response, they will continue to transpire based on the interpenetration of self and life.

Emotional intelligence is highly instructive but insufficient. Spiritual intelligence and a quantum perspective is what is needed. While this is not clear at earlier stages of development, it becomes crystal clear as we experiment with cultivating our best self and then marvel at the serendipity and witness the synchronicity that life is able to offer us.

The key is to see the shift from *Achievist* to *Synergist* as a Spectrum Stage Shift rather than take a stepping-stone approach from *Achievist* to *Catalyst*, or in other words, from the Transformational Leader to the Authentic Leader (Figure 15.4). While this is valuable, it is not sufficient to bring about transformation

Figure 15.4 The Spectrum Stage Shift from *Achievist* to *Synergist*

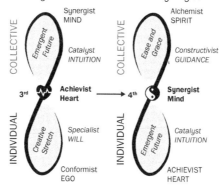

The Spectrum Stage Shift from Achievist to Synergist

in the world and indeed, leaves the person in transition, and often in discomfort, between two stages of integration. Their only natural fall-back within a conventional collective when under stress or feeling disorientated is to return to their *Achievist* perspective and focus on self rather than other.

The requirement within StageSHIFT coaching to re-engineer the collective is not part of the repertoire of developmental coaching. Neither is shadow resolution nor the radical personal accountability for life experiences commonly found within the developmental coaching paradigm. While developmental coaching is highly effective to develop authenticity, navigate political dramas, and gain a balance between work and life, professional and personal matters, it does not often go to the heart of our life experience as an integrated whole reflective of self.

The content and pathway of the transformative executive coaching program suggests that an initial focus on transforming the collective structure followed by an in-depth approach to uplifting a person's individual identity and associated self-expression is a proven pathway in later stage development to *Synergist*. The coaching outcomes suggest that the separation of these two elements commonly thought of as organisation development and leadership development are strongly intertwined and, if simultaneously present, would appear to expedite transformative vertical development.

To focus on one at the exclusion of the other occludes the opportunity and capacity to transcend the organisation's conventional operating system. Indeed, by not taking the opportunity to transcend and transform the conventional collective, leadership program participants remain entrenched in their workplace culture. This also suggests that embedding transformative executive coaching following offsite intensive leadership programs could add considerably to their efficacy in advancing their effectiveness in terms of vertical development.

VERTICAL DEVELOPMENT THEORY

Theory-building was an emergent process. It seemed that the years of reading, analysis, reflection, detachment, writing, engagement, presentation and perpetual renewal with the material were never-ending. And yet, finally a deadline loomed and a theoretical model dawned.

Consider the concept of vertical development as the evolution of a complex adaptive system that is continuously renewing itself, integrating shadow elements while embracing new aspects of one's holistic and indeed universal identity. All the while, each person's multiple selves are intertwined with each other, and interconnected with their external world of inter-systemic exchange and fusion. The exercise of conscious systemic leadership is therefore a fathomless process of oneself shaping one's world while the world shapes oneself.

Three prevailing key strategic principles emerged:

1 INTENTION: Setting purposeful evolutionary aspirational intent for self, organisation and community;
2 INTERACTION: Proactively orchestrating engagement as an essential important priority with immediate, internal and external stakeholders; and
3 INTEGRATION: Engaging with others in a space that set respectful standards based on open liberating agendas to enable disparate selves within and diverse selves across audiences to listen and learn, converse and collaborate, heal and transform.

The concerted attention given to courageously collaborate on aspirational endeavours and purposeful initiatives, was held by a sacred space of mutual inquiry, trust and transcendent meaning making led by the perspective and presence of a later stage executive coach at Synergist+. They combined to expedite and extend vertical transformation, as shown in Figure 15.5.

The Opportunity of StageSHIFT Transformative Coaching

Given that *Synergists* have been increasing as a proportion of the executive population by just 1% a decade in each of the last two decades, most leadership and coaching programs clearly fall short of the ability to facilitate the evolution to *Synergist*.

Yet if half of the executive leaders currently at *Achievist* shifted to *Catalyst*, and half of the executive leaders shifted from *Catalyst* to *Synergist*, 50% of executive leaders would be operating from the post-conventional perspective with the growing capacity to reinvent their organisations and influence

Figure 15.5 The StageSHIFT propellers of transformation

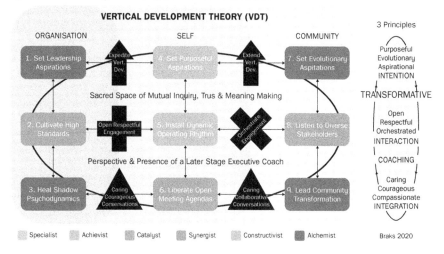

mutually beneficial social, economic, and ecological outcomes where everyone is better able to thrive and flourish in the world today.

It would be immensely valuable if more executives, coaches, and designers of leadership development interventions were aware of vertical stage leadership development and the comprehensive and interconnected nature of the drivers/propellers that have the power to generate the later stage transforming leadership capacity, presence, and effectiveness of a *Synergist*.

An overriding implication of this research study is that the vast differences in perception and understanding evident at the progressive stages of development suggest that the integration of vertical stage devleopment with executive coaching and leadership programs is a critical component to increasing the effectiveness and efficiency of developmental interventions. Without this important focus on the capacity to expedite and liberate more complex meaning-making, leadership programs are doomed to facilitate largely lateral learning with an obstinate cetnre of gravity stalled at Achievist. Given the complex and serious global concerns we face today, this would not serve society.

It is critical and urgent to foster the collaborative, innovative, and synergistic inspiring visionary leadership capacity at *Synergist* if we are to co-create a more sustainable, egalitarian world in each of the social, economic, and ecological domains of life. I invite coaches to liberate their own transformation and to share their wisdom with the individuals and collectives they serve. I invite senior executive leaders, leadership program designers, and procurers of development programs to draw upon this research.

I have experimented with and gradually integrated all aspects of the research findings to create a StageSHIFT Transformation Program for Executive Coaches, C-suite Leaders, their Executive Teams, and the strategic leaders across the organisation (Figure 15.6). There is a full suite of online programs available and customisable. In my experience, these types of interventions within 1,000-person organisations have led to a 20% increase in leadership effectiveness in one year, a 30% increase in people engagement in six months, and a 100% increase in revenues for a smaller trading company three weeks following implementation of the liberating organisational frameworks.

With personal holistic and collective strategic aspirational intent and elevated operating frameworks that invite coachees to play on a more expansive playing field, they are able to make quantum shifts in their leadership capacity, presence, and effectiveness. This approach supported by transformative executive coaching encouraged and enabled the coachees as individuals to lead effectively at the new elevated level of strategic leadership.

Over time I have come to appreciate the interpenetration of self and life while evolving into an increasingly transpersonal perspective. This has led to a way of seeing life through 4 increasingly vertical memes of the mind (Figure 15.7).

Figure 15.6 The StageSHIFT Strategic Holistic Transforming & Inspiring Leadership Programs

Figure 15.7 Four interpenetrative memes of the mind

Life is a Movie . . . A Projection of the Conscious Mind . . . *Live the Dream*
Life is a Mirror . . . A Reflection of the Subconscious Mind . . . *Love the Drama*
Life is a-Mazing . . . A Connection with the Cosmic Mind . . . *Learn to Dance*
Life is a Mystery . . . An Inception of the Universal Mind . . . *Lead the Dharma*
Antoinette J Braks

Chapter 15: Key Points

1 The *Synergist* offers a flourishing global perspective, an inner integrated identity, and the capacity to lead and sustain transformative social and economic change.

2 The coachees not only gained in their leadership capacity, presence, and effectiveness, they also won industry and state awards, and have been fortunate in realising multiple promotions in a short space of time.

3 The coachees' comments suggest that they're very aware of their new mana, their spiritual heart presence, and how differently they came to perceive others and dance with life to generate a more exciting and invigorating future.

4 The transformative StageSHIFT Coaching Model integrates four key dimensions: it is coachee-focused, the coach takes a multi-faceted role, the coaching is presence-led, and the deliberate vertical aspirational intent is transformative.

5 The two most distinguishing features of StageSHIFT Coaching are the transformation of the strategic collective at the organisational level and the transformation of the inner self at the source of identity.

6 The Spectrum Stage Shift from *Achievist* to *Synergist* is a square dance that involves a two-step process of individuation and integration from the Individual to the Collective in the Subtle Tier. Advancing to *Catalyst* stalls a person within the *Achievist's* spectrum, as they cannot reach to the next Figure-8 anchored at *Synergist* without transformative coaching with a later stage coach that includes the distinguishing features of StageSHIFT Coaching.

7 The emergent Vertical Development Theory integrates the 8 drivers of later stage development into 9 elements across the three fields of self, organisation and community, including 6 active ingredients that stimulate vertical growth and 3 key principles that underpin the vertical shift to Synergist: INTENTION, INTERACTION and INTEGRATION.

8 Given that *Synergists* amongst the executive population have only been increasing at the rate of 1% in each of the last two decades, StageSHIFT Transformative Coaching is highly recommended.

9 If half of the executive leaders currently at *Achievist* and half the current leaders at *Catalyst* all shifted to *Synergist*, 50% of executive leaders would be operating from a post-conventional paradigm.

Thank you

I hope you enjoyed reading and gained much inspiration from the stories and concepts articulated through the course of this book. It has been a 10-year journey for me culminating in an emergent Vertical Development Theory that represents the transformative pathway that enables and expedites the quantum paradigm shift from Achievist to Synergist.

Vertical development to the later stage of 4.5/Synergist is crucial to develop strategic corporate, business and political leaders to lead economic transformation and social evolution. Global, regional, national and state-based leaders hold responsibility to create more peace and harmony, shared wellbeing and better health, a flourishing society and equitable justice, a sustainable environment and flourishing planet. The more leaders there are at Synergist, the better we will be able to transcend the turmoil of disruption and cut through complexity, trust emergence to navigate uncertainty and transform the world with strategic ingenuity.

I invite you to join the shift to Synergist to realise your potential to see beyond the escalating global crises and contribute to redesigning and reengineering our economic, educational, health, justice and environmental systems and structures that underpin society today to generate a more sustainable, healthy and equitable world based on universal principles, emergent technology and community-oriented flourishing.

You can find more resources and programs at www.StageSHIFT.coach.

APPENDIX:
The Multiple Case Study Research

- Introduction to the Research
- The Nine Research Participants
- Coaching Set-up and Expectations
- The Results 12 Months Later
- The Structural Dynamics of the Stage Shift
- Three Additional Participants
- Longitudinal Research Extension
- Results of All 12 Participants
- Summary of Key Findings

Introduction to the Research

Since I formed my intention at around 33, my purpose has been to enable people to realise their potential and organisations, their aspirations. I went on to build a career as an executive leader of people and culture and a consultant in management assessment, leadership development, and org-wide transformation. Then I became an executive coach. I'm passionate about the difference executive coaching makes and how we might make an immense contribution to co-creating a better world through our transformative work with executive leaders.

I had also always propelled my own growth and was committed to making as full a contribution to the world as I was capable of. After realising that I had spent every Saturday reading a book for over a year, I decided it would be valuable to add a learning framework around my deep thirst to learn and understand more about people and the world. I embarked on a PhD. I wanted to research how effective I was as an executive coach in relation to later stage leadership development and hopefully identify some useful pointers as a result.

To be honest, I was also intrigued to discover what it was exactly that I did as an executive coach. I loved the work, enjoyed rich and intimate coaching conversations with coachees, and most were also really delighted with their coaching experience and outcomes. While I did review and reflect on my notes for each person one-at-a-time, I hadn't ever looked at lots of coaching conversations across a longish period of time such as a year. It was going to be a complete revelation, as I didn't ever plan my coaching conversations – they simply emerged.

I had discovered developmental psychology a few years earlier in 2010 when attending a workshop with Susanne Cook-Greuter. My centre of gravity turned out to be at *Synergist* with 72% of my profile at post-conventional stages. I was astonished to learn that less than 5% of executives were anchored there. *Synergist* leadership capacity was apparently essential to lead transformation. Therefore, if the world was to become more compassionate and collaborative, wiser and enlightened, healthier and environmentally stable, we needed more executive leaders at *Synergist*.

I went on to study with Bill Torbert and Terri O'Fallon. Both added immeasurably to my understanding of stage development. Bill's work was very corporate oriented and integrated power dynamics and organisational development. Terri's breakthrough research has dramatically re-engineered the structural context within which the stages are set, leading to a much better understanding of the developmental challenges for each stage.

I wanted to know if the difference I was making as an executive coach was tangible and sustainable. Were my coachees realising lateral or vertical growth to the level of *Synergist* or not? And if some were and others weren't, why was that the case? Which elements of my coaching were valuable, and which didn't matter so much. Did coachees need to have a certain level of readiness, openness, or commitment to embark on later stage growth? Was I a convenient recharging point for industrious, committed yet stressed executives or was I more than that?

The Nine Research Participants

I embarked on a research study for my PhD. It so happened that the Public Service Commission (PSC) in New South Wales, Australia, decided to invest in a psychological assessment and brief coaching program for the top 400 senior executives in the second year of their Executive Development Program. They included directors and executive directors, agency heads, C-suite leaders, and deputy secretaries across agriculture, education, environment, family and community services, finance and innovation, health, industry, planning, police, rescue services, trade, transport, and the premier's office.

I had been involved in their management assessment and had been coaching around 50 of the participants in leadership development. I emailed 25 executives, most of whom were already coachees, who I thought might be interested in joining my research project. Nineteen agreed to take up the opportunity and undertook a stage assessment with Susanne Cook-Greuter.

Of the 19, the profiles of 12 of the executives were largely at the conventional levels of *Achievist* and *Specialist*. The other seven already had more than 25% of their profile at post-conventional levels, mainly *Catalyst*. There was a very clear dividing line between the two groups. To ensure that my research would explore the potential of executive coaching to ignite as well as sustain the shift to post-conventional levels, I invited the first group of 12 to join my research study. The maximum number recommended for any case study is also 12 (Yin, 2018).

Figure A1 Assessments of the 25 potential research participants

	Gender	TWS	Primary Stage	Secondary Stage	% Profile Conventional
1	M	212	*Specialist*	*Conformist*	100%
2	M	229	*Achievist*	*Specialist*	94%
3	F	232	*Achievist*	*Specialist*	94%
4	M	233	*Achievist*	*Specialist*	97%
5	M	233	*Achievist*	*Specialist*	97%
6	M	237	*Achievist*	*Specialist*	89%
7	M	242	*Achievist*	*Specialist*	100%
8	F	242	*Achievist*	*Specialist*	81%
9	F	244	*Achievist*	*Specialist*	94%
10	M	244	*Achievist*	*Specialist*	83%
11	M	245	*Achievist*	*Specialist*	89%
12	M	247	*Achievist*	*Specialist*	89%
13	F	252	*Achievist*	*Catalyst*	75%
14	F	256	*Achievist*	*Catalyst*	75%
15	M	263	*Catalyst*	*Achievist*	64%
16	M	268	*Catalyst*	*Achievist*	53%
17	F	270	*Catalyst*	*Achievist*	47%
18	F	283	*Synergist*	*Catalyst*	33%
19	F	283	*Synergist*	*Catalyst*	31%

Nine agreed to proceed with an executive coaching program to be followed by a second stage assessment a year later. The average aggregate conventional profile of the nine purposively selected participants was 92% and each person's conventional profile was above 80%. In fact, seven of the nine had 89% or more of their profile at conventional levels. The profiles of the group are presented in Figure A1 on the basis of their total weighted score (TWS). This is a quantitative measure of their stage leadership capacity based on a weighted algorithm of the number of sentence completions at each progressive stage of development in the Mature Adult Profile (MAP). Later stages attract higher scores.

All nine research participants (three women and six men) were graduates, five had masters degrees and one a doctorate. Their average age was 52. All had significant and substantial responsibilities as strategic leaders at the levels of executive director (7) and director (2). They individually volunteered to take part in the research study and were open and committed to their own intentional development to later stages. While the PSC funded their participation, no other stakeholders were involved.

Coaching Set-up and Expectations

I adopted my standard coaching approach. To be honest, I wouldn't have been able to describe it at that point. I simply showed up, fully present, calm of mind and caring of heart. I set clear intentions to bring all the wisdom, compassion, knowledge, experience, and expertise I could access to whatever situations or events, challenges or opportunities, dilemmas or frustrations, the coachees chose to raise with me. It was definitely highly personal and very business oriented. I was often described as an uplifting, 'out-of-the-box' type of coach. However, as I said above, I had no real understanding of what I offered as a coach. At that point I had not studied various coaching approaches nor had any informed view of how my coaching approach compared with that of others.

I set up 90-minute coaching meetings in consultation with each coachee at the same time and day every four weeks for the year in advance. Most had committed to twelve months' coaching but two had a budget for just six months. I coached at 8am, 10am, 12pm, 2pm, and 4pm Monday to Friday for a fortnight. I kept the second fortnight free for consulting work. My coaching schedule was approximately 80% full. Coachees could adjust the time of their meeting for another time during that same fortnight if needed, and meetings could also be deferred to beyond the 12-month period to take account of holidays or other absences.

I took 10–15 minutes before each meeting to read last month's notes, centre myself, tune in, and set a sincere intention to be an empowering and inspiring beneficent guide for the person arriving next. I always made us both a cup of peppermint tea to enjoy during our meetings and we had water glasses and a large jug of water. Our meetings generally also ran over by about 5 minutes to complete whatever we were working on. Time was considered of the essence and was filled to the brim, mostly with dialogue in contrast to silence.

All coaching meetings were in person. The meeting room was spacious. It was on the 20th floor of an inner-city building with an enormous window overlooking Sydney harbour and parkland. The table was big enough for eight comfortable executive chairs on wheels and there was a wall-to-wall whiteboard lengthwise that I often made full use of. I took notes during our meetings and photos of whiteboard diagrams and draft content. These were sent onto the coachee later in the same day of our coaching meeting. Audio of all coaching meetings was also recorded with the written agreement of the coachees. All that took place was considered confidential and any data used for the purposes of the research study would be reported anonymously.

Previous research suggested that it took years to shift to later post-conventional stages of development. As there were few people demonstrating this level of leadership capacity, they were rarely available to be modelled in contrast to conventional levels of leadership capacity such as the micro-managing *Specialist* and high-performing *Achievist*. They were commonplace in organisations.

Needless to say, expectations were low. I really hoped that perhaps two or three of the coachees in my research study would navigate a stage shift. Then I would be able to compare their coaching conversations and developmental journeys with those who didn't move a full stage and draw some preliminary conclusions on the drivers and dynamics of development. All in all, I was simply delighted to be embarking on gaining an informed understanding of my coaching approach with a wonderful group of coachees committed to their growth as leaders, be it lateral or vertical! What I might go on to discover was, as yet, a complete mystery to me.

The Results 12 Months Later

It turned out that the coachees had an average of exactly eight coaching sessions over the 12-month period with a standard deviation of two. They ranged from five to eleven. The three who met with me between five and seven times found a bimonthly pattern more comfortable. For others, the coaching either coincided with a holiday period or it was a matter of juggling time priorities in the particular week. All coaching meetings could be freely rescheduled up to and including the week before, and were often used to extend the time period of the coaching program.

At the end of the 12-month period the participants each undertook a second stage assessment to be followed by a complementary coaching debrief. They completed their stage assessments online and sent them to me. I removed all names and other identifying information such as gender, age, role, and education and sent them off anonymously in a zip file to Susanne Cook-Greuter for assessment. I then sat back and waited very curious about the results.

I was stunned when the reports came back. Every single coachee had moved a stage! One had even made a double shift from *Achievist* to *Synergist*, and another was similarly evaluated quantitatively but their holistic assessment had moved them back slightly to late *Catalyst*. WOW! I was over the moon, very excited and thrilled to have the opportunity to discover what in the coaching approach may have enabled the shift to post-conventional leadership.

For those of you interested in statistics, a matched-pair t-test showed significant differences pre and post the coaching program over the 12-month period ($p < 0.0001$). The average shift in the TWS was 29 points, the ambit of a full stage. The change in TWS ranged from 14 points, a half stage, to 48 points, one-and-a-half stages. The group's aggregate later stage profile had shifted from 8% to 43%, an increase of 35%. Their average aggregate conventional profile dropped by this amount from 92% to 57%. The R^2 of this shift was at 0.519 with a 0.0001 and a 95% confidence interval. These results are displayed in Figure A2.

In terms of the changes in the stage distribution between the pre and post profiles, the average aggregate profile (AAP) at *Achievist* remained remarkably stable decreasing by just 4%, from 52% in the pre-assessment in

Figure A2 Pre- and post-coaching assessments for the Initial nine research participants

Participants	Total Weighted Score (TWS)			Total Protocol Rating Centre of Gravity		% Profile at Post-conventional		
	Pre-	Post-	Change	Pre-	Post-	Pre-	Post-	Change
A	242	278	+36	Achievist	Catalyst	19%	64%	+45%
B	244	265	+21	Achievist	Catalyst	6%	36%	+30%
C	245	293	+48	Achievist	Synergist	11%	81%	+70%
D	232	266	+34	Achievist	Catalyst	6%	50%	+44%
E	233	260	+27	Achievist	Catalyst	3%	31%	+28%
F	212	241	+29	Specialist	Achievist	0%	6%	+6%
G	242	265	+23	Achievist	Catalyst	0%	39%	+39%
H	247	261	+14	Achievist	Catalyst	11%	31%	+20%
I	244	271	+27	Achievist	Catalyst	17%	50%	+33%
MEAN	238	267	+29	$t =$	$p <$	Aggregate Profile Shift		
Std Dev	11.02	14.06	9.24	8.8139	0.0001	8%	43%	+35%

Year 0 to 48% in the post-assessment in Year 1. The shifts on either side were more significant. The AAP at *Catalyst* increased from 8% to 36%, an increase of 28%, and the AAP at *Specialist* decreased from 32% to 9%, a decrease of 23%. The AAP at the leading edge of *Synergist* and *Alchemist* increased 7% from 0.3% to 7.1%, and the AAP at the trailing edge of *Opportunist* and *Conformist* dropped 7% from 7.4% to 0.6%. Changes in these two profile edges were also conspicuous due to the magnitude of the change to and from close to zero.

The Structural Dynamics of the Stage Shift

Graphical representation of the results is very revealing (Figure A3). The transformative shift took place *around* the participants' largely (8/9) primary mode of operating at *Achievist*. This suggests that a person undertaking development continues to draw on a wide spectrum of stages and, in particular, continues to draw on their *Achievist* action-logic, for instance, to be decisive in the moment, while extending their reach into post-conventional stages. This is comforting to *Achievists* as they can default to a focus on goals and results when necessary while also consciously cultivating self-awareness and inquiring into the broader and deeper implications of complex situations as authentic leaders do at *Catalyst*.

This suggests that while the shift through the stages appears to be linear, the person does shift their primary centre of gravity from *Achievist* to *Catalyst*, this does not adequately explain the dynamics of the shift that took place. Their

Figure A3 Graphical representation of the stage shifts

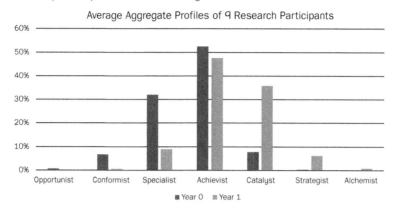

previous leading edge at *Catalyst* has developed substantially to become the new primary centre of gravity, and a new leading edge at *Synergist* has sprouted. Correspondingly, the previous secondary stage of *Specialist* has diminished substantially while the trailing edge at *Conformist* has almost disappeared. In summary, actively developing a person's leading edge while inviting them to release the constraints of earlier stages, seems to be an effective developmental strategy.

The qualitative analysis into the drivers and dynamics offers some excellent insights into this release of the *Specialist* perspective and the development of their new-found agility at *Catalyst*. Based on the scope of their coaching conversations, I've also been able to speculate on how one participant, and almost a second, navigated a double-shift of two transformations from *Achievist* to *Synergist* in the one year.

Three Additional Participants

Between 2015 and 2017, three more cases were added to the research study to test the assessment findings. I was curious to see if the results would be repeated. Of the three additional participants, one was also from the public sector and the other two were senior executives in the financial services sector. Two of the participants also had at least 80% of their initial stage profiles in conventional stages, one 83% and the other 94%. The third participant was included in the research study by way of exception to test the shift from *Catalyst* to *Synergist*. That person began with 47% of their profile at *Catalyst*.

The order of development was similar to the initial research study (Figure A4). Two shifted one stage and one transformed twice from *Achievist* to *Synergist*. Their pre-*Achievist* profiles dropped significantly (29.3%), and their

Figure A4 Pre- and post-coaching stage assessments

Participants	% Profile at Pre-*Achievist*			Total Protocol Rating Centre of Gravity		% Profile at Post-conventional		
	Pre-	Post-	Change	Pre-	Post-	Pre-	Post-	Change
J	48.0%	13.0%	−35.0%	*Achievist*	*Catalyst*	6.0%	37.0%	+31.0%
K	33.3%	16.7%	−16.7%	*Achievist*	*Synergist*	16.7%	38.9%	+22.2%
L	6.7%	0.0%	−6.7%	*Catalyst*	*Synergist*	46.7%	93.3%	+46.7%
Average	29.3%	9.9%	−19.4%			23.1%	56.4%	+33.3%

post-conventional profiles increased by a third (33.3%). The proportion of the profile at *Achievist* for the first two additional participants remained relatively stable moving only slightly from 47% and 50% to 50% and 44%, an average change of 1.3%.

The extension to the study therefore offered further evidence of the capacity of the coaching approach to enable participants to shift to post-conventional stages. While the coaching approach was adopted with greater conscious awareness of the drivers, all coaching conversations still responded specifically to the challenges and concerns, opportunities and aspirations articulated by the coachee at the beginning of each coaching meeting.

It also confirmed the nature of the transformative shift. The *Catalyst/Synergist* profile increased significantly, and the *Specialist/Conformist* profile decreased significantly. The *Achievist* profile remained relatively stable. This pattern was repeated by the two participants who transformed twice from *Achievist* to *Synergist* amongst the 12. Their shift to a primary centre of gravity at *Synergist* did see a substantial reduction in their *Achievist* profile by an average of 40.8% (41.6 % and 40%).

While this is a small sample of 12, it is very interesting to observe that a stage shift involves releasing not the stage immediately before the new centre of gravity, but the stage that is two stages before the new centre of gravity. This imitates the two-step recurring sequence of individuation followed by integration in stage development. When moving into a new individuation mode (e.g. *Catalyst*), the previous individuation mode two steps before is released (i.e. *Specialist*), and when consolidating in a new integration mode (e.g. *Synergist*), the previous integration mode also two steps before is released (i.e. *Achievist*).

Longitudinal Research Extension

Almost three years later, in March 2017, I invited all nine of the original participants to retake the stage leadership assessment. There was merit in adding a longitudinal element to the study. I was keen to discover if the leadership development they had attained had been sustained. Three of the original participants agreed to retake the assessment a third time. Interestingly, the three that did agree had been the most advanced in their second leadership assessment from amongst the nine. They seemed to be most curious about their ensuing development following the end of their coaching programs. Two of these participants had extended their coaching programs for approximately a year beyond the original research period.

The results were again unanimous. All three participants now had their centre of gravity at *Synergist*. The participant who had vaulted their way to *Synergist/Catalyst* earlier sustained this profile. Now 100% of their profile was at later post-conventional stages (previously 81%) with 63% at *Synergist* and *Alchemist* (previously 25%). The second repeat participant who had been close to *Synergist* at the end of the initial 12-month period was now operating at *Synergist/Catalyst*. Their later stage post-conventional profile had increased from 64% to 90%. The third participant had also shifted to *Synergist/Catalyst* with 73% of their responses at these two later stages compared to 50% previously. This indicative longitudinal evidence suggests that the impact of the coaching program was sustained.

It is interesting to see that the pattern of stage development was repeated. Just as the *Specialist* profile receded in the original research results where most participants shifted from *Achievist* to *Catalyst*, in this longitudinal research the *Achievist* profile diminished to give way to the *Synergist*, also two stages before the new centre of gravity.

In the transformation of their centre of gravity for all five participants to *Synergist* (Figure A5) using the three longitudinal results from Year 0 to their latest assessments, and two of the additional three participants who shifted to *Synergist*, the proportion of the aggregate profile at the earlier

Figure A5 Average aggregate profiles of the five research participants to *Synergist*

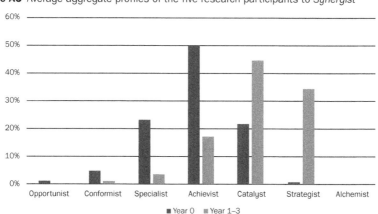

Figure A6 Average aggregate stage distribution for five participants to *Synergist*

Phase of Development	Stage	Year 0	Year 1–3	Change
Pre-conventional	*Opportunist*	0.7%	0.0%	−0.7%
	Conformist	4.6%	0.6%	−4.0%
Conventional	*Specialist*	22.8%	3.4%	−19.4%
	Achievist	49.9%	16.8%	**−33.1%**
	Catalyst	21.6%	44.7%	+23.1%
Post-conventional	*Synergist*	0.6%	34.4%	**+33.8%**
	Alchemist	0.0%	0.0%	+0.0%
Total Post-conventional		22.2%	79.1%	+56.9%

stages up to and including *Achievist* dropped by 57%, and the proportion of the aggregate profile at the new centre of gravity at *Synergist* increased by 34% (Figure A6).

Transformative development from one stage to the next again involved releasing earlier perspectives, broadening leading edge perspectives while continuing to deploy one's identity at the current perspective. It would seem that if there is sufficient lateral development within the vertical leading edge, and a release of the constraints implicit in the secondary stage and trailing edge, this results in a new centre of gravity at the person's leading edge. The starting centre of gravity lapses organically from primary to secondary.

Results for All 12 Participants

The following is a summary of the demographics, stage profile spectrum, and stage shifts of all 12 research participants (Figure A7). Most, 83%, started out with a centre of gravity at *Achiever*. Their average age was 50, ranging from 36 to 56 at the beginning of the coaching assignments when they undertook their first stage assessment. Five of the participants were women and seven men. All had university degrees; half had a master's degree, and one a doctorate. The total average of coaching meetings was 8.4, ranging from 5 to 11.

The graph of all 12 profile shifts in Figure A8 illustrates the new centre of gravity of the group of participants, largely from *Achievist* to *Catalyst*, and, three years later, onto *Synergist*. First, the *Specialist* profile fades away as the centre of gravity shifts to *Catalyst*, and then the *Achievist* profile fades away as the centre of gravity shifts to *Synergist*. The 12% average aggregate post-conventional profile in Year 0 inversed to an 88% post-conventional profile for the three longitudinal participants in Year 4.

Figure A7 Demographic summary of the 12 research participants

Participants	Total of 12	Average	Total	%
Stage	*Specialist*		1	8%
	Achievist	*Achievist*	10	83%
	Catalyst		1	8%
Age	30–39		1	8%
	40–49	50	4	33%
	50–59		7	58%
Gender	Female		5	42%
	Male		7	58%
Education	Bachelor's degree		6	50%
	Master's degree		5	42%
	Doctoral degree		1	8%
Number of Coaching Sessions		8.4	101	

Figure A8 The average aggregate profile shifts of all 12 participants

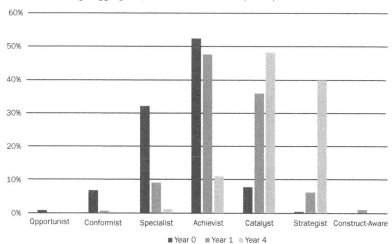

■ Year 0   ■ Year 1   ▨ Year 4

For those of you interested in statistics, a matched-pair t-test showed an extremely significant difference pre to post the coaching program for all 12 participants over the 12-month period: $p < 0.0001$. The average shift in the TWS was 29 points, the ambit of a full stage. The change in TWS ranged from 14 points, a half stage, to 48 points, one-and-a-half stages. The group's aggregate later stage profile had shifted from 11.8% to 46.3%, an increase of 34.5%. Their average aggregate conventional profile dropped by this amount from 88% to 54%. The R^2 of this shift was 0.673 with a 0.0001 at a 95% confidence interval.

Figure A9 Participants' profiles and coaching programs

	Gender	Age	Degree	Prior Sessions	MAP Year 1	Coaching Sessions	MAP Year 2	Post Sessions
A	F	54	PhD	7	7 Jun 13	8	10 Jul 14	7
B	F	48	M	3	9 Apr 13	7	11 Jul 14	1
C	M	53	M	6	23 May 13	8	12 Jul 14	9
D	F	56	B	3	12 Apr 13	5	6 Aug 14	0
E	M	56	B	5	20 Jun 13	9	5 Aug 14	1
F	M	53	MBA	6	23 May 13	10	4 Aug 14	9
G	M	46	M	5	7 Jun 13	9	5 Aug 14	1
H	M	44	B	1	11 Apr 13	11	11 Aug 14	1
I	M	56	M	4	7 Jun 13	5	5 Aug 14	1
J	M	50	M	2	1 Apr 13	5	1 Apr 16	1
K	F	42	B	1	23 Mar 17	12	21 Mar 18	1
L	F	36	B	1	24 Mar 17	12	01 Jun 18	1
Avg	42% F	50	58% M	3.7	Coaching	8.4	Sessions	2.8

Figure A9 provides a summary of the demographics together with the coaching history for each of the 12 participants in the research study.

Summary of Key Findings

The stage assessments indicate that:

The empirical evidence offered by the stage assessments pre- and post-executive coaching with 12 senior executives at an average age of 50 and a later stage coach, indicates that an average of eight 90-minute monthly coaching sessions over one year was instrumental in igniting and sustaining 10 single (83%) and 2 double shifts (17%), mostly to later stage post-conventional leadership capacity at Catalyst and Synergist.

---

1 The transformative executive coaching approach deliberately intended to liberate later stage development generated a vertical shift in stage for 100% of the participants in the 12-month research study.

2 An average of eight 90-minute monthly coaching sessions spread throughout one year was sufficient to generate a shift to later stage post-conventional leadership capacity (100% of eligible participants, i.e. 11/12 or 92%, the one exception started at *Specialist* and shifted to *Achievist*).

3 The transformative executive coaching approach also has the potential of enabling a double shift from *Achievist* to *Synergist* (2/11 or 18% of participants) in one year.

4 The longitudinal sample indicates that once a person has shifted to late *Catalyst* or *Synergist* as a primary centre of gravity, their journey continues to consolidate at *Synergist* as suggested by the two-step sequence of individuation followed by integration, indicating that once transformative shifts are attained, they can be sustained with continued coaching support, based on 100% albeit of a small sample of three participants three years later.

5 The equivalent coaching approach appears to be as relevant in expediting the subsequent integration at *Synergist* (5/12 or 42%) as it is in igniting individuation to *Catalyst* (11/12 or 92%).

6 The changing stage profiles indicate that once a person's centre of gravity shifts to the individuation collective stage of *Catalyst*, individual expression at the earlier individuation stage of *Specialist*, two stages before, diminishes significantly; similarly, as a person's centre of gravity shifts to the integration stage of *Synergist*, individual expression at the earlier integration stage of *Achievist*, also two stages before, diminishes significantly.

7 These findings are most relevant to coachees who are graduates, aged between 36 and 56, and who hold senior executive positions leading divisions with significant and substantial strategic and/or operational responsibilities.

8 A person, on average, expresses themselves and interprets their life experience across a broad spectrum of four stages simultaneously, ranging from two to five stages in total.

The assessments suggest that the shift from conventional to post-conventional stages is not a linear shift but more closely approximates a Spectrum Stage Shift where earlier individual stages are transcended, and new later collective stages of development are constructed.

References

Amen, D.G. (1998) *Change your brain, change your life*. New York: Three Rivers Press.

Askeland, M. (2009) A reflexive inquiry into the ideologies and theoretical assumptions of coaching, *Coaching: An International Journal of Theory, Research and Practice*, 2 (1): 65–75.

Athanasopoulou, A. and Dopson, S. (2018) A systematic review of executive coaching outcomes: Is it the journey or the destination that matters the most?, *The Leadership Quarterly*, 29 (1): 70–88.

Bachkirova, T. (2011) *Developmental coaching: Working with the self*. Maidenhead: Open University Press.

Bachkirova, T. (2014) Psychological development in adulthood and coaching, in E. Cox, T. Bachkirova and D. Clutterbuck (eds.) *The complete handbook of coaching* (2nd edition, pp. 131–144). London: Sage.

Bachkirova, T. and Borrington, S. (2018) The limits and possibilities of a person-centered approach in coaching through the lens of adult development theories, *Philosophy of Coaching*, 3 (1): 6–22.

Barrett, R. (2014) *Evolutionary coaching: A values-based approach to unleashing human potential*. Morrisville, NC: Lulu Press.

Baumeister, R. and Tierney, J. (2011) *Willpower: Rediscovering the greatest human strength*. New York: Penguin.

Beck, D.E. and Cowan, C.C. (1996) *Spiral dynamics: Mastering values, leadership and change*. Cambridge, MA: Blackwell.

Beckwith, M.B. (2009) *Spiritual liberation: Fulfilling your soul's potential*. New York: Simon & Schuster.

Berger, J.G. (2004) Dancing on the threshold of meaning, *Journal of Transformative Education*, 2 (4): 336–351.

Berger, J.G. (2012) *Changing on the job: Developing leaders for the complex world*. Stanford, CA: Stanford University Press.

Braks, A. (2015) *The 7 Transformations in Leadership Development*. Retrieved from: https://www.linkedin.com/pulse/7-key-transformations-leadership-part-i-antoinette-braks.

Brown, B.C. (2012) Leading complex change with post-conventional consciousness, *Journal of Organisational Change Management*, 25 (4): 560–577.

Brown, B.C. (2014) *The future of leadership for conscious capitalism*, White Paper. Sebastopol, CA: MetaIntegral Associates.

Bushe, G.R. and Gibbs, B.W. (1990) Predicting organization development consulting competence from the Myers-Briggs Type Indicator and stage of ego development, *Journal of Applied Behavioral Science*, 26 (3): 337–357.

Campbell, J. (2004) *The hero with a thousand faces* (6th edition). Princeton, NJ: Princeton University Press.

Cavanagh, M. (2006) Coaching from a systemic perspective: A complex adaptive approach, in R. Stober and A.M. Grant (eds.) *Evidence-based coaching handbook* (pp. 313–354). New York: Wiley.

Cavanagh, M. and Lane, D. (2012) Coaching psychology coming of age: The challenges we face in the messy world of complexity, *International Coaching Psychology Review*, 7 (1): 75–90.

Clutterbuck, D. (2010) Coaching reflection: The liberated coach, *Coaching: An International Journal of Theory, Research and Practice*, 3 (1): 73–81.

Cohn, L.D. (1998) Age trends in personality development: A quantitative review, in P.M. Westenberg, A. Blasi and L.D. Cohn (eds.) *Personality development: Theoretical, empirical and clinical investigations of Loevinger's conception of ego development* (pp. 133–143). Hillsdale, NJ: Erlbaum.

Cohn, L.D. and Westenberg, P.M. (2004) Intelligence and maturity: Meta-analytic evidence for the incremental and discriminant validity of Loevinger's measure of ego development, *Journal of Personality and Social Psychology*, 86: 760–772.

Cook-Greuter, S.R. (1995) *Comprehensive language awareness: A definition of the phenomenon and a review of its treatment in the postformal adult development literature*, Unpublished MA thesis, Harvard University, Cambridge, MA.

Cook-Greuter, S. (1999) *Postautonomous ego development: A study of its nature and measurement*, Doctoral dissertation, Harvard Graduate School of Education, Cambridge, MA.

Cook-Greuter, S.R. (2000) Mature ego development: A gateway to ego transcendence?, *Journal of Adult Development*, 7 (4): 227–240.

Covey, S.R. (1994) *First things first*. London: Simon & Schuster.

Cox, E., Bachkirova, T. and Clutterbuck, D. (2014) Theoretical traditions and coaching genres, *Advances in Developing Human Resources*, 16 (2): 139–160.

Csikszentmihalyi, M. (1990) *Flow: The psychology of optimal experience*. New York: Harper & Row.

Delizonna, L. (2017) High performing teams need psychological safety: Here's how to create it, *Harvard Business Review*, 24 August.

Doidge, N. (2010) *The brain that changes itself*. London: Scribe.

Dweck, C.S. (2008) *Mindset: The new psychology of success*. New York: Ballantine Books.

Eigel, K.M. (1998) *Leadership effectiveness: A constructive developmental view and investigation*, Unpublished doctoral dissertation, University of Georgia, Athens, GA.

Eigel, K.M. and Kuhnert, K.W. (2005) Authentic development: Leadership development level and executive effectiveness, in W. Gardner, B. Avolio and F. Walumba (eds.) *Authentic leadership theory and practice: Origins, effects and development* (pp. 357–385). Monographs in Leadership and Management Vol. 3. Oxford: Elsevier.

Ericsson, K.A. (ed.) (2009) *Development of professional expertise: Toward measurement of expert performance and design of optimal learning environments*. Cambridge: Cambridge University Press.

Fisher, D. and Torbert, W.R. (1991) Transforming managerial practice: Beyond the achiever stage, in R. Woodman and W. Pasmore (eds.) *Research in organizational change and development* (Vol. 5, pp. 143–173). Greenwich, CT: JAI Press.

Frankl, V. (1946) *Man's search for meaning*. New York: Rider.

Fredrickson, B. (2010) *Positivity: Discover the upper spiral that will change your life*. New York: Harmony Publications.

Fritz, R. (1984) *The path of least resistance: Learning to become the creative force in your own life*. Walpole, NH: Stillpoint Publishing.

Gallwey, T. (1999) *The inner game of work*. New York: Random House.

Goleman, D. (1995) *Emotional intelligence: Why it can matter more than IQ*. New York: Bantam Books.

Grant, A.M. (2003) The impact of life coaching on goal attainment, metacognition and mental health, *Social Behavior and Personality*, 31 (3): 253–264.

Grant, A.M. (2006) An integrative goal-focused approach to executive coaching, in D.R. Stober and A.M. Grant (eds.) *Evidence based coaching: Putting best practices to work for your clients* (pp. 153–192). New York: Wiley.

Grant, A.M. and Cavanagh, M.J. (2004) Toward a profession of coaching: Sixty-five years of progress and challenges for the future, *International Journal of Evidence Based Coaching and Mentoring*, 4 (1): 1–16.

Grant, A.M., Cavanagh, M.J. and Parker, H.M. (2010) The state of play in coaching today: A comprehensive review of the field, in G.P. Hodgkinson and J.K. Ford (eds.) *International Review of Industrial and Organizational Psychology* (Vol. 25, pp. 125–167). New York: Wiley.

Gunnlaugson, O. and Brabant, M. (eds.) (2016) *Cohering the integral space we create: Engaging collective emergence, wisdom and healing in groups*. Tucson, AZ: Integral Publishers.

Hamel, G. (2007) *The future of management*. Cambridge, MA: Harvard Business Review Press.

Harris, L.S. and Kuhnert, K.W. (2008) Looking through the lens of leadership: A constructive developmental approach, *Leadership and Organization Development Journal*, 29 (1): 47–67.

Hawkins, P. and Smith, N. (2013) *Coaching, mentoring and organizational consultancy* (2nd edition). Maidenhead: Open University Press.

Horney, K. (1950) *Neurosis and human growth*. New York: Norton.

Immordino-Yang, M.H., Christodoulou, J.A. and Singh, V. (2012) Rest is not idleness: Implications of the brain's default mode for human development and education, *Perspectives on Psychological Science*, 7 (4): 352–364.

Ives, Y. (2008) What is 'coaching'? An exploration of conflicting paradigms, *International Journal of Evidence Based Coaching and Mentoring*, 6 (2): 100–113.

Joiner, B. and Josephs, S. (2007) *Leadership agility: Five levels of mastery for anticipating and initiating change*. San Francisco, CA: Jossey-Bass.

Jones, R.J., Woods, S.A. and Guillaume, Y.R.F. (2016) The effectiveness of workplace coaching: A meta-analysis of learning and performance outcomes from coaching, *Journal of Occupational and Organizational Psychology*, 89 (2): 249–277.

Kaiser, R.B. and Kaplan, R.B. (2006) The deeper work of executive development: Outgrowing sensitivities, *Academy of Management Learning and Education*, 5 (4): 463–483.

Katie, B. and Mitchell, S. (2002) *Loving what is: Four questions that can change your life*. New York, NY: Harmony Books.

Kauffman, C. (2006) Positive psychology: The science at the heart of coaching, in D.R. Stober and A.M. Grant (eds.) *Evidence-based coaching handbook: Putting best practices to work for your clients* (pp. 219–253). New York: Wiley.

Kegan, R. (1982) *The evolving self: Problem and process in human development*. Cambridge, MA: Harvard University Press.

Kegan, R. (1995) *In over our heads: The mental demands of modern life*. Cambridge, MA: Harvard University Press.

Kegan, R., Lahey, L., Fleming, A. and Miller, M. (2014) Making business personal, *Harvard Business Review*, April: 44–52.

Kilburg, R.R. (2004) When shadows fall: Using psychodynamic approaches in executive coaching, *Consulting Psychology Journal: Practice and Research*, 56 (4): 246–268.

Kirkpatrick, D.L. (1967) Evaluation of training, in R.L. Craig and L.R. Bittel (eds.) *Training and development handbook* (pp. 87–112). New York: McGraw-Hill.

Kleitman, N. (1982) Basic rest–activity cycle – 22 years later, *Journal of Sleep Research and Sleep Medicine*, 54 (4): 311–317.

Kolb, D.A. (1984) *Experiential learning: Experience as the source of learning and development*. Englewood Cliffs, NJ: Prentice Hall.

Kohlberg, L. (1981) *The philosophy of moral development: Moral stages and the idea of justice*. San Francisco, CA: Harper & Row.

Kotter, J.P. (2012) *Leading change*. Boston, MA: Harvard Business Review Press.

Kotter, J.P. (2014) *XLR8*. Boston, MA: Harvard Business Review Press.

Kraiger, K., Ford, J.K. and Salas, E.D. (1993) Application of cognitive, skill-based, and affective theories of learning outcomes to new methods of training evaluation, *Journal of Applied Psychology*, 78 (2): 311–328.

Laloux, F. (2014) *Reinventing organizations: A guide to creating organizations inspired by the next stage of human consciousness*. Brussels: Nelson Parker.

Laske, O.E. (1999) *Transformative effects of coaching on executives' professional agenda*. Ann Arbor, MI: University of Michigan Press.

Lilienfeld, S.O., Wood, J.M. and Garb, H.N. (2000) The scientific status of projective techniques, *Psychological Science in the Public Interest*, 1 (2): 27–66.

Lipton, B. (2015) *The biology of belief: Unleashing the power of consciousness, matter and miracles*. London: Hay House.

Loehr, J. and Schwartz, T. (2004) *The power of full engagement: Managing energy, not time, is the key to high performance and personal renewal*. New York: Free Press.

Loevinger, J. (1966) The meaning and measurement of ego development, *American Psychologist*, 21 (3): 195–206.

Loevinger, J. and Wessler, R. (1970) *Measuring ego development: Vol. 1. Construction and use of a sentence completion test*. San Francisco, CA: Jossey-Bass.

Manners, J. and Durkin, K. (2000) Processes involved in adult ego development: A conceptual framework, *Developmental Review*, 20 (4): 475–513.

Manners, J. and Durkin, K. (2001) A critical review of the validity of ego development theory and its measurement, *Journal of Personality Assessment*, 77 (3): 541–567.

Marturano, J. (2014) *Finding the space to lead*. London: Bloomsbury.

Maslow, A.H. (1962) *Toward a psychology of being*. New York: Van Nostrand.

McCauley, C.D., Drath, W.H., Palus, C.J., O'Connor, P.M.G. and Baker, B.A. (2006) The use of constructive-developmental theory to advance the understanding of leadership, *The Leadership Quarterly*, 17 (6): 634–653.

Merron, K., Fisher, D. and Torbert, W.R. (1987) Meaning making and management action, *Group and Organization Studies*, 12 (3): 274–286.

Mezirow, J. (2003) Transformative learning as discourse, *Journal of Transformative Education*, 1 (1): 58–63.

Myers, A.C. and Bachkirova, T. (2018) Towards a process-based typology of workplace coaching: An empirical investigation, *Consulting Psychology Journal: Practice and Research*, 70 (4): 297–317.

Myss, C. (2007) *Entering the castle: An inner path to God and your soul*. London: Simon & Schuster.

O'Fallon, T. (2011) *STAGES: Growing up is waking up – interpenetrating quadrants, states and structures*. Paper presented at the Integral Theory Conference, San Francisco, CA.

O'Fallon, T. (2013) *The senses: Demystifying awakening*. Paper presented at the Integral Theory Conference, San Francisco, CA.

Peltier, B. (2001) *The psychology of executive coaching: Theory and applications.* Ann Arbor, MI: Sheridan Books.

Petrie, N. (2015) *The how-to of vertical leadership development – Part 2,* White Paper. Greensboro, NC: Center for Creative Leadership.

Petriglieri, G., Wood, J.D. and Petriglieri, J.L. (2011) Up close and personal: Building foundations for leaders' development through the personalization of management learning, *Academy of Management Learning and Education,* 10 (3): 430–450.

Pfaffenberger, A., Marko, P. and Combs, A. (2011) *The postconventional personality: Assessing, researching, and theorizing higher development.* Albany, NY: State University of New York Press.

PricewaterhouseCoopers (PwC) (2015) *The hidden talent: Ten ways to identify and retain transformational leaders.* Retrieved from: https://osca.co/publications/the-hidden-talent-ten-ways-to-identify-and-retain-transformational-leaders/.

Quatro, S., Galvin, B.M. and Waldman, D. (2007) Developing holistic leaders: Four domains for leadership development and practice, *Human Resource Management Review,* 17 (4): 427–441.

Redmore, C.D. and Waldman, K. (1975) Reliability of a sentence completion measure of ego development, *Journal of Personality Assessment,* 39 (3): 236–243.

Rogers, C.R. (1961) *On becoming a person.* Boston, MA: Houghton Mifflin.

Rooke, D. and Torbert, W.R. (1998) Organizational transformation as a function of CEOs' developmental stage, *Organization Development Journal,* 16 (1): 11–28.

Rooke, D. and Torbert, W.R. (2005) Seven transformations of leadership, *Harvard Business Review,* April: 66–76.

Scharmer, C.O. (2018) *Theory U: Leading from the future as it emerges.* San Francisco, CA: Berrett-Koehler.

Schwartz, T. (2010) The productivity paradox: How Sony Pictures gets more out of people by demanding less, *Harvard Business Review,* June.

Seligman, M.E.P. (2007) Coaching and positive psychology, *Australian Psychologist,* 42 (4): 266–267.

Seligman, M. (2011) *Flourish: A new understanding of happiness and well-being – and how to archive them.* London: Simon & Schuster.

Senge, P.M. (1990) *The fifth discipline: The art and practice of the learning organization.* New York: Currency Doubleday.

Sharma, B. and Cook-Greuter, S. (2012) *Polarities and ego development: Polarity thinking in ego development theory and developmental coaching.* Retrieved from: https://www.cook-greuter.com/Sharma%20Cook-Greuter%20paper%20EAIF%20SUNY.pdf.

Stelter, R. (2014) Third generation coaching: Reconstructing dialogues through collaborative practice and a focus on values, *International Coaching Psychology Review,* 9 (1): 51–66.

Stober, R. and Grant, A.M. (eds.) (2006) *Evidence-based coaching handbook.* New York: Wiley.

Strang, S. and Kuhnert, K.W. (2009) Personality and leadership developmental levels as predictors of leader performance, *The Leadership Quarterly,* 20 (3): 421–433.

Stroul, N. and Wahl, C. (2013) On becoming a leadership coach, in C. Wahl, C. Scriber and B. Bloomfield (eds.) *On becoming a leadership coach: A holistic approach to coaching excellence* (2nd edition, pp. 3–12). New York: Palgrave Macmillan.

Ten Hoopen, P. and Trompenaars, F. (2011) *The enlightened leader: An introduction to the Chakras of leadership.* New York: Wiley.

Tolle, E. (1997) *The power of now.* Vancouver, BC: Namaste.

Torbert, W.R. (1987) *Managing the corporate dream: Restructuring for long-term success.* Homewood, IL: Dow Jones-Irwin.

Torbert, W.R. (1994) Cultivating postformal adult development, in M.E. Miller and S.R. Cook-Greuter (eds.) *Transcendence and mature thought in adulthood* (pp. 181–203). Lanham, MD: Rowman & Littlefield.

Torbert, W.R. and Fisher, D. (1992) Autobiographical awareness as a catalyst for managerial and organisational development, *Management Education and Development,* 23 (3): 184–198.

Torbert, W.R. and Livne-Tarandach, R. (2009) Reliability and validity tests of the Harthill Leadership Development Profile in the context of *Developmental Action Inquiry* theory, practice, and method, *Integral Review,* 5 (2): 133–151.

Torbert, W.R., Cook-Greuter, S., Fisher, D., Foldy, E., Gauthier, A., Keeley, J. et al. (2004) *Action inquiry: The secret of timely and transforming leadership.* San Francisco, CA: Berrett-Koehler.

Vincent, N., Ward, L. and Denson, L. (2015) Promoting post-conventional consciousness in leaders: Australian community leadership programs, *The Leadership Quarterly,* 26 (2): 238–253.

Wahl, C., Scriber, C. and Bloomfield, B. (eds.) (2013) *On becoming a leadership coach: A holistic approach to coaching excellence* (2nd edition). New York: Palgrave Macmillan.

Wasylyshyn, K.M., Gronsky, B. and Haas, J.W. (2006) Tigers, stripes, and behavior change: Survey results of a commissioned coaching program, *Consulting Psychology Journal: Practice and Research,* 58 (2): 65–81.

Whitmore, J. (1992) *Coaching for performance: GROWing human potential and purpose – the principles and practice of coaching and leadership* (4th edition). London: Nicholas Brealey.

Wilber, K. (2000) *Integral psychology: Consciousness, spirit, psychology, therapy.* Boston, MA: Shambala.

Wycherley, I.M. and Cox, E. (2008) Factors in the selection and matching of executive coaches in organisations, *Coaching: An International Journal of Theory, Research and Practice,* 1 (1): 39–53.

Yin, R.K. (2018) *Case study research and applications.* London: Sage.

Zohar, D. (2016) *The quantum leader: A revolution in business thinking and practice.* New York: Prometheus Books.

Index

A

Achievists 25, 30, 31, 67
    best self cultivation 72, 73, 79
    coaching effectiveness, linking with
        stage development 165, 166, 167,
        168, 169, 172, 174, 176, 178
    distinctions between *Synergists* and
        39–41
    executive coaching research study
        54–5, 56, 57, 58, 59
    holding safe emergent space 100, 104, 105
    human faculties and energy fields,
        correlation with 156, 157, 158, 159,
        160, 161, 162, 163, 164
    leadership stage 1, 11, 12, 13, 15, 17
    multiple case study research 194, 195,
        196, 197, 198, 199, 200, 201, 202,
        203, 205
    organisational uplift 81, 86, 90, 94
    perception and perspective, attitudinal
        shifts in 121, 124, 125
    prototype 26–9, 37
        executive prototype 28–9
        needs/values 26–7
        shadow 27–8
        strengths 27
    safe expansive space, holding and
        generation of 143, 146, 147, 148,
        150, 152
    transformative coaching, key themes of
        61, 64
    Transformative STAGESHIFT™
        Executive Coaching 180, 185, 186,
        187, 188, 189, 191
    vertical development 131, 133, 134, 138,
        140–41
    shift to *Catalyst* from 140
    see also Transformation from *Achievist*
        to *Synergist*
Action-logics, Torbert's typology of 39, 41
Adult development theory, coach
        selection and 173
Adulthood, staged progression of
        growth in 3

Affective outcomes criteria 166
Alchemists
    executive coaching research study 56
    leadership transformation stages 14, 15
    multiple case study research 198, 199,
        201, 202
    prototype 35–6, 37
        executive prototype 36
        needs/values 35–6
        shadow 36
        strengths 36
    transformation from *Achievist* to
        Synergist 45, 48
Amber organisation 133
Amen, D.G. 24
AQAL Model of Integral Theory
    quadrants of 10–13, 14, 15–17
    zones adapted from 16
AQAL Model of Integral Theory (adapted)
    pathway through quadrants of, vertical
        development and 136
    vertical development and 132
Aristotle 142
Articulating a unique and inspiring living
        signature presentation (driver 7)
        64, 65, 113–16
    benchmark for 114
    case study examples 114–15
    coachees' experience with this 115
    coaching process, 12 P's of 113–14
    Compelling Signature Presentation 113,
        116
    impact on coachees of this 115
    implementation, how this is
        implemented 114
    influence, coaching process and 114
    inspire, coaching process and 113–14
    involvement, what it involves 113–14
    nature of shift activated 116
    problem or need addressed 113
    transform, coaching process and 114
    underlying principles of this 115
Askeland, M. 170, 171
Aspirational Brand Statement 77

Aspirational intent
  clarity in, need for 72
  setting of 143
Aspirational Leadership Brand
    Declaration (ALBD)
  development process examples 71
  safe expansive space, generation and
      holding of 142, 145–6, 149
  setting inspiring evolutionary
      purposeful personal aspirations
      69–70, 72, 73, 76
Athanasopoulou, A. and Dopson, S. 166
Average aggregate profiles (AAPs) 197–8,
    201, 202, 203
Awareness and engagement, Inner and
    Outer Zone of 138

B
Bachkirova, T. 170, 171
Bachkirova, T. and Borrington, S. 173
Barrett, R. 165
Barta, K. 17
Baumeister, R. and Tierney, J. 94
Beck, D. E. 6
Beck, D.E. and Cowan, C.C. 10–11, 233
Beckwith, M.B. 159
Behavioural change, coaching
    effectiveness and 167
Belonging needs 3
Berger, J.G. 173
Best self cultivation 69–80
  cultivating a positive, open, kind, and
      compassionate mind 73–9
    Aspirational Brand Statement 77
    case study examples 75–7
    coachees' experience with this 77–8
    defensiveness 74
    flaws in others (and criticism of) 74
    illumination, moments of 78
    impact on coachees of this 78
    implementation, how this is
        implemented 75
    involvement, what this
        involves 74–5
    Loving Kindness Meditation 76
    mindful leadership 79
    mindfulness practices 75–6
    nature of shift activated 79
    negative thoughts, conscious
        deletion of 75, 76

    not good enough (NGE) state of
        being 78–9
    open-mindedness 76
    positive psychology techniques 75–6
    problem or need addressed 73–4
    respectful communications 75–6
    rewind, rehearse, and record (3Rs),
        practice of 77
    self-expression, integration of
        self-awareness in 74–5
    self-protection 74
    self-transformation 77–8
    transference 73–4
    underlying principles of this 78–9
  key points 80
  setting inspiring evolutionary purposeful
      personal aspirations 69–73
    ALBD development process
        examples 71
    aspiration intention, clarity in 72
    Aspirational Leadership Brand
        Declaration (ALBD) 69–70, 72,
        73, 76
    changing life experience 71
    coachees' experience with this 71
    goals, actions and 69
    impact on coachees of this 72
    implementation, how this is
        implemented 70–71
    involvement, what this involves
        69–70
    MAGIC affirmation process to create
        the future 70
    nature of shift activated 73
    neuroscience, evidence from 73
    problem or need addressed 69
    underlying principles of this 72–3
The Biology of Belief (Lipton, B.) 102
Broad spectrum stage shift, vertical
    development and 138–40
Brown, B.C. 32, 41, 46, 48
Bullying 105
Bushe, G.R. and Gibbs, B.W. 42

C
Campbell, J. 159
Case study examples
  articulating a unique and inspiring
      living signature presentation
      (driver 7) 114–15

cultivating a positive, open, kind, and
    compassionate mind 75–7
distributing time to generate dynamic
    flow 91
engaging everyone in setting shared
    purposeful strategic direction 83–4
exploring psychodynamics to heal
    shadow and eliminate triggers
    100–101
leading wide collaboration 118
sustaining standards with courageous
    caring conversations 107–8
Catalysts
executive coaching research study 55,
    56, 57, 58, 59
leadership stage 1, 11, 12, 13, 14, 15, 17
prototype 29–31, 37
    executive prototype 31
    needs/values 29–30
    shadow 30
    strengths 30
shift to *Synergist* from, vertical
    development and 140
transformation from *Achievist* to
    Synergist 39, 41, 42, 45, 47–8, 50, 51
transformative coaching, key themes of
    61, 65
Cavanagh, M. 172
Central Stage of Integration, life
    experiences around 161
Centre of Gravity stage in personal
    profile 17
Changing life experience 71
Clustering topics of conversation 63
Clutterbuck, D. 100
Co-creative intuitive emergent
    collaboration 177
Coachee career outcomes and reflections
    182–3
Coachee experiences
cultivating a positive, open, kind, and
    compassionate mind 77–8
distributing time to generate dynamic
    flow 91–3
engaging everyone in setting
    shared purposeful strategic
    direction 84
exploring psychodynamics to heal
    shadow and eliminate triggers
    101–2

setting inspiring evolutionary
    purposeful personal aspirations 71
sustaining standards with courageous
    caring conversations 109–10
Coaching conversations 61–2, 63, 85
Coaching effectiveness
    assessment of 165, 167
    stage outcomes of 174–6
Coaching effectiveness, linking to stage
    development 165–79
adult development theory, coach
    selection and 173
affective outcomes criteria 166
assessment of coaching
    effectiveness 167
behavioural change 167
co-creative intuitive emergent
    collaboration 177
coaching interventions, diverse blend
    of 166
coaching outcomes in terms of stage
    transformations 175
cognitive-behavioural influences 166
cognitive outcomes criteria 166
collaborative meaning-making 174
current assessments of coaching
    effectiveness 165–7
developmental coaching 169–71,
    175, 176
developmental coaching, aim of 171
emotional intelligence 166
executive coaching, in-depth study
    (Wasylyshyn et al., 2006)
    166, 167
executive coaching, meta-analysis of
    impact and moderating influences
    of 165–6
experiential learning 166
Goal, Reality, Options, and Way
    forward (GROW) process 168
individual and organisational
    performance 166
intrapersonal skills criteria 166
key points 178–9
Kolb's learning cycle, transformative
    coaching in 177
learning sustainability 167
life change criteria of embrace of 166
multifaceted role of transformative
    coach 176–8

objective measurement 175
open questions, technique of 170–71
performance coaching 175, 176
person-centric counselling 170
positive psychology, influences of 166, 168–9
process consultation coaching 166
reflective observation 176
regressive behaviours criteria of overcoming 166
self-regulation criteria 166
Self-Transforming Mind 172
skill-based outcomes criteria 166
skills-based and performance coaching 168–9
skills-based coaching 175
solution-focus, influences of 166
stage outcomes of coaching effectiveness 174–6
systems-oriented approach 166
third-generation coaching approach (Stelter) 173
transformation, transformative coaching and 172–3
transformative coaching 171–4, 175, 176–7
    in Kolb's learning cycle 177
    role of transformative coach 177–8
transformative learning, Mezirow's concept of 172
versatility, expansion of 167
Coaching interventions, diverse blend of 166
Coaching meetings, multiple case study research 196
Coaching outcomes in terms of stage transformations 175
Coaching programs, executive coaching research study 55–7
Coaching set-up, expectations and 196–7
Cognitive-behavioural influences 166
Cognitive-emotional integration 49
Cognitive outcomes criteria 166
Cohn, L.D. 43
Cohn, L.D. and Westenberg, P.M. 44
Collaborating widely with stakeholders to generate synergy (driver 8) 64, 65, 116–19
    case study examples 118
    coachees' experience with this 118

Compelling Signature Presentation 116–17
impact on coachees of this 119
implementation, how this is implemented 117–18
involvement, what it involves 117
nature of shift activated 119
problem or need addressed 116–17
underlying principles of this 119
win-win-win collaborative, eco-centric solutions, generation of 117–18
'working in the orange light zone' 116
Collaboration *see* Leading wide collaboration
Collaborative meaning-making 174
Collective, re-engineering of 187
Collective action inquiry into disorienting life experiences 46–7
Collective operating system 150
Collective Quadrants 12, 13, 15, 16, 17, 138, 139
Collective Tier 12, 95, 111
Combined power of individual and collective propellers 151
Community leadership programs (CLPs) 47–8
Compelling Signature Presentation (CSP) 148
Complex meaning-making, inter-systemic complexity and 154
Concrete Collective 13, 17, 135, 146
Concrete Tier 13, 16, 17–18, 20, 22, 156
Conformists
    executive coaching research study 55
    leadership transformation stages 9, 11, 14, 17
    prototype 22–3, 37
        executive prototype 23
        needs/values 22
        shadow 23
        strengths 22
    transformation from *Achievist* to *Synergist* 45, 47
Conformity 43–4, 85
Consistency 89, 91, 94
Construct-aware stage 14, 15
Constructive developmental psychology 3, 5–6
    adult development phases 6
    concerns of 5

cultural memes and values
   development 6
faith development 6
Levels of Mind 5–6
meaning-making systems 5
moral development 6
Self-Authoring Mind 5, 6, 7
Self-Transforming Mind 5, 7
Socialised Mind 5, 7
Sovereign Mind 5, 7
subjective reality, perception of life as 5
Vertical development 131, 132, 137
worldview development 6
Constructivists
executive coaching research study 56
leadership transformation stages 14, 15,
   17
prototype 34–5, 37
   executive prototype 35
   needs/values 34
   shadow 35
   strengths 34–5
Contributions to meetings, generation of
   effectiveness in 86–7
Cook-Greuter, S. 3, 7–8, 10–11, 13,
   16–17, 18
coaching effectiveness, linking to stage
   development 171, 172
executive coaching research study 54,
   56, 57
executive prototypes, strengths and
   shadows of 21–2, 23, 26, 28, 31, 33
multiple case study research
   193–4, 197
transformation from *Achievist* to
   Synergist 43, 44, 45, 46
Corporate politics, power dynamics and 104
Corporate reputation 118
Courageous Caring Conversations (CCCs)
examples of 108, 109–10
safe expansive space, generation and
   holding of 144–5, 146
sustaining standards with courageous
   caring conversations 105–6, 107
Covey, S.R. 87
Cox, E., Bachkirova, T. and Clutterbuck,
   D. 165, 170
Creative tension, Fritz's concept of 158–9
Creativity 28, 50, 52, 79, 86, 88, 94, 134,
   135, 168

Csikszentmihalyi, M. 171
Cultivating a positive, open, kind, and
   compassionate mind (driver 2) 63,
   64, 73–9
Aspirational Brand Statement 77
case study examples 75–7
coachees' experience with this 77–8
defensiveness 74
flaws in others (and criticism of) 74
illumination, moments of 78
impact on coachees of this 78
implementation, how this is
   implemented 75
involvement, what this involves
   74–5
Loving Kindness Meditation 76
mindful leadership 79
mindfulness practices 75–6
nature of shift activated 79
negative thoughts, conscious deletion
   of 75, 76
not good enough (NGE) state of being
   78–9
open-mindedness 76
positive psychology techniques 75–6
problem or need addressed 73–4
respectful communications 75–6
rewind, rehearse, and record (3Rs),
   practice of 77
self-expression, integration of self-
   awareness in 74–5
self-protection 74
self-transformation 77–8
transference 73–4
underlying principles of this 78–9
Cultivating self, healing shadow, and
   embodying spirit 162–3
Current assessments of coaching
   effectiveness 165–7
Customer, Leadership, Integrated (with
   other stakeholders), and Project
   deliverables (CLIP) 84
Cycle for self-transformation 142–6

D
Defence of standards 105
Defensiveness 74
Delinquency 43–4
Delizonna, L. 142
Development drivers, exploration of 47

Development stages, leadership
transformation 6–9
decision-making 8
ego development, stages of 6–7, 8
holarchy of 7
individuation stage 7–8, 10, 12, 13,
15, 17
integration stage 7–8, 10, 12, 13, 15, 17
secondary integration mode 8
Washington University Sentence
Completion Test (WUSCT) 6–7, 16
Developmental coaching 169–71, 175, 176
aim of 171
Developmental psychology 3, 57, 171, 172,
193–4
see also Constructive developmental
psychology
Distinctions between *Achievists* and
Synergists 39–41
Distinctive features of STAGESHIFT™
coaching 185–7
Distinctive leadership capacity of a
Synergist 181
Distributing time to generate dynamic
flow (driver 4) 64, 86–95
case study examples 91
coachees' experience with this 91–3
consistency 94
contributions to meetings, generation
of effectiveness in 86–7
Dynamic Operating Rhythm (DOR)
89, 93
dynamic operating rhythm template
92–3
emergent state of flow, setting up of 88
generative flows, creation of 88
impact on coachees of this 93
implementation, how this is
implemented 88–91
involvement, what it involves 87–8
meeting times and timing 89
mind, pre-programming of 88
nature of shift activated 94–5
one-on-one meetings 90–91
operationalisation of strategic shift
94–5
prioritisation 87–8
problem or need addressed 86–7
Strategic Business Charter 94
strategic leadership initiatives 94–5

strategic meetings 90
time management tools 87–8
time pressures (and time management)
86–7
underlying principles of this 94
Diversity and conflict, capacity for
embrace of 118
Doidge, D. 77, 169
Draft work on Strategic Shifts 83–4
Dweck, C.S. 75, 169
Dynamic Operating Rhythm (DOR)
distributing time to generate dynamic
flow 89, 93
of engagement, generation of 82
safe expansive space, generation and
holding of 148, 149, 152
template 92–3
vertical development 134, 135

E
Early evolutionary framework 6
Efficiency, Quality, User, Income, People
(EQUIP) scorecard 82
Eigel, K.M. 42
Eigel, K.M. and Kuhnert, K.W. 42
Einstein, A. 123
Emergent Future 159
Emergent state of flow, setting up of 88
Emerson, R.W. 72
Emotional dramas in people's lives 98
Emotional intelligence 162, 169
coaching effectiveness, linking to stage
development 166
transformative STAGESHIFT™
Executive Coaching 186
Emotional triggers 162
Emotional wounds 126, 162
dealing with 97
elimination of 144
Emotions foster evolution 121, 123–4
communications that resonate 124
emotional judgements of others 123
emotional traumas and dramas 124
emotional triggers are opportunities
123
talents admired by others 124
Empowered chaotic matrix, vertical
development and 134
Energy fields of our life experience
158–9

Engagement cycle
  for inner collective 147–50
  for outer collective 151–3
Engagement fosters evolution 121, 124–6
  engagement involves thought
    generation 125–6
  everyone is a cousin 125
  everyone is doing their best 124
  feeling seen, heard, and understood
    124–5
  orange light zone 125
Engaging everyone in setting shared
    purposeful strategic direction
    (driver 3) 63, 64, 81–6
  case study examples 83–4
  CLIP (Customer, Leadership, Integrated
    (with other stakeholders), and
    Project deliverables) 84
  coachees' experience with this 84
  creativity 86
  Draft work on Strategic Shifts 83–4
  Dynamic Operating Rhythm of
    engagement, generation of 82
  EQUIP (Efficiency, Quality, User,
    Income, People) scorecard 82
  I-CARE (Integrity, Courage,
    Accountability, Respect, Energy) 82
  impact on coachees of this 84–5
  implementation, how this is
    implemented 82–3
  involvement, what it involves 82
  Key Outcomes we Aspire to 83
  nature of shift activated 85–6
  proactiveness 86
  problem or need addressed 81–2
  proven approaches, use of 82
  SCIENCE Values 84
  shared aspirational outcomes,
    realisation of 86
  Strategic Business charter
    development of 82–3
    implementation of 85
  strategic direction setting 81
  underlying principles of this 85
Entrepreneurial enterprise, vertical
    development and 134
Ericsson, K.A. 88
Evolution of
  collective context 132–5
  individual identity 131–2

Executive coaching
  in-depth study (Wasylyshyn et al., 2006)
    166, 167
  meta-analysis of impact and
    moderating influences of 165–6
Executive coaching research study 54–60
  Alchemist 56
  Catalyst 55, 56, 57, 58, 59
  coaching programs 55–7
  Conformist 55
  Constructivist 56
  key points 60
  longitudinal dimension 58
  Opportunist 55
  participants
    nine initial coachees 54–5
    profiles and coaching programs 59
    three more and assessments 57–60
  post-program assessments 57
  research question 54
  results 59
  Specialist 55
  Stages International 55
  total protocol rating (TPR) 57
  total weighted score (TWS) 54, 55,
    57, 58
  Washington University Sentence
    Completion Test (WUSCT) 54, 57
Executive distribution, statistical
    evidence of 44–6
Executive population, distribution of 45
Executive prototypes, strengths and
    shadows of 20–37
  Achievist prototype 26–9, 37
    executive prototype 28–9
    needs/values 26–7
    shadow 27–8
    strengths 27
  Alchemist prototype 35–6, 37
    executive prototype 36
    needs/values 35–6
    shadow 36
    strengths 36
  Catalyst prototype 29–31, 37
    executive prototype 31
    needs/values 29–30
    shadow 30
    strengths 30
  Conformist prototype 22–3, 37
    executive prototype 23

needs/values 22
shadow 23
strengths 22
Constructivist prototype 34–5, 37
executive prototype 35
needs/values 34
shadow 35
strengths 34–5
key points 37
Opportunist prototype 20–22, 37
executive prototype 21–2
needs/values 21
shadow 21
strengths 21
Specialist prototype 23–6, 37
executive prototype 25–6
needs/values 24
shadow 25
strengths 24
Synergist prototype 31–4, 37
executive prototype 33–4
needs/values 32
shadow 33
strengths 32–3
Experiential learning 166
Exploring psychodynamics to heal
shadow and eliminate triggers
(driver 5) 64, 65, 97–103
case study example 100–101
coachees' experience with this
101–2
emotional dramas in people's lives 98
emotional wounds, dealing with 97
GRIEF process of shadow resolution
and healing 98–100, 101, 103
growth facilitation 97
impact on coachees of this 102
implementation, how this is
implemented 98–100
interpenetrative capacity 98
interpersonal power dynamic 97
involvement, what it involves 98
MetAware Tier 103
nature of shift activated 103
power patterns in relationships
100–101
problem or need addressed 97
reflective inquiry 101–2
self-healing 102
underlying principles of this 103

F
Family dynamics foster evolution 122,
126–7
early childhood is critical 127
families include opposites 126
parents are later stage shadow
work 127
strengths distinguish families 126
wounds travel generations 126
Figure-8 Holistic Energy Operating
System 159–62
Fisher, D. and Torbert, W.R. 42
Fitch, G. 12
Flaws in others (and criticism of) 74
Flourishing global perspective 180–81
'Follow your bliss' (Campbell) 159
Fowler, J.W. 6
Frankl, V. 4
Fredrickson, B. 64, 169
Freud, S. 3
Fritz, R. 158

G
Gallwey, T. 169
Generative flows, creation of 88
Gerber, M.H. 6
Gilligan, C. 6
Goal, Reality, Options, and Way forward
(GROW) process 168
Goals 10, 32, 42, 77, 148, 149, 152, 157, 159,
181, 198
actions and 69
agreed goals 174, 175, 178
aspirations and 124
business goals 134
desired goals 170
developmental goals 69–70, 73
goal accomplishment (or achievement)
165, 167, 168, 169
goal orientation 85
performance goals 88, 137
setting goals 26, 27, 73
targets and 86
workplace goals 168
Goleman, D. 162, 169
Grant, A.M. 168, 169
Grant, A.M. and Cavanagh, M.J. 168, 169
Grant, A.M., Cavanagh, M.J. and Parker,
H.M. 171
Graves, C.W. 6

Green organisation 133
GRIEF process of shadow resolution and
    healing 98–100, 101, 103, 144
Growth facilitation 97
Gunnlaugson, O. and Brabant, M. 12, 48

H
Hamel, G. 51–2, 64
Harris, L.S. and Kuhnert, K.W. 42
Harthill Consulting 45
Harvard Business Review 56
Hawkins, P. and Smith, N. 165, 171
HeartMath Institute 64
    safe emergent space holding 103
Hero's Journey
    transformative STAGESHIFT™
        Executive Coaching 186
    vertical development 134, 136
Hierarchical organisation 134
Holistic Energy Operating System
    (whole) 163
Holistic leadership development
    importance of 163
    StageSHIFT approach to 131
Holistic self, propellers creating space
    for 143
Holistic transformation, expansive sphere
    of 154
Holists 14
Horney, K. 158
Human faculties and energy fields,
    correlation with 156–64
    Central Stage of Integration, life
        experiences around 161
    creative tension, Fritz's concept of
        158–9
    cultivating self, healing shadow, and
        embodying spirit 162–3
    Emergent Future 159
    emotional triggers 162
    energy fields of our life experience
        158–9
    Figure-8 Holistic Energy Operating
        System 159–62
    'follow your bliss' (Campbell) 159
    Holistic Energy Operating System
        (whole) 163
    holistic leadership development,
        importance of 163
    human faculties

correlated to stages of development
    156–7
    of our self-expression 156–8
    key points 164
    life experience, changing energy fields
        of 158
    MetAware Tier 157
    mind, centrality for *Synergist* of 157
    preceding and succeeding stages
        surrounding Stages of
        Integration 161
    Reactive Patterns 158, 160, 161, 162–3
    self-expression, human faculties of our
        156–8
    Spectrum Stage Shifts 156, 160–61,
        162, 163
    stages of development, human faculties
        correlated to 156–7
    Stages of Integration, preceding and
        succeeding stages surrounding
        161
    Theory U 159
    transpersonal self, emergence of 157
Humanistic psychology 3

I
I-CARE (Integrity, Courage,
    Accountability, Respect,
    Energy) 82
Identity
    authentic leadership and 131, 132
    inner integrated identity 181
Ideological values, correlation with 43–4
Illumination, moments of 78
Immordino-Yang, M.H., Christodoulou,
    J.A. and Singh, V. 94
Impacts on coachees
    cultivating a positive, open, kind, and
        compassionate mind 78
    distributing time to generate dynamic
        flow 93
    engaging everyone in setting shared
        purposeful strategic direction
        84–5
    exploring psychodynamics to heal
        shadow and eliminate triggers 102
    setting inspiring evolutionary
        purposeful personal aspirations 72
    sustaining standards with courageous
        caring conversations 110

Implementation
    cultivating a positive, open, kind, and compassionate mind 75
    distributing time to generate dynamic flow 88–91
    engaging everyone in setting shared purposeful strategic direction 82–3
    exploring psychodynamics to heal shadow and eliminate triggers 98–100
    setting inspiring evolutionary purposeful personal aspirations 70–71
    sustaining standards with courageous caring conversations 105–7
Individual and organisational performance 166
Individual Quadrant 138, 139
Individualists 1, 9, 13
Inner awareness, personal inquiry into 49–50
Inner collective
    expansive space held in 150
    propellers creating space in 149
Inner integrated identity 181
Insead 48
Inspiring Signature Presentation (ISP) 151, 152–3
Integral AQAL Model of All Quadrants, All Levels 135–6
Integrated ecosystem 134
Inter-systemic awareness of *Synergists* 40
Interpenetration 12
Interpersonal power dynamic 97
Interpretation
    interpenetrative capacity of psychodynamics 98
    interpenetrative memes of the mind 190
Intrapersonal skills criteria 166
Involvement
    cultivating a positive, open, kind, and compassionate mind 74–5
    distributing time to generate dynamic flow 87–8
    engaging everyone in setting shared purposeful strategic direction 82
    exploring psychodynamics to heal shadow and eliminate triggers 98
    setting inspiring evolutionary purposeful personal aspirations 69–70

    sustaining standards with courageous caring conversations 105
Ironists
    leadership transformation stages 14
    transformation from *Achievist* to *Synergist* 45
Ives, Y. 165, 171

J
Joiner, B. and Josephs, S. 13, 171
Jones, R.J., Woods, S.A. and Guillaume, Y.R.F. 165–6
Jung, C.G. 3

K
Kaiser, R.B. and Kaplan, R.B. 47
Katie, B. and Mitchell, S. 170
Kauffman, C. 168–9
Kegan, R. 3, 5–6, 7, 8, 9, 10–11, 13, 14, 18
    coaching effectiveness, links to stage development 172, 176
    collective vision, development of 40
    executive prototypes, strengths and shadows of 20, 21, 25, 26
    trusted relationships and community strength, espousal of 64
Kegan, R., Lahey, L., Fleming, A. and Miller, M. 40, 50, 51
Key Outcomes we Aspire to 83
Key points
    best self cultivation 80
    coaching effectiveness, linking to stage development 178–9
    executive coaching research study 60
    executive prototypes, strengths and shadows of 37
    human faculties and energy fields, correlation with 164
    leadership transformation stages 18–19
    leading wide collaboration 119–20
    organisational uplift 95–6
    perception and perspective, attitudinal shifts in 127–8
    safe emergent space holding 111–12
    safe expansive space, generation and holding of 155
    transformation from *Achievist* to *Synergist* 52–3

transformative coaching, key
  themes of 65
vertical development 141
Key Strategic Shifts (KSS) 149
Kilburg, R.R. 100
Kirkpatrick, D.L. 166
Kleitman, N. 88
Kohlberg, L. 6, 7, 8, 9, 13–14, 44
Kolb, D.A. 166, 176
  learning cycle, transformative coaching
    in 177
Kotter, J.P. 52, 81, 82, 149
Kraiger, K., Ford, J.K. and Salas, E.D. 166
Kuhnert, K. 20, 42

L
Laloux, F. 10–11, 64, 81, 94
  evolving organisations, systems and
    cultures in 133, 149
  transformation from *Achievist* to
    Synergist 47, 51, 52
Laske, O.E. 171
Later stage development
  drivers of 67–8
  dynamics of 129
  evidence of 46–52
Leadership effectiveness 39, 41–3, 81, 190
Leadership transformation stages 1–2,
    3–19
  accepting, being more 4
  Achievist leadership stage 1, 11, 12, 13,
    15, 17
  adulthood, staged progression of
    growth in 3
  Alchemists 14, 15
  AQAL Model of Integral Theory
    quadrants of 10–13, 14, 15–17
    zones adapted from 16
  astute, being more 4
  authentic, being more 4
  aware, being more 4
  belonging needs 3
  Catalyst leadership stage 1, 11, 12, 13,
    14, 15, 17
  Centre of Gravity stage in personal
    profile 17
  Collective Tier 12
  Concrete Tier 13, 16, 17–18
  Conformists 9, 11, 14, 17
  Construct-aware stage 14, 15

constructive developmental psychology
    3, 5–6
  adult development phases 6
  concerns of 5
  cultural memes and values
    development 6
  faith development 6
  Levels of Mind 5–6
  meaning-making systems 5
  moral development 6
  Self-Authoring Mind 5, 6, 7
  Self-Transforming Mind 5, 7
  Socialised Mind 5, 7
  Sovereign Mind 5, 7
  subjective reality, perception of
    life as 5
  worldview development 6
Constructivists 14, 15, 17
development stages 6–9
  decision-making 8
  ego development, stages of 6–7, 8
  holarchy of 7
  individuation stage 7–8, 10, 12, 13, 15,
    17
  integration stage 7–8, 10, 12, 13,
    15, 17
  secondary integration mode 8
  Washington University Sentence
    Completion Test (WUSCT) 6–7, 16
early evolutionary framework 6
Holists 14
humanistic psychology 3
Individualists 1, 9, 13
interpenetration 12
Ironists 14
key points 18–19
Leading Edge stage in personal profile
    17
Maslow's hierarchy of needs 3–4, 6
MetAware Tier 10, 15, 16
needs, Maslow's hierarchy of 3–4, 6
Opportunists 9, 11, 14
phases and early stages framework 8–9
phases to tiers in stage development 14
Pluralists 1, 13, 14
Rule-based stage 14, 17–18
security needs 3
self-actualising needs 3, 4
self-esteem needs 3
self-transcendence 4

shadow crashes 17–18
Specialists 12, 14, 17
spectrum stage shift 16–18
staged progression of growth in
    adulthood 3
Strategists 1, 9, 14
Subtle Tier 12, 13, 15, 16, 17
survival needs 3
Synergist leadership stage 1, 11, 12, 13,
    14, 15, 17
tiers and learning sequence 10–16
Trailing Edge stage in personal
    profile 17
Unified Tier 10
vertical development 4
Leading Edge stage in personal profile 17
Leading wide collaboration 113–20
    articulating a unique and inspiring
        living signature presentation
        113–16
    benchmark for 114
    case study examples 114–15
    coachees' experience with this 115
    coaching process, 12 P's of 113–14
    Compelling Signature Presentation
        113, 116
    impact on coachees of this 115
    implementation, how this is
        implemented 114
    influence, coaching process and 114
    inspire, coaching process and 113–14
    involvement, what it involves 113–14
    nature of shift activated 116
    problem or need addressed 113
    transform, coaching process and 114
    underlying principles of this 115
    benchmark for 114
    case study examples 114–15, 118
    coachees' experience with this 115, 118
    coaching process, 12 P's of 113–14
    collaborating widely with stakeholders
        to generate synergy 116–19
    case study examples 118
    coachees' experience with this 118
    Compelling Signature Presentation
        116–17
    impact on coachees of this 119
    implementation, how this is
        implemented 117–18
    involvement, what it involves 117

nature of shift activated 119
problem or need addressed 116–17
underlying principles of this 119
win-win-win collaborative, eco-
    centric solutions, generation of
    117–18
'working in the orange light zone' 116
Compelling Signature Presentation 113,
    116–17
corporate reputation 118
diversity and conflict, capacity for
    embrace of 118
impact on coachees of this 115, 119
implementation, how this is
    implemented 114, 117–18
influence, coaching process and 114
inspire, coaching process and 113–14
involvement, what it involves
    113–14, 117
key points 119–20
nature of shift activated 116, 119
problem or need addressed 113,
    116–17
transform, coaching process and 114
underlying principles of this 115, 119
win-win-win collaborative, eco-centric
    solutions, generation of 117–18
'working in the orange light zone' 116
Learning sustainability 167
Leximancer software 61, 62, 65
Liberating Meeting Agendas (LMAs)
    148, 150
Life change criteria 166
Life experience, changing energy
    fields of 158
Lilienfeld, S.O., Wood, J.M. and Garb, H.N.
    43, 44
Lipton, B. 102
Loehr, J. and Schwartz, T. 94
Loevinger, J. 3, 6–7, 8, 9, 10–11, 16, 18,
    43, 171
Loevinger, J. and Wessler, R. 44
Loving Kindness Meditation 76

M
Manners, J. and Durkin, K. 44, 47
Man's Search for Meaning (Frankl, V.) 4
Marturano, J. 79
Maslow, A.H. 8, 9, 18, 20, 22, 169
    hierarchy of needs 3–4, 6

Mastery, Abundance, Gratitude,
    Imagination, and Celebration
    (MAGIC)
  affirmation process to create the
    future 70
  safe expansive space, generation and
    holding of 143
Matrix of eight key drivers of
    transformative coaching 63–5
Mature Adult Profile (MAP) 195
McCauley, C.D., Drath, W.H., Palus, C.J.,
    O'Connor, P.M.G. and Baker, B.A.
    5, 44
McTaggart, L. 103
Measurement of stage development 43–4
Meeting times and timing 89
Merron, K., Fisher, D. and Torbert, W.R. 41
MetAware Tier
  exploring psychodynamics to heal
    shadow and eliminate triggers 103
  human faculties and energy fields,
    correlation with 157
  leadership transformation stages 10,
    15, 16
Mezirow, J. 47, 172
Mind
  centrality for *Synergist* of 157
  interpenetrative memes of the 190
  pre-programming of 88
Mindful leadership 79
Mindfulness 186
  practices 75–6
Moral behaviour, correlation with 43–4
Multifaceted role of transformative coach
    176–8
Multiple case study research 193–205
  additional participants 199–200
  average aggregate profiles (AAPs) 197–8
    of participants towards *Synergist*
      status 201
    shifts for all 12 participants 203
  average aggregate stage distribution
    for 4 participants to *Synergist* 202
  coaching meetings 196
  coaching set-up, expectations and 196–7
  demographic summary of 12
    participants 203
  developmental psychology 193–4
  indications from stage assessments 204
  introduction to the research 193–4

longitudinal research extension
    200–202
Mature Adult Profile (MAP) 195
  participants' profiles and coaching
    programs 204
  potential research participants (25),
    assessments of 195
  pre- and post-coaching assessments
    for added 3 participants 200
    for Initial 9 participants 198
  Public Service Commission (PSC) in
    New South Wales 194, 195
  research participants 194–5
  results
    after 12 months 197–8
    for all 12 participants 202–4
    stage shifts, graphical representation
      of 199
  structural dynamics of stage shift 198–9
  summary of key findings 204–5
  total weighted score (TWS) 195, 197, 203
  transformative development 202
Myers, A.C. and Bachkirova, T. 173
Myss, C. 103

N
Nature of shift activated
  cultivating a positive, open, kind, and
    compassionate mind 79
  distributing time to generate dynamic
    flow 94–5
  engaging everyone in setting shared
    purposeful strategic direction 85–6
  exploring psychodynamics to heal
    shadow and eliminate triggers 103
  setting inspiring evolutionary
    purposeful personal
    aspirations 73
  sustaining standards with courageous
    caring conversations 111
Needs, Maslow's hierarchy of 3–4, 6
Negative thoughts, conscious deletion of
    75, 76
Neuroscience, evidence from 73
Not good enough (NGE) state of being 78–9

O
Objective measurement 175
O'Fallon, T. 3, 10–11, 12–13, 14–15, 17, 18,
    56, 171, 185, 194

executive prototypes, strengths and
shadows of 20, 22, 23–4, 26, 29
transformation from *Achievist* to
Synergyst 44, 46
vertical development 131, 137–8
One-on-one meetings 90–91
Open-mindedness 76
Open questions
on direction, purpose, and behaviours
48–9
technique of 170–71
Operationalisation of strategic shift 94–5
Opportunists
transformation from *Achievist* to
Synergist 45
Opportunists 55
leadership transformation stages 9,
11, 14
prototype 20–22, 37
executive prototype 21–2
needs/values 21
shadow 21
strengths 21
Opportunity of STAGESHIFT™
transformative coaching 188–90
Orange enterprise 133
Orchestrated Stakeholder Collaboration
(OSC) 151, 152
Orchestrated Stakeholder Engagement
(OSE) 148
Organisational development
shifts in 50–52
spiral of 133
Organisational evolution, transport
analogy of 134
Organisational uplift 81–96
distributing time to generate dynamic
flow 86–95
case study examples 91
coachees' experience with this 91–3
consistency 94
contributions to meetings, generation
of effectiveness in 86–7
Dynamic Operating Rhythm (DOR)
89, 93
dynamic operating rhythm template
92–3
emergent state of flow, setting
up of 88
generative flows, creation of 88

impact on coachees of this 93
implementation, how this is
implemented 88–91
involvement, what it involves 87–8
meeting times and timing 89
mind, pre-programming of 88
nature of shift activated 94–5
one-on-one meetings 90–91
operationalisation of strategic
shift 94–5
prioritisation 87–8
problem or need addressed 86–7
Strategic Business Charter 94
strategic leadership initiatives 94–5
strategic meetings 90
time management tools 87–8
time pressures (and time
management) 86–7
underlying principles of this 94
engaging everyone in setting shared
purposeful strategic direction 81–6
case study examples 83–4
CLIP (Customer, Leadership,
Integrated (with other
stakeholders), and Project
deliverables) 84
coachees' experience with this 84
creativity 86
Draft work on Strategic Shifts 83–4
Dynamic Operating Rhythm of
engagement, generation of 82
EQUIP (Efficiency, Quality, User,
Income, People) scorecard 82
I-CARE (Integrity, Courage,
Accountability, Respect,
Energy) 82
impact on coachees of this 84–5
implementation, how this is
implemented 82–3
involvement, what it involves 82
Key Outcomes we Aspire to 83
nature of shift activated 85–6
proactiveness 86
problem or need addressed 81–2
proven approaches, use of 82
SCIENCE Values 84
shared aspirational outcomes,
realisation of 86
Strategic Business charter,
development of 82–3

Strategic Business charter,
  implementation of 85
  strategic direction setting 81
  underlying principles of this 85
  key points 95–6
Outcomes of coaching, reflections on 182
Outer collective, expansive space
  held in 153

P
Pacific Integral 48
Pathway through quadrants 135–7
Peltier, B. 170
Perception and perspective, attitudinal
  shifts in 121–8
  emotions foster evolution 121, 123–4
    communications that resonate 124
    emotional judgements of others 123
    emotional traumas and dramas 124
    emotional triggers are opportunities
      123
    talents admired by others 124
  engagement fosters evolution 121,
    124–6
    engagement involves thought
      generation 125–6
    everyone is a cousin 125
    everyone is doing their best 124
    feeling seen, heard, and understood
      124–5
    orange light zone 125
  family dynamics foster evolution 122,
    126–7
    early childhood is critical 127
    families include opposites 126
    parents are later stage shadow work
      127
    strengths distinguish families 126
    wounds travel generations 126
  key points 127–8
  self-work fosters evolution 121, 122–3
    life is a miracle 123
    masterpiece in progress 122
    recurring life events 122
    from self-conscious to conscious
      self 122
    we can transform relations
      unilaterally 123
Performance coaching 175, 176
Person-centric counselling 170

Personal concerns, correlation with 44
Personal Development Elective in Insead
  MBA program 48
Personality characteristics, correlation
  with 43–4
Petrie, N. 48
Petriglieri, G., Wood, J.D. and Petriglieri,
  J.L. 48, 50
Pfaffenberger, A., Marko, P. and
  Combs, A. 49
Phases
  early stages framework and 8–9
  movement to tiers in stage
    development 14
Piaget, J. 176
Positive psychology
  influences of 166, 168–9
  techniques of 75–6
Post-conventional growth 49, 50
Post-program assessments 57
The Power of Now (Tolle, E.) 159
Power patterns in relationships 100–101
Preceding and succeeding stages
  surrounding Stages of
  Integration 161
Precision in measurement 44
Preoccupations, correlation with 44
PricewaterhouseCoopers (PwC) 21, 23,
  26, 28, 31, 33, 45
Prioritisation 87–8
Proactiveness 86
Problems or needs
  cultivating a positive, open, kind, and
    compassionate mind 73–4
  distributing time to generate dynamic
    flow 86–7
  engaging everyone in setting shared
    purposeful strategic direction 81–2
  exploring psychodynamics to heal
    shadow and eliminate triggers 97
  setting inspiring evolutionary
    purposeful personal aspirations 69
  sustaining standards with courageous
    caring conversations 104
Process consultation coaching 166
Proven approaches, use of 82
Public Service Commission (PSC) in New
  South Wales 194, 195
Purposeful Strategic Scaffolding (PSS)
  134, 135, 137

Q
Quatro, S., Galvin, B.M. and Waldman, D. 49

R
Rail transport system, large hierarchical
    organisation 133–4
Reactive Patterns 158, 160, 161, 162–3
Red organisation 133
Redmore, C.D. and Waldman, K. 43
Reflective inquiry 101–2
Reflective observation 176
Regressive behaviours, criteria of
    overcoming 166
Reinventing Organisations (Laloux, F.)
    11, 133
Research question 54, 57
Research studies *see* executive coaching
    research study; multiple case
    study research
Respectful communications 75–6
Rewind, rehearse, and record (3Rs),
    practice of 77
Rogers, C.R. 170
Rohm and Haas Company 167
Rook, D. and Torbert, W.R. 29, 42–3, 45,
    48, 50
Rooke, D. 45
Rule-based stage 14, 17–18

S
Safe, secure, and sacred spaces,
    standards for maintenance of
    144–5
Safe emergent space holding 97–112
  exploring psychodynamics to heal
    shadow and eliminate triggers
    97–103
    case study example 100–101
    coachees' experience with this
    101–2
    emotional dramas in people's
    lives 98
    emotional wounds, dealing with 97
    GRIEF process of shadow
    resolution and healing 98–100,
    101, 103
    growth facilitation 97
    impact on coachees of this 102
    implementation, how this is
    implemented 98–100

interpenetrative capacity 98
interpersonal power dynamic 97
involvement, what it involves 98
MetAware Tier 103
nature of shift activated 103
power patterns in relationships
    100–101
problem or need addressed 97
reflective inquiry 101–2
self-healing 102
underlying principles of this 103
HeartMath Institute 103
key points 111–12
sustaining standards with courageous
    caring conversations 104–11
    bullying 105
    case study examples 107–8
    coachees' experience with this
    109–10
    corporate politics, power dynamics
    and 104
    Courageous Caring Conversation
    (CCC) 105–6, 107
    Courageous Caring Conversation
    (CCC), examples of 108, 109–10
    defence of standards 105
    impact on coachees of this 110
    implementation, how this is
    implemented 105–7
    involvement, what it involves 105
    nature of shift activated 111
    problem or need addressed 104
    standing your ground 106–7
    tolerance of inappropriate
    behaviour 105
    Truth, the Implications, and turning
    Point (TIP) 105–6
    'truth will set you free' 110
    underlying principles of this 110
Safe expansive space, generation and
    holding of 142–55
    aspirational intent setting 143
    Aspirational Leadership Brand
    Declaration (ALBD) 142,
    145–6, 149
    collective operating system 150
    combined power of individual and
    collective propellers 151
    Compelling Signature Presentation
    (CSP) 148

complex meaning-making, inter-systemic complexity and 154
contrasting expansive space held by *Synergist* 147
Courageous Caring Conversations (CCCs) 144–5, 146
cycle for self-transformation 142–6
Dynamic Operating Rhythm (DOR) 148, 149, 152
emotional wounds, elimination of 144
engagement cycle
for inner collective 147–50
for outer collective 151–3
expansive space around the *Synergist* 146–7
expansive sphere of transformation 153–5
GRIEF process 144
holistic self, propellers creating space for 143
holistic transformation, expansive sphere of 154
inner collective
expansive space held in 150
propellers creating space in 149
Inspiring Signature Presentation (ISP) 151, 152–3
key points 155
Key Strategic Shifts (KSS) 149
Liberating Meeting Agendas (LMAs) 148, 150
Mastery, Abundance, Gratitude, Imagination, and Celebration (MAGIC) 143
Orchestrated Stakeholder Collaboration (OSC) 151, 152
Orchestrated Stakeholder Engagement (OSE) 148
outer collective, expansive space held in 153
safe, secure, and sacred spaces, standards for maintenance of 144–5
self, recalibration of identity and 154
self-awareness, critical judgement becoming 143
serendipity 143
shadow, illumination of 144
strategic scaffolding 148–9

supporting, empowering, and encouraging people, coachees' appreciation of 144
symmetry 151, 153
Synergist, expansive space held by 146
synthesis 152, 153
Transformative Strategic Agenda (TSA) 148, 149
Truth, Implications, Point (TIP) approach 145
Scharmer, C.O. 50–51, 64, 72, 159
Schwartz, T. 88
SCIENCE Values 84
Security needs 3
Self, recalibration of identity and 154
Self-actualising needs 3, 4
Self-Authoring Mind 39
Self-awareness, critical judgement becoming 143
Self-esteem needs 3
Self-expression
human faculties of our 156–8
integration of self-awareness in 74–5
Self-healing 102
Self-protection 74
Self-regulation criteria 166
Self-transcendence 4
Self-transformation 77–8
Self-Transforming Mind 172
Self-work fosters evolution 121, 122–3
life is a miracle 123
masterpiece in progress 122
recurring life events 122
from self-conscious to conscious self 122
we can transform relations unilaterally 123
Seligman, M.E.P. 64, 75, 76–7, 169
Senge, P.M. 159
Serendipity 143
Setting inspiring evolutionary purposeful personal aspirations (driver 1) 63, 64, 69–73
ALBD development process examples 71
aspirational intention, clarity in 72
Aspirational Leadership Brand Declaration (ALBD) 69–70, 72, 73, 76
changing life experience 71
coachees' experience with this 71
goals, actions and 69

impact on coachees of this 72
implementation, how this is
    implemented 70–71
involvement, what this involves
    69–70
MAGIC affirmation process to create
    the future 70
nature of shift activated 73
neuroscience, evidence from 73
problem or need addressed 69
underlying principles of this 72–3
Shadows
    illumination of 144
    shadow crashes 17–18
    shadow resolution 186
Shared aspirational outcomes, realisation
    of 86
Shared direction, shared values 134
Sharma, B. and Cook-Greuter, S. 50
Shift to *Synergist,* invitation to join 192
Skill-based outcomes criteria 166
Skills-based and performance coaching
    168–9
Skills-based coaching 175
Socrates 170
Solution-focus, influences of 166
Specialists
    executive coaching research study 55
    leadership transformation stages 12, 14,
        17
    prototype 23–6, 37
        executive prototype 25–6
        needs/values 24
        shadow 25
        strengths 24
    transformation from *Achievist* to
        Synergist 41, 45, 47
Spectrum Stage Shifts 186–7
    from *Achievist* to *Synergist* 187
    human faculties and energy fields,
        correlation with 156, 160–61,
        162, 163
    leadership transformation stages
        16–18
Spiral Dynamics (Beck, D.E. and Cowan,
    C.C.) 10–11, 133
Spiritual intelligence 186
Spiritual Liberation (Beckwith, M.B.) 159
Stage development, linking coaching
    effectiveness to 165–79

Stage outcomes of coaching effectiveness
    174–6
Stage shifts, graphical representation
    of 199
Stages International 55
Stages of development, human faculties
    correlated to 156–7
Stages of Integration 161
STAGESHIFT™
    Drivers 63–5
    Executive Coaching Matrix
        transformative coaching, key themes
        of 64
        vertical development 137
    propellers of transformation 189
    Strategic Holistic Transforming &
        Inspiring Leadership
        Programs 190
    Transformative Coaching Model 184
Standing your ground 106–7
Stelter, R. 165, 173
Stober, R. and Grant, A.M. 169, 170
Strang, S. and Kuhnert, K.W. 42
Strategic Business Charter
    development of 82–3
    distributing time to generate dynamic
        flow 94
    implementation of 85
Strategic direction setting 81
Strategic leadership initiatives 94–5
Strategic meetings 90
Strategic scaffolding 148–9
Strategists
    leadership transformation stages 1, 9, 14
    transformation from *Achievist* to
        Synergist 45
Stroul, N. and Wahl, C. 177
Structural dynamics of stage shift 198–9
Subtle Collective 132, 138
Subtle Tier transformations 185
Supporting, empowering, and
        encouraging people, coachees'
        appreciation of 144
Survival needs 3
Sustaining standards with courageous
        caring conversations (driver 6)
        64–5, 104–11
    bullying 105
    case study examples 107–8
    coachees' experience with this 109–10

corporate politics, power dynamics
and 104
Courageous Caring Conversation
(CCC) 105–6, 107
Courageous Caring Conversation
(CCC), examples of 108, 109–10
defence of standards 105
impact on coachees of this 110
implementation, how this is
implemented 105–7
involvement, what it involves 105
nature of shift activated 111
problem or need addressed 104
standing your ground 106–7
tolerance of inappropriate
behaviour 105
Truth, the Implications, and turning
Point (TIP) 105–6
'truth will set you free' 110
underlying principles of this 110
Symmetry 137, 151, 153, 174, 183, 190
Synergists 67, 70, 72, 73, 75, 79, 129
coaching effectiveness, linking to stage
development 165, 166, 167, 172,
173, 174, 176, 177
contrasting expansive space
held by 147
distinctions between *Achievists* and
39–41
distinctive leadership capacity of 181
executive coaching research study 54,
55, 56, 57, 58, 59, 60
expansive space around 146–7
expansive space held by 146
human faculties and energy fields,
correlation with 156, 157, 158, 159,
160, 161, 162, 163
inter-systemic awareness of 40
leadership stage 1, 11, 12, 13, 14,
15, 17
leading wide collaboration 113, 116,
117, 119
multiple case study research 193–4,
195, 197, 198, 199, 200, 201, 202,
204, 205
organisational uplift 81, 85, 86, 88, 95
perception and perspective, attitudinal
shifts in 121, 124, 127
presence and capacity of 180–82
prototype 31–4, 37

executive prototype 33–4
needs/values 32
shadow 33
strengths 32–3
safe emergent space holding 98, 102,
103, 105, 106, 111
safe expansive space holding 142, 144,
146, 147, 150, 151, 152, 153
shift to, invitation to join 192
transformative coaching, key themes of
61, 65
Transformative STAGESHIFT™
Executive Coaching 180, 181, 182,
183, 184, 185, 186, 187, 188, 189,
191, 192
vertical development 131, 133, 134, 135,
137, 138, 140
see also transformation from *Achievist*
to *Synergist*
Synthesis 152, 153
Systems-oriented approach 166

T
Teal evolutionary purpose-led
organisation 133–4
Ten Hoopen, P. and Trompenaars, F. 156
Thematic analysis 61–2
Thematic relational analysis
(Leximancer) 62
Theory U 159
Third-generation coaching approach
(Stelter) 173
Tiers 13, 16, 17–18, 20, 22, 156
Collective Tier 12, 95, 111
learning sequence and 10–16
MetAware Tier 10, 15, 16, 103, 157
movement to tiers in stage
development 14
Subtle Tier 12, 13, 15, 16, 17
transformations in subtle tier 185
unified Tier 10
Time management tools 87–8
Time pressures (and time management)
86–7
Tolerance
correlation with 43–4
of inappropriate behaviour 105
Tolle, E. 159
Torbert, W.R. 17, 40, 43, 50, 172, 173, 194
Torbert, W.R. and Fisher, D. 46, 50

Torbert, W.R. and Livne-Tarandach, R. 44
Torbert, W.R., Cook-Greuter, S., Fisher, D.,
    Foldy, E., Gauthier, A., Keeley, J.
    et al. 32, 46–7, 171, 172
Total protocol rating (TPR) 57
Total weighted score (TWS)
    executive coaching research study 54,
        55, 57, 58
    multiple case study research 195,
        197, 203
    transformation from *Achievist* to
        Synergist 44
Trailing Edge stage in personal
    profile 17
Transference 32, 75, 79, 143, 177,
    178, 181
    cultivating a positive, open, kind, and
        compassionate mind 73–4
Transformation from *Achievist* to
    Synergist 39–53
    action-logics, Torbert's typology of 39, 41
    Alchemists 45, 48
    Catalyst to *Synergist* transformation 50
    Catalysts 39, 41, 42, 45, 47–8, 51
    cognitive-emotional integration 49
    collective action inquiry into
        disorienting life experiences 46–7
    community leadership programs
        (CLPs) 47–8
    Conformists 45, 47
    conformity, correlation with 43–4
    delinquency, correlation with 43–4
    development drivers, exploration of 47
    distinctions between *Achievists* and
        Synergists 39–41
    executive distribution, statistical
        evidence of 44–6
    executive population, distribution of 45
    Harthill Consulting 45
    ideological values, correlation with 43–4
    inner awareness, personal inquiry into
        49–50
    inter-systemic awareness of
        Synergists 40
    Ironists 45
    key points 52–3
    later stage development, evidence of
        46–52
    leadership effectiveness increases at
        later stages 41–3

measurement of stage development
    43–4
moral behaviour, correlation with 43–4
open questions on direction, purpose,
    and behaviours 48–9
Opportunists 45
organisational development, shifts in
    50–52
Pacific Integral 48
personal concerns, correlation with 44
Personal Development Elective in
    Insead MBA program 48
personality characteristics, correlation
    with 43–4
post-conventional growth 49, 50
precision in measurement 44
preoccupations, correlation with 44
Self-Authoring Mind 39
Specialists 41, 45, 47
Strategists 45
tolerance, correlation with 43–4
total weighted score (TWS) 44
vertical development, polarities and
    later stages of 50
VUCA (volatile, uncertain, complex,
    and ambiguous) world,
    transformation of 46
wariness, correlation with 43–4
Washington University Sentence
    Completion Test (WUSCT) 43, 44
Transformations
    expansive sphere of 153–5
    in subtle tier 185
    transformative coaching 171–4, 175,
        176–7
Transformative change, source of 137
Transformative coaching
    in Kolb's learning cycle 177
    role of transformative coach in 177–8
Transformative coaching, key themes of
    61–5
    articulating a unique and inspiring
        living signature presentation
        (driver 7) 64, 65
    Catalyst 61, 65
    clustering topics of conversation 63
    coaching conversations 61–2, 63, 85
    collaborating widely with
        stakeholders to generate synergy
        (driver 8) 64, 65

cultivating a positive, open, kind,
and compassionate mind (driver 2)
63, 64
distributing time to generate dynamic
flow (driver 4) 64
engaging everyone in setting shared
purposeful strategic direction
(driver 3) 63, 64
exploring psychodynamics to heal
shadow and eliminate triggers
(driver 5) 64, 65
key points 65
Leximancer software 61, 62, 65
matrix of eight key drivers 63–5
setting inspiring evolutionary
purposeful personal aspirations
(driver 1) 63, 64
StageSHIFT Drivers 63–5
StageSHIFT Executive Coaching
Matrix 64
sustaining standards with courageous
caring conversations (driver 6) 64–5
thematic analysis 61–2
thematic relational analysis
(Leximancer) 62
word cluster analysis (Leximancer) 62
Transformative development 202
Transformative leadership capacity 182
Transformative learning, Mezirow's
concept of 172
Transformative STAGESHIFT™
Executive Coaching 180–92
coachee career outcomes and
reflections 182–3
collective, re-engineering of 187
distinctive features of STAGESHIFT™
coaching 185–7
distinctive leadership capacity of a
Synergist 181
emotional intelligence 186
flourishing global perspective 180–81
Hero's Journey 186
inner integrated identity 181
interpenetrative memes of the mind 190
mindfulness 186
opportunity of STAGESHIFT™
transformative coaching 188–90
outcomes of coaching, reflections on 182
presence and capacity of the *Synergist*
180–82

shadow resolution 186
shift to *Synergist,* invitation to
join 192
Spectrum Stage Shift 186–7
Spectrum Stage Shift from *Achievist* to
Synergist 187
spiritual intelligence 186
STAGESHIFT™ propellers of
transformation 189
STAGESHIFT™ Strategic Holistic
Transforming & Inspiring
Leadership Programs 190
STAGESHIFT™ Transformative
Coaching Model 184
subtle tier transformations 185
transformations in the subtle tier 185
transformative leadership capacity 182
Transformative STAGESHIFT™
Coaching Model 183–5
vertical development 191–2
vertical development theory 188
strategic principles 188
www.StageSHIFT.coach for resources
and programs 192
Transformative Strategic Agenda (TSA)
148, 149
Transpersonal self, emergence of 157
Truth, the Implications, and turning
Point (TIP)
safe expansive space, generation and
holding of 145
sustaining standards with courageous
caring conversations 105–6
'Truth will set you free' 110

U
Underlying principles
cultivating a positive, open, kind, and
compassionate mind 78–9
distributing time to generate dynamic
flow 94
engaging everyone in setting shared
purposeful strategic direction 85
exploring psychodynamics to heal
shadow and eliminate triggers 103
setting inspiring evolutionary purposeful
personal aspirations 72–3
sustaining standards with courageous
caring conversations 110
Unified Tier 10

V
Versatility, expansion of 167
Vertical development 131–41
    Achievist, shift to *Catalyst* from 140
    amber organisation 133
    AQAL model (adapted) 132
        pathway through quadrants of 136
    awareness and engagement, Inner and
        Outer Zone of 138
    broad spectrum stage shift 138–40
    Catalyst, shift to *Synergist* from 140
    Collective Quadrant 138, 139
    Concrete Collective 135
    constructive developmental psychology
        131, 132, 137
    Dynamic Operating Rhythm (DOR) 134,
        135
    empowered chaotic matrix 134
    entrepreneurial enterprise 134
    evolution of collective context 132–5
    evolution of individual identity 131–2
    green organisation 133
    Hero's Journey 134, 136
    hierarchical organisation 134
    holistic leadership development,
        StageSHIFT approach to 131
    identity, authentic leadership and
        131, 132
    Individual Quadrant 138, 139
    inner and outer zones of eight
        drivers 139
    inner and outer zones of leadership
        137–8
    Integral AQAL Model of All Quadrants,
        All Levels 135–6
    integrated ecosystem 134
    key points 141
    leadership transformation stages 4
    orange enterprise 133
    organisational development, spiral
        of 133
    organisational evolution, transport
        analogy of 134
    pathway through quadrants 135–7
    polarities and later stages of 50
    Purposeful Strategic Scaffolding (PSS)
        134, 135, 137
    rail transport system, large hierarchical
        organisation 133–4
    red organisation 133
    shared direction, shared values 134
    StageSHIFT Executive Coaching
        Matrix 137
    Subtle Collective 132, 138
    teal evolutionary purpose-led
        organisation 133–4
    transformative change, source of 137
    transformative STAGESHIFT™
        Executive Coaching 191–2
    strategic principles 188
Vincent, N., Ward, L. and Denson, L. 47
VUCA (volatile, uncertain, complex, and
        ambiguous) world,
        transformation of 46

W
Wahl, C., Scriber, C. and Bloomfield, B. 172
Wariness, correlation with 43–4
Washington University Sentence
        Completion Test (WUSCT)
    executive coaching research study
        54, 57
    transformation from *Achievist* to
        Synergist 43, 44
Wasylyshyn, K.M., Gronsky, B. and Haas,
        J.W. 166–7
Whitmore, J. 168
Wilber, K. 10, 131–2, 135
Word cluster analysis (Leximancer) 62
www.StageSHIFT.coach for resources
        and programs 192
Wycherley, I.M. and Cox, E. 173

Y
Yin, R.K. 194

Z
Zohar, D. 56